Date Due

Demco 38-297

Big
Business
Economic Power in a Free Society

Big Business

Economic Power in a Free Society

Advisory Editor
LEON STEIN

Editorial Board
Stuart Bruchey
Thomas C. Cochran

A NOTE ABOUT THIS BOOK

Davis, an outstanding authority on corporations, depicts the clash between inherited political concepts and institutions and the impatience of new economic forces. The history of the Union Pacific is the case in point. The Credit Mobilier scandal it spawned reached into the United States Senate, uncovering influence and payoffs that shocked the nation. The race for industrial and economic power had outstripped the nation's power of restraint and, according to Davis, "afforded convincing proof of the obscurity in which the relations of social principles are involved."

THE

UNION PACIFIC RAILWAY

A STUDY IN RAILWAY POLITICS, HISTORY,
AND ECONOMICS

BY

JOHN P. DAVIS

ARNO PRESS

A New York Times Company

New York / 1973

Reprint Edition 1973 by Arno Press Inc.

Reprinted from a copy in
  The University of Illinois Library

BIG BUSINESS: Economic Power in a Free Society
ISBN for complete set: 0-405-05070-4
See last pages of this volume for titles.

Manufactured in the United States of America

———◆———

Library of Congress Cataloging in Publication Data

Davis, John Patterson, 1862-1903.
    The Union Pacific Railway.

    (Big business: economic power in a free society)
    Reprint of the 1894 ed. published by S. C. Griggs,
Chicago.
    1. Union Pacific Railroad. I. Title. II. Series.
HE2791.U55.D2 1973   385'.0978   73-2501
ISBN 0-405-05082-8

THE

UNION PACIFIC RAILWAY

A STUDY IN RAILWAY POLITICS, HISTORY, AND ECONOMICS

BY

JOHN P. DAVIS, A.M.

"I think there is a history about that matter which ought to be published to the country."— E. B. WASHBURNE.

"The public interest urges prompt and efficient action."— PRESIDENT CLEVELAND

CHICAGO

S. C. GRIGGS AND COMPANY

1894

The Lakeside Press

R. R. DONNELLEY & SONS CO., CHICAGO

TABLE OF CONTENTS.

CHAPTER IV.— THE CHARTER.

CHAPTER V.—DONE!

CHAPTER VI.—CREDIT MOBILIER.

CHAPTER VII.— THURMAN ACT.

CHAPTÉR VIII.— PRESENT AND FUTURE.

INTRODUCTION.

THE work of the student of history has heretofore been confined almost wholly to the political, religious and literary development of peoples; their industrial development has been subjected to inexcusable neglect. Yet the pillars of the dominance of the Anglo-Saxon race are its superior industrial attributes. What a people accomplishes industrially and how it accomplishes it go far to determine how it will be governed, what it will think and feel, and what it will write. The freedom of the individual that was the product of the eighteenth century has been more emphatically manifested in the field of industry than in any other field of human activity. The growth of constitutional government in England is easily traced to the want of harmony between the old political status and the newly developed industrial status of English society. The increasing tendency to submit international disputes to arbitration is attributable not so much to a more enlightened repugnance to warfare as to the mere human fear of destruction of wealth and interference with industries occasioned by it. The Annapolis Convention had its origin in the desire of the American states "To consider how far a uniform system in their commercial relations" might "be necessary to their common interests." The slavery question was largely an industrial question, and its solution was industrial, not political or moral; the event of the Rebellion was not a decision that Webster was a more skillful interpreter of the Constitution than was Calhoun, or that slavery was morally wrong and freedom morally right, but simply that the North was stronger than the South, that a form of society based on free labor was stronger than one based on slave labor, and had produced greater material results. If the political, religious and literary conditions of the present day may be understood aright, it is only by studying them in the light of past and present industrial conditions. From this point of view, the study of the origin, growth and present status of the Union Pacific Railway as a type of the transcontinental railway systems of the United States—the result, and reactively the cause of industrial conditions of the greatest moment—can hardly fail to be productive of more than passing benefit. The internal development of the Union Pacific and its relations to the individual citizen have been so similar to those of other American railways that little space will be given to them in these pages; its relations to the whole people and to the United States, the political embodiment of the people, will receive most attention.

It will be found that the Union Pacific is an exceptional manifestation of a rapidly expanding people's economic need of industrial instruments, and of its willingness to overleap political barriers to obtain them and strain legal principles to control them. The agencies through which this particular instrument was obtained and applied to use will be found seriously out of harmony with settled political and moral principles, and the latter distended and strained to subserve unusual industrial purposes. Finally, settled principles of law will be found to have been inadequate in this case to attain the ends of abstract justice, and the term justice itself to have been offered a new and strange definition in response to the demand of a dangerous industrial outgrowth. In the uncertain groping of statesmen, jurists and "industrial captains," manifestoes and edicts in place of laws and judgments, and "manipulations" in place of free individual activity, have afforded convincing proof of the obscurity in which the relations of social principles are involved.

The present practical question of the Pacific railway debt is of the highest importance in that it involves the possible loss to the United States of one hundred and twenty-five millions of dollars, with the dangerous alternative of a radical departure from the previous industrial policy of the government and people of the United States. If one hopes to discover a true solution of the question, it is only by a scientific study of the subject in its origin, development and present status.

CHAPTER I

GENESIS OF THE PACIFIC RAILWAY.

THOUGH the idea of uniting the Atlantic and Pacific by a railway, or system of railways, or connecting railways and waterways, may have occurred to several minds in different places at about the same time, and though it was the natural result of industrial and political conditions, it was probably first given public expression in the *Emigrant*, a weekly newspaper published at Ann Arbor, Michigan (Territory) from November 18, 1829, to December 1, 1834. The writer of the article, found in the editorial columns of number XII. of Volume III., issued February 6, 1832, is unknown, though it should probably be accredited to Judge S. W. Dexter, the publisher and one of the editors of the paper. Under the title of "Something New," the unknown writer, after a quite profuse apology for suggesting a scheme that might be regarded by an incredulous public as chimerical and visionary, and after consoling himself with the reflection that "it is nobler to fail in a great undertaking than to succeed in a small one," elaborates his proposed scheme in the following paragraphs :

"The distance between New York and the Oregon is about three thousand miles,—from New York we could pursue the most convenient route to the vicinity of Lake Erie, thence along the south shore of this lake and of Lake Michigan, cross the Mississippi between forty-one and forty-two of north latitude, cross the Missouri about the mouth of the Platte, and thence on by the most convenient route to the Rocky Mountains, near the source of the last named river, thence to the Oregon, by the valley of the

13

south branch of that stream, called the southern branch of Lewis' river."[1]

"We hope the United States will not object to conducting this national project. . . . . . But if the United States would not do this . . . . . Congress would not, we presume, object to the organization of a company and a grant of three millions of acres for this purpose."

This article was to be the first of a series of articles,[2] but the succeeding articles, if published, cannot be found, though many of the later issues of the paper are lost or destroyed and the writer's intention may have been executed.[3]

Soon after the appearance of the article in the *Emigrant*, Samuel Bancroft Barlow, a practising physician at Granville, Massachusetts, contributed to the *Intelligencer*, a newspaper published at Westfield, Massachusetts, an article in which he proposed the execution of the project of a railway to the Pacific by the following means:

" I have a method to propose by which this work can be accomplished by our general government at the expense of the Union." " Let preliminary measures be taken for three years to come, such as making examinations, surveys, lines, estimates, etc., etc., at the end of which time, the public debt being paid, the national treasury overflowing (I presume also that the present duties and taxes, indeed every source of revenue, be continued at their present rates), then let the work proceed with all possible and prudent speed and vigor, to a speedy and perfect completion, and let six, eight, ten, twelve, or fifteen millions

---

[1] It is remarkable how closely this suggested line has been followed in later days. Beginning at New York, the line would be by the Erie or New York Central and Hudson River to Buffalo, the Lake Shore to Chicago, one of the Chicago-Omaha lines to Omaha, and the Union Pacific and its Oregon short line to Ogden and Portland. See map (1) at end of volume.

[2] The article concludes, "we shall examine this subject more in detail in some future number."

[3] The original files of the *Emigrant*, or such of them as it has been possible to find, are among the collections of the Washtenaw County Pioneer Association, at Ann Arbor, Michigan.

of dollars of the public money be appropriated to defray the expense annually until it is finished."[1]

Lewis Gaylord Clarke, in an article in the *Knickerbocker Magazine*, in 1836, claimed the honor of having originated the idea of a Pacific railway.

The claim of Lalburn W. Boggs, once governor of Missouri, has been advanced by his son, W. N. Boggs, of California, who has an article written by his father in 1843 for the *Saint Louis Republican*, but never published, in which the author urged the building of a Pacific railway and presented an estimate of the cost.[2]

In a speech delivered in Saint Louis in 1844, Thomas H. Benton predicted that men full grown at that time would yet see Asiatic commerce crossing the Rocky Mountains by rail.[3]

In *Hunt's Merchants' Magazine* for January, 1845 (Volume XII., page 80), the editor, in discussing the commercial relations between England and China, predicts, "Those persons are now

---

[1] Dr. Barlow's article may be found quoted in full in E. V. Smalley's History of the Northern Pacific Railway, pages 52-56. The first paragraph is as follows : " An able writer in the *Emigrant*, ... in a series of numbers of which it has fallen to my lot to see only the first, is endeavoring to draw the attention of the public to the scheme of uniting New York and the mouth of the Columbia River by railroad." But with reference to the priority of the two articles in the *Emigrant* and *Intelligencer*, Mr. Smalley observes : " Evidently the article was written as early as 1834 and perhaps in 1833, and the articles in a Michigan paper to which it refers are supposed to have been called out by others previously written by him." (History of Northern Pacific Railway, page 52). And later he adds : " Perhaps there were earlier advocates of a Pacific railway than Dr. Barlow, but if so, the author of this volume has not been able to identify them, and therefore accords to him the first place." In the face of Dr. Barlow's own acknowledgment, however, it is difficult to find a justification of Mr. Smalley's statement. To this unwarranted conclusion by Mr. Smalley, attention was also called by General Granville M. Dodge in a valuable paper on Transcontinental Railways, read by him before the Society of the Army of the Tennessee at its twenty-first annual reunion at Toledo, Ohio, September 15, 1888.

[2] Bancroft, History of California, Volume VII., page 500, note.

[3] Ibid.

living who will see a railroad connecting New York with the Pacific, and a steam communication from Oregon to China."[1]

In 1835, Rev. Samuel Parker, a missionary sent out by a Presbyterian church in Ithaca, New York, to convert the Indians in Oregon and on the Pacific coast, wrote in his journal after he had crossed the Rocky Mountains : "There would be no difficulty in the way of constructing a railroad from the Atlantic to the Pacific Ocean, there is no greater difficulty in the whole distance than has already been overcome in passing the Green Mountains between Boston and Albany ; and probably the time may not be far distant when tours will be made across the continent, as they have been made to Niagara Falls to see Nature's wonders."[2]

In 1838, the idea of a Pacific railway had ceased to be novel and the execution of the project was freely suggested, predicted, and urged in newspapers and magazines from that time.

The timidity with which the project of a Pacific railway was suggested by the early writers may be pardoned when it is considered that the Stockton and Darlington railway had been open only since 1825, and the Liverpool and Manchester railway only since 1829, that there was not a mile of railway in New England until 1834, and that the Baltimore and Ohio was still considered an experiment in 1840.[3]

In a memorial presented by Robert Mills to Congress in 1845,

[1] See also Volume XVII., page 385 (October, 1847), of the same magazine, where reference is made to the efforts of Whitney to accomplish the object.

[2] Quoted in History of Northern Pacific Railway, E.V. Smalley, pages 43-44.

[3] The following table shows the number of miles of railway built in the United States in each year before 1836 :

	1830	1831	1832	1833	1834	1835	Total.
Maine	....	....	....	....	....	2.00	2.00
Massachusetts	....	....	....	....	31.60	64.55	96.15
New York	....	22.20	21.41	10.59	36.61	20.82	111.63
New Jersey	....	....	34.17	15.07	27.00	....	76.24
Pennsylvania	14.80	30.00	41.04	3.00	91.64	4.20	184.68
Maryland and District Columbia	15.00	46.50	11.00	....	12.00	31.00	115.50
Virginia	....	....	31.68	27.32	....	....	59.00
South Carolina	10.00	....	52.00	75.00	....	....	137.00
Ohio	....	....	....	....	...	15.25	15.25
Total	39.80	98.70	191.30	130.98	198.85	137.82	797.45

in which the author asked Congress to appropriate money for testing the qualities of an improved form of roadway, he claimed to have " had the honor of being perhaps the first in the field to propose to connect the Pacific with the Atlantic by a railway from the head navigable waters of the noble rivers disemboguing into each ocean " in a book published in 1819. In his memorial, he discouraged the use of railways as being expensive to build, unable to ascend steep grades, and slow ; in place of them he proposed the building of improved public roads, over which " steam carriages " as well as other vehicles might be propelled or drawn. In his memorial he advocated the construction of such a road from the mouth of the Platte River over the Rocky Mountains near the source of the Missouri River and thence to the head of navigation on the Columbia River. He can hardly be regarded as the advocate of a Pacific *railway*.

Bancroft is authority for the statement that, in 1832, Hartwell Carver, of Rochester, New York (grandson of Jonathan Carver, the early explorer of the Northwest), published articles in the New York *Courier and Enquirer* in favor of a transcontinental railway with its western terminus on the Columbia River, and that he afterwards memorialized Congress in behalf of such a project from 1835 to 1839. He is said to have asked Congress to grant him and his associates a perpetual and exclusive charter for a railway and telegraph from Lake Michigan to the South Pass and branches to San Francisco and the Columbia River, with a sufficient land grant and the privilege of purchasing eight millions of acres of selected public lands at $1.25 per acre, to be paid for in stock of the company as fast as the railway and telegraph should be completed ; the time of travel from New York to San Francisco was estimated at five days, and the trains were to be provided with sleeping cars sixteen feet long, and saloon and dining cars.[1] An article on the subject by Carver is found published in the *Courier and Enquirer* in 1837.

[1] See Bancroft's History of California, Volume VII., pages 498–499. This claim appears to have been made later by Carver himself, and is doubtful of verification. Smalley, in his History of the Northern Pacific, rejects it (page 52). The proceedings of Congress contain no record of the alleged memorials.

2

John Plumbe, of Dubuque, Iowa, advocated in a pamphlet in 1836, a railway from Lake Michigan to Oregon, and a meeting of his townsmen was held in March, 1838, for the consideration of his scheme. On the anniversary of that meeting, another meeting, held in Dubuque in 1847, and presided over by Plumbe himself, resolved "that this meeting regard John Plumbe, Esquire, our fellow-townsman, as the original projector (about nine years ago) of the great Oregon railroad."[1] In 1840, Plumbe is said to have visited Washington with a memorial from the legislature of Wisconsin, praying for an appropriation of alternate sections of public land on each side of a prospective railway to be constructed by a company composed of all who should desire to participate in the work, with a capital of $100,000,000.00 divided into 200,000 shares of $500.00 each, payable in installments of twenty-five cents as often as needed until the railway should be completed at the rate of one hundred miles per annum ; this scheme is said to have been defeated by the opposition of Southern representatives.[2]

The history of great and novel projects is much the same. First is the timid suggester, expressing his ideas cautiously, regarded by most people as hair-brained, and giving vent to his innovations in articles in obscure publications ; next in line is the zealous agitator, overstepping in his enthusiasm the bounds of common sense, moving about among the people and advocating ridiculous means of promoting the projects ; then last comes— sometimes slow, but always sure—the great mass of humanity with a consensus of opinion not far from the right and with the energy to enforce it.

In this study of the Union Pacific Railway, the period of *invention* or *inception*, exemplified in the writer in the *Emigrant*, has been passed, and the period of *agitation* and *ferment*, exemplified in Asa Whitney, will properly follow in the next chapter.

[1] Bancroft, History of California, Volume VII., page 499.

[2] Ibid, pages 499-500.

CHAPTER II.

ASA WHITNEY.

A NARRATIVE of the life of Asa Whitney from 1840 to 1850 is the history of the development, during that period, of the Pacific Railway project. The aim and object of his life was the building of a railway from Lake Michigan or the Mississippi River to the Pacific Ocean, and he devoted his fortune and energies to that aim and object with all the zeal and persistence of a fanatic. He was a merchant in New York City, and had spent some years in China, Japan and the East. In the second memorial presented by him to Congress in 1846, he says that while riding on the Liverpool and Manchester Railroad in England, in 1830, and observing the speed and facility with which its work was done, he foresaw the great future of railways, and predicted the important part they would perform in abbreviating the distance between China and the markets of England. In 1842, while on a voyage to China, his attention was more forcibly called to the matter by information of the recent conclusion of a peace with China, and the opportunity afforded by it for a more extensive commerce. He spent about two years thereafter in China, during which time he accumulated much information concerning the commerce of the East; and in 1844 he returned to America fully impressed with the importance of constructing a Pacific railway.

Whitney did not look upon his scheme purely and simply as a business project, but crowned it with the halo of an enthusiastic's fancy. In a pamphlet published by him in 1849, he describes his attitude in the following words: "My desire and object have been to carry out and accomplish this great work for the motives, as here and everywhere else by me declared, to give my

19

country this great thoroughfare for all nations without the cost of one dollar; to give employment to and make comfortable and happy millions who are now destitute and starving, and to bring all the world together in free intercourse as one nation. If it is feared that the remuneration will be disproportionate to the extent and importance of the work, then I am ready to relinquish any claim I may have for compensation, and let the people give me anything or nothing, as they please. If they will but allow me to be their instrument to accomplish this great work, it is enough; I ask no more. I am willing to have my acts scanned, but I feel that I ought not to be doubted when I say that what I have done, and what I propose to do, is not for the gain of wealth, or power, or influence, but for the great good which I am persuaded it must produce to our whole country. I have undertaken this mighty work because I know someone's whole life must be sacrificed to it."[1]

He first brought the project to the attention of Congress, January 28, 1845, in a memorial presented by him to the Senate through Senator Dickinson, and to the House of Representatives through Congressman Pratt. Whitney's plan, as set out in this memorial, was to build a railway from Lake Michigan to the mouth of the Columbia River in Oregon, though he afterwards modified his plan, when Wisconsin had become a state, so that it should begin at Prairie du Chien and end at Puget's Sound; and he was even willing to modify it in later days, when California had become a part of the United States, so that it should begin at almost any point on the Mississippi and end at San Diego, San Francisco, the mouth of the Columbia, or Puget's Sound, on the Pacific Coast.[2] His plan for building the railway was unique and visionary. He estimated that the railway would cost $50,000,000.00, and that incidental expenses and expenses of management till completion would amount to $15,000,000.00. The public domain was to be the source of the means needed for

[1] Quoted in Report of Committee on Roads and Canals, H. R. Reports, 1st Session, 31st Congress, 140.

[2] See map (1) at end of volume.

the work, and the railway, when completed, was to be Whitney's private property, but practically free, though such tolls and fares were to be charged as would be sufficient to pay the expenses of maintenance and management. Whitney's idea of the ownership of his railway was peculiar. He expected that for some years the railway would not pay expenses, but was willing to undertake its management until it should pay expenses, and then submit it to the control of the general government; if there should be any surplus of earnings over expenses, he expected it to be devoted to educational and other public purposes. "Your memorialist is induced to pray," he concludes, "that your honorable body will grant to himself, his heirs and assigns, such tract of land[1] the proceeds of which to be strictly and faithfully applied to the building and completing the said railroad, always with such checks and guarantees to your honorable body as shall secure a faithful performance of all the obligations and duties of your memorialist, and that, after the faithful completion of this great work, should any lands remain unsold, any money due for lands, or any balance of moneys received for lands sold, and which have not been required for the building of this road, then all and every of them shall belong to your memorialist his heirs and assigns forever."

The weakest point in Whitney's scheme was the colonization feature of it, by which he expected to make his land-grant produce the means of building the railway. "It is proposed," he dreams, "to establish an entirely new system of settlement, on which the hopes of success are based, and on which all depends. The settler on the line of the road, would, as soon as his house or cabin were up and a crop in, find employment to grade the road. The next season, when his crop will have ripened, there would be a market for it at his door by those in the same situation as himself the season before. If any surplus, he would have the road at low tolls to take it to market ; and if he had in the first instance paid for the land, the money would go back, directly or indirectly,

[1] A strip of land sixty miles wide, thirty miles on each side of the railway, from Lake Michigan to the Pacific.

for labor and materials for the work; so that in one year the settler would have his home, with settlement and civilization surrounding, a demand for his labor, a market at his door for his produce, a railroad to communicate with civilization and markets, without having cost one dollar. And the settler who might not have means in money to purchase land, his labor on the road and a first crop would give him that means; and he would in one year have his home, with the same advantages, and equally independent."

When Whitney's scheme was cast in the form of proposed legislation, as in the bill favorably reported by the Committee on Roads and Canals in the House of Representatives in March, 1850, the following were the principal provisions: Whitney was to have the right of way of two hundred feet through the public lands from any point he should select on Lake Michigan or the Mississippi River to any point on the Pacific Ocean at which a good harbor could be secured, and the railway was to be built as nearly as possible in a straight line. A strip of public land sixty miles in width (thirty miles on each side of the railway) was to be withdrawn from sale and to be sold to Whitney for ten cents per acre, and as fast as each section of ten miles of railway should be completed, Whitney was to have power to contract for the sale of the first strip of sixty miles by five miles (*i.e.*, one half of the first ten-mile strip of his grant) and the government was to issue patents to the purchasers; but if the price at which Whitney should sell the land should net an average of seventy-two cents per acre, and should exceed the outlay for the construction of the ten miles of railway, the excess was to be held by the government for application on the construction of the railway where the lands should prove to be less valuable. And whenever sums realized from the sale of the first strips of five by sixty miles, together with any accumulated excess, should prove insufficient to pay the expenses of constructing the railway, enough of the second strips should be sold in like manner to reimburse Whitney's actual outlay, and this latter sale should be by public auction in lots of from forty to one hundred and sixty acres, under the direction of a commissioner of the government. The railway and all machinery and other property connected with it should be forfeited by Whitney if he should fail to complete his work. While the work should be in progress, United States mails (but not foreign mails) should be carried free of charge, while for private passengers and freight only such tolls should be charged as were charged on the principal railways of the United States, to be established and regulated by Congress. Upon the completion of the railway, all unsold lands in the strips granted to Whitney were to be held by the government as a pledge for the operation of the railway for ten years, or until such time as the tolls of the railway should pay its expenses. "After said road shall be completed, the Congress of the United States shall have power to establish and regulate its tolls or charges for freight or passengers forever after, and it being intended that this road shall be a free public highway, as far as practicable, for the equal and common benefit of all the people of the United States, the rates of said tolls shall be such as to yield a reserve merely sufficient to keep said road in repair, and to defray the necessary expenses of its operation, superintendence and other charges, including the sum of four thousand dollars per annum to be allowed said Whitney and his assigns for the care and superintendence of said road." "All that part of the route for said road which is not within a state, but territory of and under the jurisdiction of the United States, the said road, its machinery, and appurtenances, shall be exempt from taxation forever; and this exemption shall be continued on admitting any of such territory to be a state of this Union." The interests of the government were to be protected and represented by a commissioner appointed by the President; in case of disagreement between Whitney and the commissioner, each was to select a competent engineer whose decision should be final; in case of a disagreement between the engineers, they were to select a third engineer whose decision should be finally final. Whitney was to be permitted to cut timber and get stone, fuel and other materials from any unsold government lands convenient to the railway. Whitney and his assigns were to locate and survey at least two

hundred miles of railway from the eastern terminus, and to complete at least ten miles of the railway, within two years; and the
entire route was to be located and surveyed, and one-third of the
railway completed, within nine years from the passage of the act;
one other third should be made and completed within six years
thereafter; and the entire railway should be completed and ready
for use within twenty-five years from the passage of the act.[1]

The first memorial was presented to Congress too late for any
action, and Congress adjourned without having considered Whitney's scheme. Soon afterwards Whitney, with a party of seven
young men, went on an exploring expedition from Prairie du Chien
westward across the great bend of the Missouri and southward
and eastward down the Missouri to Saint Louis, where he arrived
September 20, 1845, more enthusiastic than ever in the prosecution of his project. He now began a systematic bombardment
of Congress directly and indirectly through every available means
of affecting public opinion. He conversed with every public man
that he could reach, and wrote letters to others out of reach,
sought the general public through published letters and newspaper articles, and spent much effort in Washington in personal intercourse with everyone that would take an interest in his great project. He prevailed on the learned and studious in magazine articles and pamphlets. Each session of Congress found his scheme
bobbing up in each House. He visited all the great cities in the
country from Boston to Saint Louis and Memphis and held public meetings in them.

The nature of these public meetings is well shown by William
D. Kelley, in his description of a meeting held in Philadelphia,
on the 23d day of December, 1846 (found in an address
delivered in the Academy of Music, June 12, 1871, on the "New
Northwest" in the interest of the Northern Pacific Railway, and
published in the "Speeches, Addresses, and Letters on Industrial
and Financial Questions, by William D. Kelley, M. C.").

"The grandeur of the subject inspired me, and my enthusiasm
for the great project induced Mr. Whitney, despite the disparity

[1] House of Representatives Reports, 31st Congress, 1st Session, 140.

of our years, to favor me with frequent conferences, and to bring to my attention whatever information relating to the subject he obtained. Early in the year 1846, I felt justified, by the growth of sentiment in its favor, in undertaking to secure him an opportunity to present his subject to a public meeting of the citizens of Philadelphia.

"To induce a sufficient number of the citizens to act as officers of the meeting was the work of time. I found but few who took an interest in the subject, or believed in the feasibility of the project. Some said that a railroad so far north would not be available for as many months in the year as the Pennsylvania canals were; that it would be buried in snow more than half the year. Others cried, 'What madness to talk of a railroad more than two thousand miles long through that wilderness, when it was impossible to build one over the Alleghanies!'

"As I went from man to man with invaluable collections of facts and figures Mr. Whitney had gathered, I found that the doubts with which the work must contend were infinite in number; and it was not until six months had elapsed that a sufficient number of well-known citizens to constitute the officers of the meeting had consented to sign the call for a meeting and to act as such.

"Yet the cause had gained adherents, and, as I find by reference to the papers of that day, the meeting for which I had so long labored was held in the Chinese Museum on the evening of December 23, 1846.

"His Honor, John Swift, then mayor of the city, acted as president; Colonel James Page, Hons. Richard Vaux, William M. Meridith, and John F. Belstering, together with Mr. David S. Brown and Mr. Charles B. Trego, acted as vice-presidents; and Senator William A. Crabb and William D. Kelley, acted as secretaries. The speakers at the meeting were Messrs. Whitney, Josiah Randall, Peter A. Brown, and William D. Kelley.

"Mr. Whitney stated with great clearness his project and the advantages that would result from it. It was, he said, to be a railroad from Lake Michigan to Oregon. He believed it would be constructed on a line about 2400 miles in length, and he and his associates hoped to be able to build it in twenty years if the government would grant sixty miles breadth of land for the whole distance.

"In answer to the question how he could make land in that remote wilderness available for building a road, he dwelt upon the contrast between the climate of that country and that with which dwellers east of the Mississippi were familiar, and asserted fearlessly that a railroad through that section would be less disturbed by snow than one through central New York or Pennsylvania, and proceeded to disclose his plan, which involved a large annual emigration from Europe and the cities of the eastern states. His plan was to employ these emigrants in the construction of the road, and to pay them, in part, in land, and to detail a sufficient number to prepare small portions of the farm of each for cultivation and occupation, so that they who worked upon the road one year should dwell upon its borders as farmers thereafter. By this method he believed that by the time the road should be built the line of it should be tolerably well settled, and a large local traffic created.

"Josiah Randall, Esq., submitted to the meeting a series of resolutions which were heartily adopted, and from which I quote the following :

"'Whereas, the completion of a railroad from Lake Michigan to the Pacific would secure the carrying of the greater portion of the commerce of the world to American enterprise, and open to it the markets of Japan and the vast empire of China, of all India, and of all of the islands of the Pacific and Indian Oceans, together with those of the western coast of Mexico and South America ;

"'And, whereas, we have in our public lands a fund sufficient for and appropriate to the construction of so great and beneficent a work ; and the proposition of Asa Whitney, Esq., of New York, to construct a railroad from Lake Michigan to the Pacific for the grant of a strip of land sixty miles wide, offers a feasible and cheap, if not the only, plan for the early completion of an avenue from ocean to ocean ; therefore,

"'Resolved, that we cordially approve of the project of Asa Whitney, Esq., for the construction of a railroad to the Pacific, and respectfully petition Congress to grant or set apart, before the close of the present session, the lands prayed for by Mr. Whitney, for this purpose.'"

Of a meeting held in New York City, on the 4th day of January, 1847, the *Courier and Enquirer*, then the principal newspaper of that city, had to say : " The public meeting advertised to be held in the Tabernacle last evening for the purpose of considering the expediency of commending to the consideration of Congress the projected railroad to the Pacific, was turned into a bear-garden tumult by a packed party of Agrarians, National Reformers, Fourierites, etc., who seem to think that the public lands of the United States have no other legitimate use or purpose than to be distributed without money and without price among the landless of the Universe, who may come here to clutch a portion of the plunder."[1] With reference to the same meeting, E. V. Smalley (in his History of the Northern Pacific Railroad, page 59) adds : " Whitney had hardly begun speaking when he was interrupted with calls for Shepherd, a young lawyer then popular with the turbulent classes. Ryckman, then a candidate of the National Reformers for some city office, mounted the platform and began a harangue denouncing Whitney's project, and claiming the public lands as the property of the people, not to be given over to any set of speculators.

" There was a great uproar in the audience, and the mayor and the vice-president prudently seized their hats and overcoats, and escaped by a back door, Mr. Whitney presumably following after. The mob had the hall to themselves for a time, until at last the gas was turned off, amid the shoutings of an Irish agrarian orator named Comerford."

And William D. Kelley, on the same subject, says : "On the

[1] Quoted on page 59, E. V. Smalley's History of the Northern Pacific Railroad.

4th of January, 1847, he addressed an immense meeting in the Tabernacle, New York, which was presided over by the mayor and participated in by the leading men of that city. His remarks were listened to, but at their close a mob took possession of the hall and denounced the project as a swindle, declaring that it was an attempt on the part of a band of conspirators to defraud the people by inducing the government to make an immense grant of land for an impracticable project."[1]

In May, 1845, *Niles' National Register*[2] was willing to concede that Whitney's scheme was "seriously entertained by some of the public journals;" and when he began his exploration, in 1845, of the country west of Prairie du Chien, the same journal[3] denominated him "that prince of projectors." Senator Bell testified of him in Congress when assailed by Benton, that he had "conversed with him (Whitney) and had found him modest and intelligent." Even the London *Times* gave serious consideration to his project, though without endorsing it. Whitney had visited and memorialized nearly every state legislature in the country, and had secured from them resolutions in support of his plan that were later presented to Congress by the senators and representatives of the several states ; and in 1850 he was able to boast that his memorial to Congress was backed by the favorable resolutions of Maine, New Hampshire, Vermont, Rhode Island, Connecticut, New York, New Jersey, Pennsylvania, Ohio, Michigan, Maryland, Tennessee, Kentucky, and Indiana, as well as by resolutions of public meetings at Jefferson (Indiana), Cincinnati, Louisville, Terre Haute, Indianapolis, Dayton, Wheeling, and Philadelphia.

But after all, Whitney's scheme was visionary and could not be successful ; mature public opinion finally passed judgment on it and rejected it, though it retained all that was good in it in the plan that was finally carried into effect. What was really accomplished by Whitney seems to have been fully appreciated

[1] Speeches, Addresses, and Letters, by William D. Kelley, M. C., page 458.
[2] Volume 68, No. 11.
[3] Volume 68, No. 20.

and expressed in the report of the Committee on Roads and Canals of the House of Representatives in 1850 : " Mr. Whitney has been unremittingly engaged at his own expense since 1841, in collecting information on this subject, as well in Asia as in our own country ; and we are indebted to him for the origination of the project, for the maturity of the first plan, for the large amount of practical information that is brought to bear on the subject, and for awakening public attention to its importance.[1]"

In the 28th Congress, in January, 1845, Mr. Whitney's first memorial was presented to both houses of Congress by Representative Zadock Pratt, of Prattsville, New York, an enthusiastic convert to Whitney's project, but no action was taken on it.[2]

In the 29th Congress, a second memorial was presented by Whitney to Congress, and in the Senate was referred to the Committee on Public Lands (Senator Breese, Chairman), from whom a bill was reported in favor of Whitney's project on the 31st of July, 1846.[3] In the House of Representatives, the Committee on Roads and Canals, to whom Whitney's memorial and other communications of divers persons had been referred, reported that " while the prudent and sober-minded would, probably, be unwilling to see the revenues or the property of the nation pledged or in any way committed to the construction of a

[1] House of Representatives Reports, 31st Congress, 1st Session, Number 140.

[2] See " Zadock Pratt's Letter to the People of the United States," published in the *National Intelligencer* and *The Union*, at Washington, and in *Hunt's Merchants' Magazine* for October, 1847 (Volume XVII., page 385). In the *American (Whig) Review* for April, 1845 (Volume I., page 424) is an exhaustive consideration of the memorial presented to Congress by Whitney. The writer says : "We have no more of doubt but that Mr. Whitney's project will be realized, than we have that steam is now amongst the great agents of human power, or that Clinton's canals are now amongst the great highways of our country. In fine, we have lived to hear street-corner wits amusing themselves on the folly of railroads ; but, though we cannot hope to enjoy such a jaunt, many, we have no doubt, are the children now in life, who will pass on railroads from the tide-margin of the Atlantic to the tide-margin of the Pacific."

[3] The Breese report is considered with approval in *Hunt's Merchants' Magazine* for November, 1846 (Volume XV., page 477).

costly railroad, ... it is believed that they would cheerfully assist to open an eligible avenue, if one could be assured at a small cost compared to the object to be realized."

In the first session of the 30th Congress, on January 17, 1848, Senator Felch presented Asa Whitney's third memorial to Congress, and it was referred to the Committee on Public Lands; on the 26th of June, 1848, this committee reported a joint resolution for a survey and exploration of one or more routes for a railroad from the Mississippi below the Falls of St. Anthony to the Pacific Ocean, under the direction of the Secretary of War. On the next day (June 27, 1848) Senator Niles, having learned that the Committee on Public Lands would not report a bill in favor of the Whitney project, introduced a bill in favor of the grant of land prayed for, and had it referred to a select committee of Senators Niles, Corwin, Lewis, Dix and Felch; the bill was favorably reported back to the Senate with amendments on the 7th of July, 1848. Senator Niles moved for the consideration of the bill, but the motion was lost by a vote of 27 to 21, largely through the "boisterous and unparliamentary" opposition of Senator Benton. In the same session, a select committee in the House of Representatives reported a bill similar to the Niles bill in the Senate, but it was referred to the Committee of the Whole, and nothing further was done.[1] In the second session of the 30th Congress, January 29, 1849, Senator Niles succeeded in getting his bill up for

[1] See letter of Asa Whitney to Freeman Hunt, editor of *Hunt's Merchants' Magazine*, published in November, 1848, in Volume XIX. (page 527) of that periodical. He asserts that "Should the bill be passed at the early part of the coming session of Congress, the work may be carried out, though not without great difficulties, much increased by the large amount of lands sold or taken up during the present year. After another season it would be impossible. Therefore with the failure of this bill must end forever all hope for the accomplishment of this great work," on his plan. This letter also contains a review by Whitney of the work of the first session of the 30th Congress, and a defense against the violent and unjustifiable attack made by Benton on his project and the motives of the projector. See also exhaustive review of the report of this select committee of the House (Pollock, Chairman) in the *Democratic Review* for November, 1848, (Volume XXIII. page 405).

consideration, but before a vote was reached it became apparent that the local interests of the senators would not permit the passage of the bill; and on the 7th of February, 1849, Benton introduced a rival bill for a "National Central Highway" from Saint Louis to San Francisco, with a branch to Oregon west of the Rocky Mountains. Benton's scheme was for the reservation of a strip of land one mile in width from Saint Louis to San Francisco, and one thousand feet wide for the Oregon branch, on which were to be built railways and wagon roads to be paid for by the receipts from the sales of public lands, seventy-five per cent being reserved for that purpose from sales in California and Oregon, and fifty per cent from all other sales of lands. The railway was to be leased to such persons as should by contract with the government undertake to carry persons and articles at reasonable rates, to be agreed upon. In the same session Senator Houston introduced a bill authorizing the Galveston and Red River Railroad Company to construct and extend a railway to the coast of the Pacific Ocean in California. Nothing beyond reference to committees was done with these bills. It had become painfully plain that the local and sectional question of the eastern terminus of the Pacific railway would make it impossible to unite the majority of members of either House of Congress on a single line of railway, and would make any project on which a majority could be united too extensive to receive the support of conservative statesmen. A resolution introduced by Davis (Mississippi) late in the session for the survey of routes from the Mississippi to the Pacific was not acted on, but in the Army Appropriation bill at the end of the session $50,000 was appropriated for that purpose; the appropriation was not used, however, and was allowed to lapse.

The year 1849 was the year of great railroad conventions, and marks the high-water mark of Whitney's project. The agitation of the conventions simply crystallized sectional and local interests, while liberal bounty laws disposed of the public land on which the success of Whitney's plan was based. In this year he published a book in which was embodied, in a complete form, all his accumulated information on the subject of a Pacific railway and all the details of his plan.[1]

In the 31st Congress (1st session) all the memorials, petitions and bills presented in Congress were referred to the Committee on Roads and Canals in each House, and each Committee made an exhaustive report in favor of the grant (or sale on nominal terms) of land to Asa Whitney for the construction of his railway. But sectional feeling had become too strong to permit action on either report. The two reports, however, received ample attention from the country.[2]

[1] *Project for a Railroad to the Pacific*, by Asa Whitney, of New York. Printed by George W. Wood, Number 15 Spruce street, New York. See article on "The Great Pacific Railroad" in the *American (Whig) Review*, for July, 1849 (Volume X., page 6), which is really a favorable review of Whitney's book, and concludes (of his plan) "its boldness, feasibility, simplicity, and economy must commend it to universal favor." In the September number of the same periodical (Volume X., page 311) is an extended comment on the recent meeting of the New York Chamber of Commerce, in which a preference for Whitney's plan over others had been expressed in a memorial to Congress; the burden of the article is that Whitney's plan is commendable as "keeping the railroad out of politics," and that the feature of it which provides a possible profit for the projector is not objectionable. In *Hunt's Merchants' Magazine* for July, 1849 (Volume XXI., page 72) is a long article by Senator Niles in favor of the Whitney project; one in August, 1849 (Volume X., page 94) by William Derby, (author of a "*Universal Gazetteer*") in the same vein; and a third in December, 1849 (Volume X., page 616) by an "an officer of engineers" in vigorous support of a line from Texas to the Gulf of Lower California through Mexico. The route from the Gulf of Mexico to the junction of the Gila and Colorado rivers, and thence to San Francisco is also advocated in the February (1850, Volume XXII., page 146) number of the same magazine. That Whitney's project was not a "party question" (at least in the north) at this time appears from the hearty support given to it by the *Democratic Review* in September, 1849 (Volume XXV., page 243). The article particularly recommends the project as avoiding "the great evils of extending the patronage of the Government—of creating a gigantic debt, or of giving life to a corporation of dangerous magnitude."

[2] See *Democratic Review* for December, 1850, Volume XXVII., page 536, and *American (Whig) Review* for November, 1850, Volume XII., page 539. In *DeBow's Southern and Western Review* for December, 1850 (Volume IX., page 601) is an ingenious argument for the Whitney project from a Southern and slavery standpoint. "The South have generally favored Mr. Whitney's

The growth of sectionalism appeared in a modified Whitney bill reported in the 32d Congress on April 1, 1852, by the Senate Committee on Post-office and Post-roads, and providing for the setting apart and sale to Whitney of a portion of the public land to enable him to build a railway from the Mississippi to the Pacific, not north of Memphis and San Francisco, and reaching California by way of the Rio del Norte. This was the end of the Whitney project of a Pacific railway.

Whitney's entire fortune is said to have been spent in the attempt to realize his dream of a Pacific railway, and the "prince of projectors" to have kept a dairy and sold milk in Washington for a livelihood in his declining years.

The next ten years were to see the construction of a Pacific

scheme, ... but since the acquisition of California, and the increased agitation of the slavery question, she has felt a strong desire to have the road located as far south as possible. . . . . . Philanthropically and nationally, there could be no hesitancy in our opinion; and did peace and harmony exist between the North and South, the latter we believe would, with one voice, say Amen to Mr. Whitney's proposition. But as it is, the North continually aggressing upon the South, we may justly hesitate before we enter into further partnership concerns with partners whom we know to be opposed to us in every feeling and interest." Though "the route proposed [by Whitney] is all on what is termed free soil," and "the building of the road would greatly accelerate the settlement of the entire line to the Pacific, [a result that would be] prejudicial to the South, by increasing a population hostile to our institutions," yet "there is left . . . . . no choice, except to decide between Mr. Whitney's plan and no road at all," for "there is no other route which can furnish an adequate amount of land to induce Mr. Whitney to undertake the work," and "were the work to be done by the Government, ... there would arise a controversy for the location of the route that would more likely defeat all." The Southern cities could connect with the Whitney road near Chicago by the Mississippi Valley so as to "give to the South an advantage over the North." As to the new population in the West, they "being agriculturists, and desiring no protective legislation," their wants and their interests [would] be more directly connected with the South than with the North and East, ... and they would . . . . . support and strengthen the South." "In case of dissolution, the South would hold all the lands now on any Southern route; and if they could be made available for the means to build a railroad to the Pacific, it would no doubt be done, so that we cannot see how Mr. Whitney's project should be made to conflict with a Southern one or with Southern interests."

3

railway delayed and hindered by the reluctance of the Federal government to extend aid (except by grants of land) to private projectors, by the constitutional objection to the accomplishment of the work by the government itself, and by the mutual jealousies of the sections of the country contending for the eastern terminus of the railway. These tendencies, it will be found, were finally overcome only by the realization of the overwhelming necessities of the country, and an appreciation of the part to be performed by a Pacific railway in the preservation of the national existence.

CHAPTER III.

SECTIONALISM AND LOCALISM.

No SOONER was a clearly-defined Pacific railway project in existence than the particular interests of sections and localities began to interfere with its practical accomplishment. When the plan of Asa Whitney was first presented to the country, it was regarded as a distinctly national scheme, and in his view the matter of an international highway from Japan, China and Eastern Asia to England and Western Europe was the most important feature of it. Pacific coast territory of the United States in 1845 was bounded on the south by the parallel of 42° north (the southern boundary of the present state of Oregon) and was claimed by the government to extend north to the parallel of 54° 40′. California, Nevada, Utah, Arizona, New Mexico, and Texas, and portions of Colorado and Wyoming, were still a part of the territory of Mexico, and a Pacific railway built in United States territory would have had to be built along the northern route (now followed substantially by the Northern Pacific Railroad) or the route by way of South Pass, suggested in the *Emigrant* article (and now followed substantially by the Union Pacific Railway and its Oregon Short Line), and as it was regarded largely as an international highway, the natural connection would be with the Great Lakes or the system of east-and-west railways terminating at the head of Lake Michigan. Thus it is that, on the earliest map presented by Asa Whitney in explanation of his plan, the routes of the proposed railway are indicated by almost straight lines from Saint Joseph, Michigan, to the mouth of the Columbia River, one through the South Pass.[1]

When the scheme was first proposed, there was no rivalry for

[1] See Map (1) at end of volume.

the western terminus ; indeed, the population of the Pacific coast was not sufficient in numbers and strength to exert an appreciable influence on the question of route, and the question of route and western terminus became a question of expediency, within territorial limits, under the control of the projector. This was likewise true of the eastern terminus, for a time, partly because in the public mind the international highway feature of the railway was exaggerated, and its local importance not fully appreciated.[1]

But in 1845, Texas was admitted to the Union ; in 1846, the "Oregon question" was settled by establishing the boundary of the United States at the parallel of 49° north—6° 40' (or four hundred and fifty miles) south of the boundary claimed by the government of the United States. In 1848, by the territory ceded in the treaty of Guadaloupe Hidalgo, the Pacific coast line was trebled in length, and the extent of the national territory was increased towards the south so as to extend the coast line from the parallel of 31° 28' north to that of 49° north. In 1847, gold was discovered in California, and in the three years following, such a stream of population and property poured into the territory, and such a vast amount of wealth was drawn from its soil, that, in 1850, the territory became a state, and San Francisco with its superior harbor became the principal commercial center on the Pacific coast. The direct effect of this development on the project of a Pacific railway was to make it inevitable that the western terminus should be at San Francisco.[2] In the decade from 1850 to 1860, in which sectionalism and localism were engaged in "drawing and quartering" the Pacific railway scheme,

[1] For an appreciation of the different light cast on the Pacific railway by the development of the western states and territories, compare Whitney's and Benton's ideas, as so often expressed, with the ideas of E. H. Derby, set out in his article on "The Pacific Railway" in *Hunt's Merchants' Magazine* for December, 1856 (Volume XXXV., page 659).

[2] See two interesting articles in *Hunt's Merchants' Magazine*, Volume XVIII., pages 497 and 592, May and June, 1848, to the effect that Monterey or San Francisco would be a better western terminus than Puget's Sound or the Columbia River.

and at the East a score of large cities, a dozen states, and the two great national sections were contending for the political and industrial advantage of controlling the eastern terminus of the great highway, the question of a western terminus was not raised. Oregon had no territorial government until 1848, and had no voice in Congress as a state until near the end of the decade, in 1859. San Francisco was assumed without contention to be the proper western terminus, and if the interests of Oregon were considered, they were assumed and conceded to be fully served by a branch line from the trunk of the system; during the decade the senators and representatives of California were occupied with the almost hopeless task of harmonizing and balancing the contending interests of the North and South, and of the several states and great cities east and south of the territories, while the nation as a whole was fully convinced of the political and industrial necessity of a closer connection between the Mississippi valley and the Pacific coast than was afforded by the long and dusty emigrant trail, "liberally strewn with the bleaching bones of draft-animals and the wrecks of prairie-schooners."

The prime objection to the building or initiative control of railways by a republican state, instead of by individuals, is that local and sectional demands (political as well as industrial) will cause the system built to be either too extensive or lacking in continuity and proper correlation of members. A vote of a legislative body representing an agglomeration of the contending and opposing views of numerous sections, localities, and industrial centers will always present a heterogeneous and irrational scheme for a railway system. This is particularly the case in a nation of such diversified and intensified interests as the United States, while it is only less true in centralized and unified France, England, and Belgium; in Russia, where the Czar, when asked by one of his ministers for directions as to the route of a proposed government railway, laconically indicated his desire by placing a rule upon a map, drawing a pencil line along the edge from one terminus to the other, and saying, "you can construct

the line so,"[1] homogeneity and escape from " over-building "
may be expected, but not in America, where every subject is a
sovereign, and every citizen a law-maker. This lesson is taught
by the building of the Union Pacific Railway, as that system was
planned, and, in one sense, built by the government—and that,
too, under the most favorable conditions, in many respects, for
government railway building under a republican form of government.

The decade from 1850 to 1860 was the " storm and stress "
period of the history of the Union Pacific Railway, and a review
of the course of events in Congress during that time will show
how the project was tossed about on the legislative sea by the
contending storms of local and sectional interests. But, before
entering upon a detailed review of the work in Congress, it may
be advisable to consider the separate contending interests and
their condition at the beginning of the decade.

I.

(1) What might be called the Eastern interest was the strongest interest represented. The wealth and influence of Boston,
New York, Philadelphia and Baltimore were almost a unit upon
such a location of the Pacific Railway as would make them the
outlets of its business on the Atlantic sea-board. Whitney had
been a merchant in New York City, and his scheme had received
active support from prominent public men in New York,
Pennsylvania and Massachusetts. The earliest advocates of a
Pacific railway had contemplated its connection with the east
through the railways terminating at the head of Lake Michigan.
George Wilkes, of New York, in a memorial to Congress and else-
where, had strongly advocated a route due west from Chicago
to the South Pass and thence to Oregon, differing from Whitney's
only as to the form of management under which the railroad
should be built and operated; according to his scheme, the land-

[1] This is related by D. Mackenzie Wallace, in his *Russia* (Volume I., pages
3 and 4) of the railway from Saint Petersburg to Moscow, four hundred miles
of track.

grant feature was to be discarded, and the government was to build and own the railroad and operate it through commissioners elected by the legislatures or the people of the United States. In 1849 a Pacific railway convention had been held in Chicago, in which Wilkes' plan had been indorsed in a letter from William H. Seward. Dr. Hartley Carver, an adherent of the New York interests, had published newspaper articles in favor of a Pacific railway, and in January, 1849, was an applicant to Congress for a charter under which to construct a railway from Lake Michigan to San Francisco by way of the South Pass. In January, 1850, Daniel Webster had called the attention of the Senate to the enthusiasm of the people of Boston for the project. The completion of the Erie Canal, and the building of the Pennsylvania, New York Central, New York and Erie, Baltimore and Ohio, Michigan Southern and Michigan Central railways had given this interest a strong prestige.

(2) The most persistent opponent of the Eastern interest was the Saint Louis interest, represented by the indefatigable Thomas H. Benton. His idea was that the natural point for the distribution of goods and persons transported from the west was at the head of navigation on the Mississippi River. As early as December, 1846, on motion of Senator Semple, the Committee on Roads and Canals of the Senate had been instructed to inquire into the expediency of incorporating a company to construct a railway from some point on the western border of the state of Missouri to the mouth of the Columbia River. Later William Bayard & Company, of New York, presented a memorial to Congress, in which they asked for a grant of land to enable them to build a railway from Saint Louis to California by way of the Rio Grande and Gila River. In February, 1849, Benton himself had introduced in the Senate a bill for a Pacific railway.[1] On March 20, 1850, in the discussion of one of Whitney's bills, he was openly accused of being actuated by "sectional motives" in his persistent opposition to the Whitney measure. A convention held at Saint Louis on the 16th of October, 1849, with delegates from

[1] Supra, page 31.

several states, and presided over by Stephen A. Douglas, had condemned Whitney's scheme and presented a memorial to Congress in favor of the Saint Louis interest. This convention had had a stormy session. Benton, led by John C. Fremont, had advocated a line from Saint Louis to cross the Rocky Mountains and Sierra Nevada, between the 38th and 39th parallels, but had been defeated by the wing of the convention, led by a lawyer named Loughborough, in favor of the South Pass route; the convention had adjourned to meet in Philadelphia the following year.[1] The Saint Louis interest also found some support in the plan of P. P. F. Degrand, endorsed at a meeting of "friends of a railroad to San Francisco," held in Boston in April, 1849; by this plan a company chartered by Congress, after paying in $2,000,000.00, should have a right of way (a strip of land, ten miles wide, on the north side of the track) and a loan of not more than $98,000,000.00 in government bonds secured by mortgage on the road; the route was to be from Saint Louis by the South Pass to San Francisco.

(3) Memphis was supported by a strong party, with Arkansas

[1] The work of the Philadelphia convention, held in April, 1850, is instructive. Fourteen states, of which Virginia and Texas were the only Southern states, were represented. A committee on resolutions, composed of one delegate from each state represented, could agree on no resolution having reference to routes or to means or manner of construction or control. The memorial to Congress that represented the work accomplished by the convention emphasized " the fact, that the convention has avoided all reference to particular plans . . . . . The delegates . . . . . . , . believed that a railroad from the navigable waters of the valley of the Mississippi to those of the national territory on the Pacific ocean, is practicable. That the expenditure necessary to accomplish it is within the compass of national means ; . . . . that the advantages, political, military, and commercial, to result . . . . . would be more than commensurate with the outlay required. They desire to call the early and earnest attention of [Congress] to the subject . . . . . It was the general sentiment . . . . . that the route of this great work . . . . . should be such as an impartial examination of the result of a full and accurate survey of all the lines . . . . . shall indicate as most eligible, and that the plan under which it shall be prosecuted, should be such as Congress, in its wisdom, may deem most advantageous." Conventions were as much dominated by sectional and local motives as Congress.

and Tennessee behind it. February 22, 1849, a call was made for a general convention to be held on the 4th of July following, at which were to be one hundred and twenty-five delegates from South Carolina, one hundred from Georgia, and numbers from other states. " The favorite project of these conventions (at Saint Louis and Memphis) was a grand trunk line from Fort Independence, with three branches to the Mississippi, one to Saint Louis, one to Memphis, and one to Chicago."[1]

(4) Charleston was early in the field as a seeker of the benefits of a terminus of the Pacific railway. The Mississippi party were in favor of Charleston as a terminus. In October, 1845, Colonel Gadsden, by whom the Mexican boundary was settled in behalf of the United States, in 1853, and who was a member of one of the aristocratic families that controlled the political and industrial influences of South Carolina, urged upon the people of Charleston the building of a railway to California on the route of the 32d parallel. And in the next year a formidable movement was begun by the people of Natchez to build a railway from Vidalia to Alexandria in Louisiana, as the first link in a railway from Charleston to Mazatlan in Mexico, on the Gulf of California. A modification of this scheme was promoted by Professor Forshey, who made the eastern terminus Vicksburg instead of Natchez. Whitney vigorously contested Forshey's position in an article in *DeBow's Commercial Review*,[2] in commenting on which the editors of *Niles' National Register*[3] agreed with Whitney that " the route through the South Pass is the only one which can be adopted with an equal regard to the interests of all parts of the country."

(5) Texas not only had a scheme for a railway from Corpus Christi or some other point on the Gulf of Mexico to San Francisco by way of Paso del Norte,[4] but was eager to be in the path of the

---

[1] Report of Committee on Roads and Canals, House of Representatives Reports, 31st Congress, 1st Session, Number 140.

[2] October, 1847.

[3] Volume 73, Number 8.

[4] *Niles' National Register*, Volume 73, Number 21 (1848).

railway and have a Gulf branch from the trunk line if a Mississippi river terminus should be decided on.   In January, 1849, the "citizens of the State of Texas" petitioned Congress for a "right of way" from the Rio Grande, on the western border of the state, through the national territories to the Pacific on any line south of 36° 30′ north latitude.   In the next month (February, 1849) Senator Houston introduced a bill authorizing the Galveston and Red River Railway Company to construct a railway to the Pacific Ocean in California.

Behind and beyond the separate sectional and local interests that were crystallized in the forms described, were the great political and industrial divisions of the North and South.   The South had not been slow to appreciate the advantages of railways.   The first railway in the country had been built and operated in South Carolina.   At the time when the Pacific railway project was first brought to the attention of Congress (in 1845) the United States, under the influence of Southern statesmen, were annexing Texas and giving to the South the means of extending slave territory and maintaining the equilibrium of slave states and free states in the Senate.   The historians are undoubtedly justified in concluding that the Missouri Compromise opened the eyes of the Southern leaders to the necessity of acquiring more territory in a section having an industrial soil in which the institution of slavery might be expected to take root.   Oregon and the northern part of the Louisiana Purchase and the Northwest Territory were unsuited to the purpose.   Slavery is essentially extensive and not intensive; the North had thus developed in the line of manufactures and small farming, while the South had been given over to large plantations.   Hemmed in on three sides by the Northern States, the Atlantic Ocean and the Gulf of Mexico, the further increase of slave territory and slave states had to be to the west and southwest.   "It was precisely the struggle over the Missouri question which paved the way, in the South, for the recognition of the fact that it would have to break through the southwest boundary, drawn by the Florida treaty, if it would maintain as

strong a representation in the Senate as the North."[1]   After the
acquisition of the territory, the next step was to bind it more closely
by the industrial bonds of railways.   The Pacific railway was reasonably expected to have a great influence on the growth and development of the parts of the country through which it passed ; and
the South, having already observed the superior wealth-producing
power of free labor, as compared with slave labor, and having seen
the population and wealth of the great cities of the North doubled
and the fertility of its farms increased by free labor, while the plantations of the South were "worked out" by slave labor, was anxious
positively for the stimulus of the immense trans-continental traffic
expected, and negatively, unwilling that the overbalance of the
North should be increased by it.   Suffice it to say, that in 1850, at
the beginning of the decade of "storm and stress" in Pacific railway history, the effort to make California a slave state or to divide
it into two states, a free and a slave state, was a failure.   The South
was ready to urge the repeal of the Missouri Compromise and the
North was ready to yield to it.   The decade, from a political standpoint, was to be given to a contest of freedom and slavery, in the
territories—the part of the nation to which a Pacific railway was to
give its greatest impetus—and at the end of the decade, the contest
was to be transferred from the halls of Congress to the battle fields
of the Rebellion.   In 1850, the interests of the South as a section
had already become concentrated ; the interests were rather local
than sectional.   But from 1850 to 1860, the history of the Pacific
railway can hardly be understood or appreciated without bearing
in mind the acute interest that the South had in the route and
eastern termini of the Pacific railway.

These concrete interests have been dwelt upon at some length
because it is only by holding them constantly in mind that the
development (or more properly, perhaps, the failure of development) of the Pacific railway project from 1850 to 1860 can be made
intelligible or instructive.

[1] Von Holst, Constitutional History of the United States, Volume II., page 551.

II.

In the second session of the 32d Congress (1851-1853) the Senate gave more time and attention to the subject of a Pacific railway than to any other subject. A bill "for the protection of the emigrant route and a telegraphic line, and for an overland mail between the Missouri River and the settlements in California and Oregon," reported by the Committee on Territories in the preceding session of Congress, was made a special order and taken up January 13, 1853; thereupon a bill introduced by Senator Gwin, of California, was substituted for it, the latter being "to authorize the construction of a railroad and branches, for establishing a certain postal communication between the shores of the Pacific and the Atlantic within the United States, for the protection and facilities of travel and commerce, and for the necessary defences of the country."

This bill provided for a trunk line from San Francisco through "Walker's Pass" and Albuquerque and along the Red River to Fulton in the southwest corner of Arkansas. From this trunk line a Saint Louis branch was to be extended to Independence, Missouri, from a point south of Santa Fé. From the Saint Louis branch a Dubuque branch for connection with Chicago and the Lakes was to be extended from the point where it crossed the Arkansas River. From Fulton branches were to be built to Memphis and New Orleans, and to make connection for Charleston. A Texas branch was to extend from the source of the Red River through Austin to Matagorda. An Oregon branch was planned from a point in California to Puget's Sound. The length of the trunk and branches was estimated at 5115 miles.[1] Through the territories the road was to be built by contractors designated by the President, and they were to enjoy the road for such time as should be specified in their contracts, and then surrender it to the government; through the states, the states themselves were to have the control of the construction. To provide means for the work, the contractors in the territories

[1] See map (1) at end of volume.

and the state of California were to receive alternate sections (odd numbers) for twenty miles on each side of the road.[1] If any state should not accept its grant of land and undertake the construction of the part of the road within its borders before the expiration of one year, the general government, through the President, with the consent of the state, should undertake the work in like manner as in the territories.

The first trouble with this bill was that the system contemplated by it was too extensive, and the bill had been framed to satisfy sectional and local demands. A slight consideration of the provisions of the bill will show that every one of the five great local interests had been consulted and fairly satisfied. But the mark had been overshot. Not only was the contemplated system too extensive, but the " state rights" spirit had been aroused by the effort to give the Federal government control over improvements within the " sovereign states." The ghost of the Cumberland Road stalked in the Senate. The constitutional question united with the practical question to " kill" the bill. Lewis Cass voiced the general sentiment when he said in the Senate, "No man estimates the value of this road higher than I do, and within the constitutional powers of this government all our efforts should be devoted to its construction. But . . . . it is . . . . apparent now and will yet be more apparent from day to day, that there is danger of frittering away our strength on mere local questions as to the terminations of the road. With respect to the general idea of a railroad to the Pacific, I am in favor of it, and I shall vote for it most cheerfully ; but I think I cannot vote for this bill as it is. It is entirely too magnificent for me. I want a road and for the present I want one road, and only one road, for one is all we can get now."[2] That fully describes the situation : the road was generally regarded as a necessity ; the means of building it were by the majority of the

---

[1] The bill was afterwards made to provide that to Texas, in lieu of land, should be paid the sum of $12,000.00 for each mile of the railway built within its borders. *Congressional Globe*, 32d Congress, 2d Session, page 516.

[2] Ibidem, 32d Congress, page 285.

dominant political party regarded as unconstitutional; localism was its practical weakness ; the effort to satisfy local interests had made it too extensive ; it was too " magnificent."

The bill was read section by section in Committee of the Whole, so as to permit amendments to be offered. The first amendment offered (by Adams) provided for striking out the provision for branches, to be followed, as promised by the mover, by an elimination of the provisions for a definite and settled route ; Chase made matters worse by suggesting that the amendment simply change the Eastern terminus from Fulton to some point " on the Missouri River, not below Independence, nor above Kanesville " (Council Bluffs). The amendment received only seven votes and was rejected, the contest over the routes of the railway and location of its terminus was resumed by the formal offering of the amendment already suggested by Chase, that the railway be " from San Francisco in California, by the most direct and feasible route, to some point on the Missouri River, not below Independence in Missouri, nor above Kanesville (Council Bluffs) in Iowa."[1] Saint Louis and the Eastern party were fairly content with this proposition, but it was naturally unsatisfactory to Memphis and the Southern parties, as shown by the amendment offered by Bell (Tennessee) : " That with the view of securing the speedy construction of a railroad and branches connecting the Mississippi River with the Pacific coast, at suitable points, the President of the United States is hereby authorized, with the lights afforded by the several official explorations and reconnoissances, and others which have been heretofore made, and with the aid of any such further examinations and surveys of particular mountain passes or sections of country, supposed to present obstructions of a serious nature, as he may think proper to be made hereafter, to designate the terminus and general direction of the route of a railroad to connect the valley of the *Missouri* with the state and territory of the United States on the Pacific coast, keeping in view, in making such designation, economy in cost and distance, easy grades, and at the same time the greatest

[1] See Map (1) at end of volume.

facilities for branch roads on or connections *with Lake Michigan,*
with Saint Louis, with Memphis, with New Orleans, with Mata-
gorda, and with some safe and commodious harbor on the coast
of Oregon."[1] Senator Bell frankly admitted that his reason for
submitting such an amendment was to satisfy the whole country,
though he knew that the choice of the President would necessarily
be in favor of the Memphis route.[2] His words on the amendment
are prophetic: "I trust . . . . that we shall try the question
whether we are to have one road or two, because I think I foresee
that, unless we do something of this kind, we shall at this Congress do nothing. By and by we shall be forced by dire necessity,
by the condition of the country, in the midst of difficulties, to
construct a road, wherever it may be, north or south."[3]

On the 1st day of February, 1853, the bill "for the protection
of the emigrant route, and a telegraphic line, and for an overland mail between the Missouri River and the settlements in
California and Oregon,"[4] having been referred to a Select Committee and reported back with a proposed amendment, was substituted for the bill under discussion as the special order. The
amendment proposed by the Select Committee was the substitution of a bill (the Rusk bill) differing from the Gwin bill in providing that the President, after having ascertained by the aid of
the army and civil engineers the most practicable route, should
designate the route and terminus of the railway, and should contract for the construction of it by contractors who should constitute a corporation under the name of "The Pacific Railroad and
Telegraph Company." The land grant was to be increased to

---

[1] The italicised word "*Missouri*" was afterwards changed by Senator Bell,
the author of the amendment, to "*Mississippi,*" for the obvious reason that the
restriction of the Eastern terminus to the Missouri River would militate against
Memphis. The italicised words "*with Lake Michigan, with Saint Louis, with
Memphis, with New Orleans, with Matagorda,*" were replaced, upon an application of Adams (Miss.) to have Vicksburg added to the list, by the words "*with
the Atlantic and Gulf Railroads, now completed, or in progress, or projected.*"

[2] *Congressional Globe,* 32d Congress, 2d Session, page 341.

[3]. Ibidem.

[4] Supra, page 44.

alternate sections (odd numbers) on each side of the railway for
six miles in the states and twelve miles in the territories. Twenty
millions of dollars in United States bonds, bearing interest at five
per cent. and maturing in fifty years, were to be issued in aid of
the construction of the railway, and *pro rata* payments of the whole
sum were to be made to the corporation of contractors upon the
completion of each section of fifty miles of the road. The provisions of the act proposed to be substituted were to have no force
or effect within the states without the consent of their legislatures.
There was no provision for branch lines except that Congress
might authorize individuals, companies or states to form connections between it and any other road; and the trunk lines and telegraph were to connect the valley of the Mississippi with the Pacific Ocean. The company were to afford all railway and telegraph
facilities to the government free of charge, and the government
was to have the right to require the surrender of the property and
appurtenances after thirty years from its completion, upon the
payment of the actual cost of it, with interest at ten per cent., less
the amount of bonds advanced to it. The provisions of this bill
were intended to meet all the objections that had been proposed
to the former measures. Those conservative Senators like Davis,
Brodhead, and Borland, who had complained that sufficient scientific information of the extreme West was not at hand for the establishment of the route and the terminus of the railway, would find
in the bill a provision for preliminary surveys. Sectional and local
interests were expected to be obviated by having the selection of
the route and terminus in the hands of the "representative of
the whole people." The Democratic disbelievers in government
initiative in internal improvements were to be satisfied with the
creation of a corporation for the building, owning and operating
of the railway. Statesmen like Bradbury (Maine) who had inveighed
against devoting to a western railway a portion of the public
domain greater than all New England, could not with good grace
complain of the decreased grant of *six* and twelve sections per
mile. Far-sighted Senators like Brooke and Hale, who had early
foreseen that the public domain could not be relied on for the

construction of the railway, and that soon or late the national government would have to put its own money into the project, could find in the grant of twenty millions some reasonable expectation of success. State-rights Democrats could not urge against this bill the constitutional objection that the federal government could not construct internal improvements within the limits of the "sovereign states" without their consent. But the more the amendment was discussed, the more it became apparent that the sectional and local interests involved would not permit the final passage of a Pacific railway bill, at that session of Congress. The interests in the central and northern part of the country might have been made almost unanimous if it had not been for the opposition of the extreme northern Democrats like Lewis Cass, who insisted they would never vote for a bill that gave the President such extensive powers, or permitted the expenditure of the money of the nation in furtherance of internal improvements within the states. Some extreme state-rights Senators from the South, like Mason of Virginia, openly declared they would never vote for a Pacific railway bill, as a project with which the national government had no concern. And Southern Senators in favor of the road would not vote for its location by a Northern President, even if he were a Democrat; besides, as was to be expected, Whigs and Democrats, as political parties, each wished the other to assume the responsibility of the practical carrying out of the project. A failure of such an undertaking and a great waste of public land or money, or the creation of an overtowering autocratic corporation, or the location of the route so as to unduly favor a particular section or locality, would be certain to redound to the serious injury of the party upon whom the responsibility could be placed. The memory of the Cumberland Road and the Bank of the United States "made cowards of them all." For that reason, the resistance of the Democrats to the imposition of such duties on the President was fully justified as a matter of practical politics. Franklin Pierce, by trying—however conscientiously—to execute the law, might have compassed the complete destruction of his party. When the Pacific Railway finally came to be built, by the

4

aid of the government, it was at a time when the project was more
or less justly identified with the great effort to preserve the national
life, the people had unfortunately become accustomed to the expenditure and waste of vast sums of money in national enterprises,
and what had threatened in 1853 to become the most important
sectional and partisan measure in American politics, was in 1862
and 1864 only a minor and subsidiary question of politics, concealed and hidden by the overshadowing question of national life
or death. The Cumberland Road and the Bank of the United
States had made and unmade political parties for thirty years,
but the Pacific Railway and the National Banks of 1862 and 1864
were comparatively unimportant matters; the mountains had
dwindled into comparative mole-hills beside so much greater
mountains.

Matters were even more complicated by a "corporation"
amendment offered by Senator Brooke (Mississippi), which he
moved to be substituted for the Gwin bill after the enacting clause,
providing for the issuance of United States bonds in the sum of
$30,000,000, to run thirty years, in aid of the construction of a rail-
way from the Mississippi River to San Francisco, by "the Atlantic
and Pacific Railroad Company," a corporation to be organized
under the laws of any state. If the company could not get the
consent of California, Iowa, Missouri, or Texas to build the road
through either of those states, then the road was to terminate at
the eastern or southeastern boundary of California on the west,
and at the northern boundary of Texas, or western boundary of
Iowa, Missouri or Arkansas on the east, in the discretion of the company. When the company should have finished and equipped fifty
miles of the road, it was to receive $750,000.00 in money or in the
bonds issued in its aid; and for each succeeding section of fifty
miles, until five hundred miles had been constructed and equipped,
it was to receive a like sum; and thereafter, for each five hundred
miles until the road should be finally completed, the company
was to receive $1,500,000.00. The sum thus paid to the company
was to be repaid to the government, with interest, at any time
during the thirty years; the mails were to be carried free of charge,

but all other services performed for the government should be charged for at the rate charged to individuals; the government retained the right to become the owner of the property at any time after the expiration of twenty years from its completion, upon payment to the company of the actual cost of it (less the amount due from the company to the government). No land was granted to the company except enough for the right of way and other necessary purposes of construction and operation.

But it was plain that public opinion in 1853 demanded some action on the subject of a Pacific railway, and many Senators gradually went over to the small wing of the Senate which had insisted that a properly conservative view of the subject justified Congress in going no further at that session than to provide for such surveys of the western country, between the Missouri River and the Pacific Ocean, as might be of future assistance in determining the natural and best route and terminus, whether finally determined by Congress or otherwise. Such an amendment had been offered by Brodhead (Pennsylvania) to the bill (commonly called the Rusk bill and reported by the Select Committee) proposed as a substitute for the Gwin bill, but the amendment was rejected on the 18th of February, 1853, by a vote of 22 to 34.

A crisis was reached on the following day (February 19, 1853) when Shields (Illinois) offered an amendment providing . . . . "That no portion of the $20,000,000.00 to be advanced by the United States, shall be expended in, or deemed to apply to, a road within the limits of any existing state of the Union; and so much of said road, if any, as shall be located within any state of this Union, shall be made under the authority thereof, to be derived from the state legislature, and not otherwise." This was held up as the embodiment of good Democratic doctrine, and the party lash was applied to such good purpose and with such good effect that the amendment was adopted by a vote of 22 to 20, the only Democrats voting against the amendment being from the states of the Mississippi valley and directly interested in the routes not south of Memphis. Thereupon Rusk and Gwin dramatically proclaimed that their bill was "disjointed," "destroyed," and " dead," and announced their intention of deserting the dismembered corpse of their bill without tarrying to give it decent burial. On the Monday (February 21, 1853) following the adoption of the amendment and the "death" of the bill, there was a general desire to prove that as a matter of truth, the bill was not "dead"— but still lived, and was made even stronger by the amendment. The Senators that considered the bill really "dead" hastened to lay the responsibility of the murder on other shoulders, and as the result of the efforts to shift the responsibility, the vote on the amendment was then rejected, Miller, (California), and the two Missouri Senators changing their votes. Yet a new amendment, having practically the effect to limit the application of the $20,000,000.00 to the construction of railway exclusively in the territories, was proposed by Weller (California) and adopted. Then the friends (or mourners) of the bill discovered after all they were right when they had taken the bill for "dead," and that on this last day they had mistaken galvanic twitches for evidences of vital activity. The adoption of the amendment restricting the application of the bonus to construction in the territories had made it practically impossible for the road to be built on the line through Texas and Arkansas followed in the original Gwin bill; the contractors would get no bonus for such portion of their work as passed through Texas, California, or Arkansas. The eastern terminus would have to be Independence, Saint Louis, Saint Joseph, or Council Bluffs; thus the opposition of the Texas, Memphis, Mississippi, Charleston, and New Orleans parties was again aroused, and the Senate proceeded with its wake over the corpse of the Pacific railway bill. Seward comforted and cheered the mourners by moving an amendment for the payment of $600.00 per mile per annum for carrying the mails on the portions of the line within the states, but the rest of the time was consumed by the Senators in "explaining their positions," and nothing more was heard of the Rusk bill after the adjournment of the Senate on the 22d of February.

On the following day, when the Army Appropriation Bill was taken up by the Senate, an amendment offered by Gwin (being identical with the Brodhead amendment[1]) was adopted by the Senate and afterwards concurred in by the House of Representatives on the 1st day of March, 1853. The Army Appropriation Bill was approved by the President on the last day of the session, and the sum total of the Pacific railway legislation of the 32d Congress was the provision in it added by the Gwin (or Brodhead) amendment, as follows :

" And be it further enacted, that the Secretary of War be, and, he is hereby, authorized, under the direction of the President of the United States, to employ such portion of the corps of Topographical Engineers and such other persons as he may deem necessary, to make such explorations and surveys as he may deem advisable, to ascertain the most practicable and economical route for a railroad from the Mississippi River to the Pacific Ocean, and that the sum of $150,000.00 or so much thereof as may be necessary, be, and the same is hereby, appropriated out of any money in the treasury not otherwise appropriated, to defray the expense of such explorations and surveys.

" That the engineers and other persons employed in said explorations and surveys shall be organized in as many district corps as there are routes to be surveyed, and their several reports shall be laid before Congress on or before the first Monday in February, 1854."

III.

In his annual message to Congress (first session of 33d Congress) in 1853, President Pierce referred to the Pacific railway project to the extent of a column in the *Congressional Globe*, but without saying much except by way of general recommendation of the subject to the early consideration of Congress. It is true the President made an effort to lay down some good Democratic doctrine in his message, but he qualified it with a fairly clear intimation that a strict construction of the Constitution, or the proper maintenance and protection of state rights, was not incompatible with donations of land or money, or both, by the

[1] Supra, page 51.

government to aid in the construction of a Pacific railroad, on the ground of its power " to -establish post-offices and post-roads," and " to provide for the common defence and general welfare of the United States."

In the Senate a Select Committee of nine members was appointed, with Gwin as chairman, for the consideration of all bills, propositions and communications concerning a Pacific railway ; this committee reported a bill in preparing which they had, according to Gwin, " endeavored carefully to exclude everything that might give rise to eonstitutional doubt or objection or tend in any manner to create local or sectional prejudices," and had framed a bill that "established no eastern terminus," and " gave no preference to any state in the great valley of the Mississippi—no advantage to any particular locality, except that given by nature herself." But nothing was done with this bill in the first session, and nothing serious was evidently intended by Gwin, beyond satisfying his constituents. The explorations and surveys under the supervision of the Secretary of War, according to the provisions of the Army Appropriation Act, passed at the preceding Congress, were in progress, and there was a general disposition to allow the whole matter to rest until they should be completed.

The course of matters in the House of Representatives during the session was much the same as in the Senate ; a Select Committee of thirteen members was appointed for the control of Pacific railway matters, and reported a bill, under the influence of McDougall of California, for the construction by the government of two railways, one to be not north of 37° north latitude, and the other from Lake Superior or the Mississippi River in Minnesota to the Pacific Ocean. Such a bill could not have become a law, even if seriously urged by McDougall ; nothing was done with the bill, except to arouse bitter opposition to it from the members representing Indiana, Michigan, Ohio, and New York, and the other states interested in the Eastern party.

By this time, some change had taken place in the attitude of the several parties. The influence of the Mississippi River and the Allegheny Mountains on the problem must be understood in order to get any benefit from a review of the events in Congress during the last half of the sixth decade. It was assumed by many people that when the Pacific coast products reached the Mississippi River they would leave the railways and follow the river, unless they should reach it above the head of all-the-year navigation, generally considered to be at Saint Louis. Up to 1855, it would have been difficult for members in either House of Congress to understand how commerce would come to disregard the great rivers, and bridge and cross them instead of following them (except as to a few lines of products). In the second session of the 32d Congress, Senator Underwood was an enthusiastic advocate of the mouth of the Ohio (Cairo) as the eastern terminus of the Pacific railway, and it was not entirely because he had the interests of his own state of Kentucky at heart. He argued that that point was the natural point of distribution for Pacific coast products and the natural point of accumulation of eastern products, destined for Pacific coast and Asiatic markets. " There is a point lower down the river [than Saint Louis] where the terminus should be. Nature has made the point. I suggested it a week or two ago, but I am afraid it will not be carried, because there is no influence in behalf of that point here. It will sink below zero in consequence of Saint Louis on the one side and Memphis on the other. But why is that the point in a commercial attitude ? It is because when you bring this commerce from the Pacific you can thence distribute it by water, you can go down the Mississippi River, or if the Missouri be open, you can ascend it by steamboats, which is a cheaper mode of transportation than railroads. You can ascend the Ohio to Pittsburg. You can branch away and reach Paducah, and go up the Tennessee to the falls, twelve miles, and reach Florence. You can go up the Cumberland River to Cumberland, passing Nashville, and when at a little distance above, at Shawneetown, you can turn to the left and go to Terre Haute by ascending the Wabash. There is no such concentration of waters on the face of the world as at that point. In the making of a railroad for commercial purposes, you ought to regard the point from which you can distribute this important trade and commerce with the greatest facility, with the greatest cheapness, over the whole valley of the Mississippi ; and that point is at the head of perpetual navigation upon the Mississippi River, which is at or near the mouth of the Ohio ; because from the concentration of waters there you may have the Gulf trade in Gulf streams from that point all the year."[1] And he was not answered as the merchant or railway manager of the present decade would have answered him, to the effect that the natural path of commerce would be east and west in spite of rivers, lakes, and mountains, and that the magnetic poles of commerce would be shifted by the truly wonderful magnetic commercial currents of railway transportation from the North and South to the East and West, that the railways would climb over the mountains or tunnel through them, but not go around them, and that they would bridge over and ferry across rivers and lakes, but not yield up their burdens of wealth to be carried by them ; on the contrary, Underwood's argument was met by a denial of his premises, and not by a denial of the conclusions that he drew from them. Senator Borland's words in reply were : "So far from attacking the argument made by the Senator from Kentucky (Underwood) the other day, I shall, without attempting a new one, adopt his argument in support of my own views, but starting upon another state of facts. I shall adopt his course of argument precisely, for to my mind it was conclusive ; but I shall start from different premises, and from what I think are the well ascertained and established facts of the case."[2] But the great extension of east and west lines from Boston, New York, Philadelphia, and Baltimore to Prairie du Chien, Dubuque, Burlington, Hannibal, Saint Louis, Memphis, and Vicksburg in the first half

---

[1] *Congressional Globe*, Volume 26 (32d Congress, 2d Session), page 355. There are some geographical inaccuracies in this quotation, that Senator Underwood saw fit to correct a few days after the remarks were made. The correction is found in *Congressional Globe*, Volume 26, page 421. As the idea and point made by the speaker are perfectly plain, the correction of the geographical inaccuracies will not be attempted here.

[2] Ibidem, page 421.

of the decade, had brought the keener commercial mind of the Eastern party to a partial realization of the fact that even if the Pacific railway should terminate at Saint Louis, the great mass of its freight would not be transferred to Mississippi River steamboats, but would, of its own accord and by its own inclinations, follow the lines of east and west railways terminating on the North Atlantic seaboard, and the east and west water route by the Great Lakes and Erie Canal to New York. Thus it became possible for the Eastern party to support the Saint Louis terminus. It was supposed for a time that freight from the Pacific coast was restricted by the barrier of the Alleghenies to two outlets from the upper Mississippi valley, the one north by way of the Great Lakes and Erie Canal, or the contiguous system of railways, the other by the Mississippi River. But in the next Congress (33d), in recognition that the Alleghenies were not insuperable obstacles to railway engineers, that transcontinental freights would naturally prefer the east and west railway east of the Mississippi to the north and south route by the river, and that the river was not the only outlet from the lower Mississippi valley to the Atlantic, Seward will be found saying: . . . . "I deem only one terminus material to be fixed, and that is the western terminus, which, I believe, ought to be at San Francisco. In regard to the eastern terminus, while I have my opinion about what would be the most expedient, and proper, and advantageous location of that terminus, I am prepared to surrender my convictions on that point for the purpose of obtaining harmony in Congress in regard to the passage of some bill that will accomplish the object. So far as the state which I represent is concerned, I feel entirely confident that her geographical position and commercial advantages will make the city of New York the eastern terminus of any and of all roads which may be made across the plains to the Pacific Ocean."[1]

The intrusion of the scheme for a line from Lake Superior

[1] *Congressional Globe*, Volume 30, page 750, 33d Congress, 1st Session.
Seward had said in the debate on the Rusk bill in the second session of the 32d Congress, "To me, ... a northern or a southern route are as nearly equal as may be. You may make a route across the continent wherever you

to the Pacific into the Pacific railway question in the 33d Congress was due to two considerations :

(1) The great increase in population and wealth in Oregon and Washington and in Minnesota and Wisconsin, the superiority of the soil of the intervening territory over that of the " Great American Desert " further south, and the digging of the Sault Sainte Marie Canal gave the world a foresight of the future importance of the extreme North and of the future need of a transcontinental railway in that section ; Jefferson Davis, as Secretary of War, under the law of 1853, had given these facts additional importance by assigning one of his five surveying parties to the region between the 47th and 49th parallels ; and the work of Governor Stevens and McClellan had been, on the whole, better done than the work on any other of the five divisions. Jefferson Davis himself had been so impressed by the result of the survey of the Northern route and the probable cheapness of railway construction on it that he deliberately changed the estimated cost of construction by increasing it in his report about 30 per cent. above the cost estimated by the engineers.[1]

please, there will be but two terminals of that road—one in the east, at New York, and the other on the west, at San Francisco. . . . . It is for this reason that I have been satisfied not to raise the question about the location of the road." *Congressional Globe*, Volume 26, page 766.

[1] From $117,121,000.00 to $150,871,000.00. Senate Executive Documents, 33d Congress, 2nd session, No. 78, Volume I., page 11.

In 1852, Edwin F. Johnson, a noted railway engineer, prepared for publication a work on Pacific railways, in which he insisted that the future Northern Pacific route was the best of all for a transcontinental railway. When Jefferson Davis heard of the proposed book through Robert J. Walker, a fellow-member of the cabinet, he went to New York and borrowed the manuscript of Johnson. When he returned the manuscript, after a few days, he tried to convince Johnson that his conclusions were unjustified. His efforts were unsuccessful, however, and on his return to Washington he pushed through Congress the Act of 1853 for the general surveys. It is further charged that when he afterwards assigned engineers to the several routes, he assigned to the Northern route Stevens and McClellan, with whom he had most influence and from whom he expected to be able to get an unfavorable report. See Life of Thomas Hawley Canfield, page 17.

(2) The McDougall-Gwin bill was a Southern measure, and represented a combination of California, Texas, Memphis, and Arkansas, Mississippi, and New Orleans against Saint Louis ; the Northern Pacific scheme was intended to create a defection in the Eastern party from the Saint Louis combination. In the words of Representative Davis (Indiana), " It is plain and palpable . . . . . that the intention of constructing two roads is to divert our attention from and finally defeat the Central route. ' Not north of the thirty-seventh parallel' means the Gila, or extreme Southern route."[1]

IV.

Under the law of 1853, Jefferson Davis, as Secretary of War, sent into the field five corps of engineers, scientists and surveyors, and the region between the Mississippi and the Pacific was divided into five divisions, corresponding to the five general routes that had been urged by Pacific railway advocates. These routes were designated as (1) the route of the 47th and 49th parallels, or the Northern route ; (2) the route of the 41st and 42d parallels, "Overland route," "Central route" or "Mormon Trail ; " (3) the route of the 38th and 39th parallels, or the "Buffalo Trail ;" (4) the route of the 35th parallel ; and (5) the route of the 32d parallel, or Southern route. The separate reports were sent to Congress from time to time but not in a complete form until January, 1855, and Secretary Davis' final report on the surveys was made on the 27th day of February, 1855. The reports are in eleven large octavo volumes, amply supplied with maps, profiles, tables, and engravings. Not only was the topography of the country exhaustively described, but the geology, botany, ornithology, zoölogy and anthropology of the various parts of the Great West were dealt with so exhaustively as to afford an excuse for embellishing the reports with copious illustrations of cactus plants, sage brush, birds of gay plumage, rattlesnakes, jack rabbits, prairie-dogs, and Root Digger Indians. The

[1] Appendix to *Congressional Globe*, Volume 29, page 962, 33d Congress, 1st session.

$150,000.00[1] of government money, appropriated for the purpose of the surveys, had to be expended, and the result of the expenditure was a mass of scientific information simply confirming the belief, common before the surveys were made, that there were several practicable railway routes across the plains and over the Rocky Mountains. Jefferson Davis, being from the South, and particularly from Mississippi, could be pardoned by the public for concluding in his report that "the route of the 32d parallel is of those surveyed the most practicable and economical route for a railroad from the Mississippi River to the Pacific Ocean," "the shortest route," and the easiest to build.[2] The public understood from the reports, however, that a dozen routes were practicable, and members of Congress had now no excuse for further delay in satisfying the general demand of the public for a Pacific railway. The second session of the 33d Congress began in December, 1854, and the battle of the sections and localities was renewed with increased vigor, each member of Congress urged and pushed on by a clamoring constituency, and vying with his fellow Congressmen in his efforts to overcome the centrifugal force of sectionalism and localism by the superior force of the attraction of the national center.

V.

In the second session of the 33d Congress, the work was taken up where it had been left at the end of the first session. The Select Committee was continued in each House of Congress. The efforts to secure some positive legislation on the subject of the

---

[1] In May, 1854, a deficiency appropriation of $40,000.00 was made, and in August, 1854, was followed by a further appropriation of $150,000.00 for continuing the explorations and surveys, and "for completing the reports of surveys already made."

[2] Senate Executive Documents, 33d Congress, 2d session, No. 78, Volume I, page 29. See also De Bow's Review for September, 1855 (Volume XIX., page 336). The surveys made under Secretary Davis' authority were critically discussed in De Bow's Review for December, 1856 (Volume XXI., page 555) and even by that representative periodical of Southern industry the conclusions of the Secretary were not endorsed.

Pacific railway were exerted in a more systematic form. The two committees, after extended conferences within themselves and with each other, finally reached a compromise on the Douglas plan, which first made its appearance in the Senate; there it was introduced in the form of a bill by Stephen A. Douglas on the 9th day of January, 1855, and referred to the Select Committee of the Senate. On the 15th day of the same month, it was reported back to the Senate with amendments as a proposed substitute for the Gwin bill (for two roads) left over from the preceding session.

The Douglas bill, as reported with amendments by the Select Committee, provided for the construction of three lines of railway, (1) one from the western border of the state of Texas to the Pacific Ocean in California, to be known as the Southern Pacific railroad, (2) one from the western border of Missouri or Iowa to the Bay of San Francisco, to be known as the Central Pacific railroad, and (3) one from the western border of Wisconsin, in the territory of Minnesota, to the .Pacific Ocean in Oregon or Washington Territory, to be known as the Northern Pacific railroad. The three lines were to be constructed in the following manner: The Secretary of the Interior, the Secretary of War and the Postmaster General were to advertise for and receive "sealed and separate proposals for the construction of each or either of said lines . . . . . stating . . . . . whether it be for the Southern, Central, or Northern lines, and also,—First, the time in which the parties proposed to construct . . . . . the road . . . . . Second, the time in which such . . . . . . parties will surrender and transfer, free of cost to the United States, ... said road with its appurtenances . . . . . and Third, the sum, not exceeding $300.00 per mile per annum, for carrying the United States mails daily both ways on said road . . . . . for a period of fifteen years from the completion of the road; and while in course of construction, for the portion in use and at what rate per mile, for a like period, and on the portions in use while being constructed, they will carry on said road . . . . . freights . . . . . for government purposes . . . . . . and from and after the expiration of

said period of fifteen years, said transportation . . . . .
for government purposes, shall be . . . . . performed on
said road . . . . . at reasonable prices, not exceeding those
usually paid for the time being on other first class roads, to be
ascertained by Congress in the event of disagreement between the
government and the owners of the road." A quantity of land,
"equal to the alternate sections for the space of twelve miles on
each side of said roads" was to be conveyed to the constructors
of the roads, together with a right of way of two hundred feet and
the right of taking material for construction from adjoining government lands. The Secretary of the Interior, the Secretary of
War and the Postmaster General, under direction of the President, were to enter into contracts with the contractors whose proposals should be accepted, and the contractors were to deposit a
guaranty of $500,000.00 in bonds of the United States or of the
states, with the Secretary of the Treasury, to be withdrawn by
them in sums of $5,000.00 upon showing that like sums had been
expended on the lines. The roads, right of way, and property
were to be forfeited to the government upon the failure of the contractors to comply with their contracts. "Whenever . . . . .
said roads shall be surrendered to the United States, ...
so much of said roads as may lie within any of the states, shall with
their consent . . . . . become the property of the . . .
. . states within the limits of which the same may be located,
subject to the use of the United States for . . . . . government services . . . . . and to such regulations as Congress
may prescribe, restricting the charge for transportation thereon.
And all other states . . . . . admitted into the Union
thereafter shall acquire the same rights." "No road shall be made
. . . . . in the state of California without the authority of
the legislature of that state, and then only by virtue of the
authority of such state." If no proposals should be received on
the first advertisement, new advertisements were to be issued "once
in each year, until each of said . . . . . lines shall be put
under contract . . . . . unless Congress shall otherwise

order and direct." The route and termini were to be located by the contractors, within the limits proposed by the bill.[1]

The only serious amendment offered in the Senate was by Mason (Virginia), who proposed that instead of permitting the three cabinet officers to make definite contracts for the construction of the roads, the bill should require them to communicate proposed plans and contracts to Congress for ratification. This was done by Mason for the sole purpose of causing defections from the ranks of the supporters of the bill. Mason was in the forefront of the state-rights and strict construction opposition to Pacific railway legislation, and had repeatedly said that he would vote for no road at all.[2] That had been a favorite mode, on the part of Southern Senators, of opposing Northern and Western measures. Frequently, when the advocates of a Pacific railway had seemed to approach unanimity, the Southern members had separated them by offering some amendment that would precipitate a quarrel between the New Orleans, Vicksburg, Memphis, and Saint Louis parties. In this instance Mason caused the defection of Chase and the Pennsylvania members, and Geyer (Missouri) had taken fear lest the "Wall Street influence" (prominent by reason of the fact that the selection of the route and termini had been left to the contractors) should act against the interests of Saint Louis, and favor the Iowa, Illinois and Lake roads, owned by the Eastern party;[3] yet there was strength enough left to push the bill through and it was passed in the Senate on the 19th of February, 1855, by a vote of 24 to 21.

[1] *Congressional Globe*, Volume 30, page 749, 33d Congress, 2d Session. See map (1) at end of volume.

[2] Supra, page 49.

[3] In debate, Geyer charged that California (desiring as much mileage as possible), the Southern Pacific contractors (necessarily controlled by California and Texas), and the Eastern capitalists controlling Illinois, Iowa and the Northwest were united against Saint Louis, and his charge was not denied. "When Wall Street, and the other interests I have named, are brought into competition with a state that relies exclusively upon her own resources to build her roads, as they are by this bill, the result is certain against the state," he complained. Appendix to *Congressional Globe*, Volume 31, page 200. 33d Congress, 2d Session.

In the House of Representatives, the Douglas bill had a stormy and thrilling parliamentary experience. Some unconsidered Pacific railway bills had been left over from the first session in the House of Representatives, and on the 16th of January, 1855, the Douglas bill, in accordance with the arrangements entered into by the Select Committees of the two Houses, was moved by Dunbar (Louisiana), as a substitute for the pending bill. Then the House of Representatives proceeded to compress into one week of the session all the parliamentary tangles that the wit and ingenuity of members could contrive. Several unimportant amendments were offered but rejected, until one of more moment was offered January 18, by Davis (Indiana) to strike out of the Douglas bill the provision for three roads and to substitute for it a provision for one trunk line from San Francisco to the western border of Missouri or Iowa, between the parallels of 39° and 41°, afterwards changed to 36° and 43°, north latitude, with branches to Memphis and Lake Superior from some point between the meridians of 103° and 105° west longitude. When this amendment was proposed, McDougall, Chairman of the Select Committee and the mainstay of the Douglas bill, exclaimed, "If this amendment is adopted, it will destroy the bill." This was the signal for a profuse display of parliamentary pyrotechnics. The air was full of motions of every character, from motions to strike out enacting clauses, to frequent motions to adjourn, and the previous question was called for at every step. The Davis amendment was adopted and the Douglas bill, as amended, was substituted for the pending bill. A motion for a final vote was sustained and then the vote reconsidered. Then a motion to recommit the bill to the Select Committee was defeated and the vote reconsidered, and the next vote to recommit was a tie of 103 to 103, decided by the casting vote of Speaker Linn Boyd against recommitting. Then the bill was passed by a vote of 109 to 97. After the bill was passed and the agony apparently over, Mace (Indiana), on January 22, stated that he was "paired off" with Edmunson (Virginia), but had nevertheless, by some misunderstanding, participated in the vote on the passage of the bill; he asked leave to withdraw his vote; thereupon his attention was called to the fact that, by the same misunderstanding, he had participated in the tie vote on the motion to recommit; the vote on the passage of the bill and the tie vote were therefore reconsidered, and the motion to recommit was sustained by a vote of 105 to 91. On the following day, January 23, 1855, a motion to reconsider the last vote to recommit was laid on the table by a vote of 95 to 94. Later in the session, the 20th of February, when the Douglas bill, passed by the Senate,[1] was sent to the House of Representatives from the Senate for its action, nothing was done with it— the adverse sentiment of the House had already been expressed.

Thomas H. Benton, aided by some Indiana and Ohio representatives, was responsible for the defeat in the House of Representatives. The Saint Louis influence insisted on either the one central road or no road at all. And the year 1855 was not a time when public confidence in Douglas or his measures was strong. So many northern people and such a remarkably large foreign population of Germans had been added to Saint Louis, that it had ceased to be a stronghold of slavery. Maryland and Delaware might be whipped into line on the Kansas-Nebraska bill, but Thomas H. Benton was one of the two representatives that voted against it. Douglas had been responsible in the Senate for the abortive Gwin-McDougall bill providing for two roads, one not north of the 37th parallel and the other from Lake Superior to the Pacific Ocean—a direct blow at Saint Louis. After that it was not difficult for Benton to consider any Pacific railway bill emanating from Douglas a suspicious affair; and particularly when the making of the contracts and location of route and termini were to be left with three cabinet officers (of whom two were from the South) under the direction of Pierce, "the New Hampshire paradox." Benton could say nothing worse of the Douglas bill than that it was an "administration measure," and the student of this decade will find in Benton's estimation of the bill a sufficient reason for his opposition to it.

The most distinct development in the 33d Congress was that

[1] Supra, page 63.

5

of what might be called, for want of a better term, "individual confidence." The development that had taken place in the states was duplicated in the single example of a national railway. Between 1830 and 1835, railway building was little above a succession of local experiments; by 1835, it was a "condition and not a theory"; from 1835 to 1845, some of the states (like Michigan and Pennsylvania) built and managed railways as public industries, but by 1845, state building of railways had ceased, and the states sold their railways to corporations; from 1845 to 1860, the railways were built by corporations with the aid of the states. Finally, after 1870, railways were built by corporations without aid from the states, but with their own means, supplemented by donations from directly interested local communities, who looked upon the new railway rather as a private benefit to the community than a public benefit to society. A step has been taken even beyond this in the last decade of the century, and now when a railway corporation wishes to build a railway, it builds it just as an individual establishes a grocery,—not as a public enterprise, aided by public or private bonuses, but as a private project, with the projector's own means, and for the profit expected by the projector from the operation of the business.

Up to 1850 the controlling idea was that the Pacific railway was to be a "national highway," and ought to be built by the national government or under its direct initiation and control. The theory on which Asa Whitney acted was that he was simply an agent of the nation for the purpose of accomplishing a national object ; he was not projecting a private enterprise, which, on account of incidental advantages to the nation, was deserving of aid and stimulus from the nation—he was projecting a national enterprise, that could only be accomplished through the medium of individual effort, and in his view, when the project should become a fact, the railway would be only a public or national instrument, requiring individual effort and agency in its manipulation and use. From 1850 to 1855 the national view of the project was still predominant, though the individual feature, while not fully understood and appreciated, was yet felt and con-

sidered. And as the commercial spirit of the North (or rather of
the East) was keener and quicker than that of the South (partly
on account of the repressive influence of slavery), this "individual"
feeling is first shown in isolated passages in the speeches of
Northern statesmen. Seward, Chase and Douglas discussed the
personal, individual factor in the problem before 1855, but in
that year, in the debates in both Houses on the Douglas bill,
the idea seems to have sprung up in a night. The theory of the
Douglas bill was that anyone that wished to build a Pacific railway should have the opportunity to do it. The grant of land was
considered as the contribution of a prudent landlord to a project
that would make the rest of the land more valuable. The contemplated payments for carrying the mail may have been a trifle
high, but after all they were simply to be payments for services
rendered. The Douglas bill was individualistic in a great degree.
The industrial growth had given the railway builder confidence
in himself, and as " people have confidence in those who have
confidence in themselves," Congress had confidence in the "contractors." The money centers were full of individuals, companies and corporations, willing to undertake the building of
Pacific railways. Benton had taken a northern and eastern
speech-making trip during the fall of 1854, and when the
Douglas bill came up in the House, he had facts that justified
him in saying :

" I have turned my attention to private enterprise, and have
found solid men who are willing to take the preliminary steps
now, preparatory to the final assumption of the work, Congress
granting the necessary authority and confirming the right of way
through its territories, one mile wide on each side of the road.

" I would have preferred that Congress should have made the
road, as a national work, on a scale commensurate with its
grandeur and let out the use of it to companies, who would fetch
and carry on the best terms for the people and the government.
But that hope has vanished, and the organization of Kansas having opened up the country to settlement, ... a private
company has become the resource and the preference. I embrace

it as such, utterly scouting all plans for making private roads at national expense, of paying for the use of roads built with our land and money, of bargaining with corporations or individuals for the use of what we give them. " [1]

Geyer was apprehensive of " Wall Street influence " and was sure that it was behind an anti-Saint Louis project. [2]

Texas, Louisiana, Mississippi, New Orleans and Memphis were satisfied with a provision for a line from the western border of Texas to the Pacific, though they had been found in vigorous opposition to it on the dramatic death and resurrection of the Rusk bill at the hands of Shields and Douglas, because they thought they needed the opportunity to build and not the means to build. " Wearied with the delay incident to a government appropriation for this project, individual capitalists, particularly those of the South, are earnestly considering the propriety of a road to connect San Diego with Charleston in South Carolina . . . . From Charleston to Shreveport in Louisiana a line of Railway connections already exists, or is in a state of progress. The offer of alternate sections of land from Marshall on the eastern limit of Texas to its western border, through the best lands of the state, presents a strong inducement to capitalists to construct such a road. . . . . Although no serious objection appears to exist to the prosecution of this enterprise, yet further consideration may diminish the confidence with which the project is now regarded. The gradual progress of public sentiment, as it becomes enlightened by a better acquaintance with the facts of the case, will in a few years, at furthest, determine definitely the course which this great achievement of modern science and enterprise must pursue. " [3]

The theory of the Douglas bill was expressed concisely and perfectly by Congressman Bliss when he argued : "The people

---

[1] Thomas H. Benton, Appendix to *Congressional Globe*, Volume 31, page 73, 33d Congress, 2d Session.

[2] Supra, page 63 and note.

[3] Historical Collections of the Great West, Volume II., page 448. By Henry Howe. Published at Cincinnati in 1855.

of the southern portion of the Confederacy have confidence enough in themselves to believe that they could construct the road, through their section of the country, if Congress will give them the privilege of competing in that matter. The people of the central portion of the Union have confidence that they could do it, and just such confidence inspires the people of the North." "I admit that the passage of this bill does not give a certainty that the three lines will be constructed. I do not care whether it will be so or not. We cannot legislate against nature. If the lynx eye of capital cannot perceive an advantage in constructing a railroad at the north, the enterprise will not be engaged in. If the natural advantages of the central line of railroad are not sufficient to justify its construction, that line will not be put under contract ; and so of the other line ; why, then, let people experiment for themselves upon all these routes ; and if they do not succeed in building them all, I ask, in the name of reason, what is the objection ? What objection can there be to the construction of a northern railroad, if it can be accomplished ? What objection, under like circumstances, can there be to the central or the southern? No gentleman can reasonably object to it. "[1]

It was freely conceded that eventually there would be Pacific railways to accommodate all localities and sections; the contention of the sections and localities was now not which should be the terminus of the *only* Pacific railway, but which should be the terminus of *the first* Pacific railway. The progress of railways east of the territorial line had been remarkable. The constitutional scruples of the Virginia school had been overcome by the industrial development of the West. Railways had been or were soon to be completed to Saint Paul, Sioux City, Council Bluffs, Saint Joseph, Independence (Kansas City), the southwest corner of Missouri, and Fulton (Arkansas), and southern capital was ready to build across Texas.[2]

The country west of the Mississippi was being rapidly settled,

[1] George Bliss, January 19, 1855. *Congressional Globe* Volume 30, page 329.
[2] Supra, page 68.

and the argument that "if the government would give the right of way, the 'lynx-eyed capitalist' would do the rest" had much force. The annexed table[1] shows the rapid expansion of railway building after 1850, and in it may be found a proof that the spirit of the Douglas bill was only a reflection of the spirit of the people in 1855. It must be noted that in 1855 the country was on the threshold of one of its periodic outbursts of railway building, and that most of the building was in the Mississippi valley.[2]

VI.

The 34th Congress (1855–1857) was well-nigh a blank in Pacific railway legislation, as in everything else. True, the Select Committee in each House was maintained, and a few bills were referred to them. But no committee report or bill was taken up or considered. The strength of Pacific railway legislation had been in the Whig party assisted by Northern Democrats and the Democrats of the lower Mississippi valley, and there had

	1850	1851	1852	1853	1854	1855	1856	1857	1858	1859	1860
[1]Number of miles constructed.	1656	1961	1926	2452	1360	1654	3642	2487	2465	1821	1846
No.of miles in operation at end of year.	9021	10982	12908	15360	16720	18374	22016	24503	26968	28789	30635

[2] See the *Democratic Review* of 1852 (Volume XXX., page 229), for a clear expression of the *laissez faire* theory of building a Pacific road. That influential periodical had formerly looked with favor on the Whitney project, but in this article it deserted it, as giving to an individual too extended control of a large part of the public domain. The article referred to was an argument for the construction of the road as a business enterprise (with the aid of a moderate grant of land) by eastern railway companies interested in it, as contrasted with individual or governmental ownership; and it expresses the spirit that dominated Congress in 1855.

See also *DeBow's Southern and Western Review* for May, 1854 (Volume XVI., page 506). "Exploration has convinced everyone that there are several ways of connecting the waters of the Atlantic and Pacific by ordinary railways. The obstacle to be surmounted is, not the location of a route, but what route to choose of the number already located; not the question of practicability, but the combined one of availability and expediency. None will doubt the utility always been a majority in each House of Congress in favor of the general project of a Pacific railway, in spite of the opposition of extreme state-rights Democrats like Lewis Cass in the North and Mason and Hunter in the South. As frequently explained, the dissensions had arisen over the particular projects, every one of which was either too "magnificent" or failed to satisfy some local or sectional interest. Mason frankly admitted, in 1853, when it was proposed to survey routes to the Pacific : "I appeal to Senators if this project can be fairly and legitimately destroyed, to destroy it for the present session ; and I know of no way of doing it, inasmuch as there is a fixed majority here in favor of making a railroad from some point on the Mississippi River, to some point on the Pacific Ocean, but by getting up an internecine war among the friends of the measure; that is the way we fortunately succeeded in defeating the friends of the measure upon the bill itself." In the later treacherous days of the 33d Congress — the Congress of the repeal of the Missouri Compromise — even steadfast friends of the project, like Benton, could not have confidence in bills that apparently aimed at the satisfaction of all sectional and local interests, when the execution of the law would be left in the hands of adherents of particular sections and localities, like President Pierce, Stephen A. Douglas, and Jefferson Davis. The reaction in the North against the repeal of

of the contemplated measure; but all may very justly find exception to forming a monopoly, or determining a line that shall contribute mainly to the benefit of a section.

"The chief difficulty, therefore, which besets the proposition is the reconciling of conflicting interests, and adapting preferred claims to a general emergency. . . .

"Meanwhile, individual interest improves the opportunity of doing what it can towards forwarding its own views. It associates itself into a company, and casts about for means and appliances to accomplish the stupendous undertaking. It virtually attempts to take out of the hands of the government the construction of the gigantic scheme; and under the name, style, or title of "the Northern Pacific," the "Central Atlantic and Pacific," or the "Southern Pacific and Mississippi" Railroad Company, boldly offers to do the work which the nation is too timid or too negligent to engage in, or which furnishes politicians but too dangerous a platform. . . ."

the Missouri Compromise in the preceding Congress (May 30, 1854) had disrupted the Whig party, and it was left helpless. The contests of the fall of 1856, though they resulted in the election of Buchanan and a majority of Democrats in each House, had unseated many members of both Houses, and there was a resulting feeling of inertia that produced no positive legislation of importance. Politicians were too much occupied in watching the contest in Kansas to discuss Pacific railway bills.

VII.

The outlook for Pacific railway legislation in 1857 was, on the surface, favorable.

In June, 1856, at their national convention at Cincinnati, the Democratic party had as a plank in their platform : " Resolved, that the Democratic party recognizes the great importance, in a political and commercial point of view, of a safe and speedy communication by military and postal roads through our own territory between the Atlantic and Pacific coasts of this Union, and that it is the duty of the Federal Government to exercise promptly all its constitutional power to the attainment of that object."[1]

In the same month, in Philadelphia, the delegates of the Republican party had resolved : " That a railroad to the Pacific Ocean by the most central and practicable route, is imperatively demanded by the interests of the whole country, and that the Federal Government ought to render immediate and efficient aid in its construction, and, as an auxiliary thereto, the immediate construction of an emigrant route on the line of the railroad."[2]

In a letter written by Buchanan to the Chairman of the Democratic State Central Committee of California, the candidate for the Presidency had expressed himself in a few of his diplomatic

[1] McKee's Platforms and Parties, page 55.

[2] Ibidem, page 59.

phrases as being "decidedly favorable to the construction of a Pacific railroad."[1]

In his inaugural address, President Buchanan had intimated : "It might also be wise to consider whether the love for the Union which now animates our fellow citizens on the Pacific coast may not be impaired by our neglect or refusal to provide for them, in their remote and isolated condition, the only means by which the power of the states on this side of the Rocky Mountains can reach them in sufficient time to protect them against invasion."[2]

In his first annual message, Buchanan had gone fully into the subject of a Pacific railway, and had said in explanation of his

[1] The letter is found quoted in full by Senator Gwin (*Congressional Globe*, Volume 41, page 44, 35th Congress, 2d Session) and is as follows :

"Wheatland, September 17, 1856.

SIR : I have received numerous communications from sources in California entitled to high regard in reference to the proposed railroad. As it would be impossible for me to answer them all, I deem it most proper and respectful to address you a general answer in your official capacity. In performing this duty to the citizens of California, I act in perfect consistency with the self-imposed restriction contained in my letter accepting the nomination for the Presidency, not to answer interrogations raising new and different issues from those presented by the Cincinnati convention, because that convention has itself adopted a resolution in favor of this great work.

"I then desire to state briefly, that, concurring with the convention, I am decidedly favorable to the construction of the Pacific railroad, and I derive the authority to do this from the constitutional power 'to declare war,' and the constitutional duty 'to repel invasions.' In my judgment, Congress possesses the same power to make appropriations for the construction of this road, strictly for the purpose of national defense, that it has to erect fortifications at the mouth of the harbor of San Francisco. Indeed, the necessity, with a view to repel foreign invasion from California is as great in the one case as in the other. Neither will there be danger from the precedent, for it is almost impossible to conceive that any case attended by such extraordinary and unprecedented circumstances, can ever again occur in our history.

"Yours, very respectfully,

"JAMES BUCHANAN.

"To B. F. Washington, Esq., Chairman State Central Committee, California."

[2] Quoted by Senator Gwin, *Congressional Record*, Volume 41, page 49, 35th Congress, 2d session.

constitutional attitude, "Long experience has deeply convinced me that a strict construction of the powers granted to Congress is the only true, as well as the only safe, theory of the constitution. Whilst this principle shall guide my public conduct, I consider it clear that under the war-making power, Congress may appropriate money for the construction of a military road through the territories of the United States when this is absolutely necessary for the defense of any of the states against foreign invasion. The constitution has conferred upon Congress power 'to declare war,' 'to raise and support armies,' 'to provide and maintain a navy,' and 'to call forth the militia to repel invasions.' These high sovereign powers necessarily involve important and responsible public duties, and among them there is none so sacred and so imperative as that of preserving our soil from the invasion of a foreign enemy. The constitution has, therefore, left nothing on this point to construction, but expressly requires that 'the United States shall protect each of them (the states) against invasion.' Now, if a military road over our own territories be indispensably necessary to enable us to meet and repel the invader, it follows as a necessary consequence, not only that we possess the power, but it is our imperative duty to construct such a road. It would be an absurdity to invest a government with the unlimited power to make and conduct war, and at the same time deny to it the only means of reaching and defeating the enemy at the frontier. Without such a road it is quite evident we cannot 'protect' California and our Pacific possessions 'against invasion.' We cannot by any other means transport men and munitions of war from the Atlantic states in sufficient time successfully to defend these remote and distant portions of the Republic."

In a later paragraph of the same message, Buchanan betrayed the spirit that has made American statesmen bend and conform constitutional dogmas to the material welfare of the people, has given the American manufacturer protection on the pretext that it is merely an incident of taxation and a "regulation of commerce," and has seen fit to inspect the butter that the American *pater familias* is to use on his breakfast table on the pretext that the government is only taxing an imitation product known as oleomargarine. And in the same paragraph Buchanan betrayed the baneful influences under which his administration was to be conducted and the close connection they were to have with the evolution of the great industrial desideratum. He continued:

"The difficulties and the expense of constructing a military railroad to connect our Atlantic and Pacific states have been greatly exaggerated. The distance on the Arizona route, near the thirty-second parallel of north latitude, between the western boundary of Texas on the Rio Grande and the eastern boundary of California on the Colorado, from the best explorations now within our knowledge, does not exceed four hundred and seventy miles, and the face of the country is, in the main, favorable. For obvious reasons, the government ought not to undertake the work itself, by its own agents. This ought to be committed to other agencies, which Congress might assist, either by grants of land or money, or by both, upon such terms and conditions as they may deem most beneficial to the country. Provision might thus be made not only for the safe, rapid and economical transportation of troops and munitions of war, but also of the public mails. The commercial interests of the whole country, both east and west, would be greatly promoted by such a road, and, above all, it would be a powerful additional bond of union. And although advantages of this kind, whether postal, commercial or political, cannot confer constitutional power, yet they may furnish auxiliary arguments in favor of expediting a work which, in my judgment, is clearly embraced within the war-making power.

" For these reasons, I commend to the friendly consideration of Congress the subject of the Pacific railroad, without finally committing myself to any particular route."[1]

The commendation of the President was supported by the annual report of the Secretary of War (Floyd, of Virginia) who assumed that " in the opinion of competent judges, there is now no

[1] Message of the President, Appendix to *Congressional Globe*, Volume 40, page 6, 35th Congress, 1st Session.

controversy as to the most eligible route for the railroad. . . .
The route from El Paso to the Colorado, besides being the shortest
of all yet surveyed, possesses very decided advantages over others
in several important particulars . . . ; so that, in selecting a
railroad route between the Pacific and the valley of the Mississippi, as far as our present information goes, that by El Paso
would be chosen, but the consummation of this project, freed from
all other difficulties, would require immense sums of money and
a great length of time."

The Postmaster General (Aaron V. Brown, of Tennessee) had
been accused by Congressmen of favoring the South by having
the overland mail carried from Saint Louis and Memphis by way
of Springfield (Missouri) and El Paso, instead of by the usually
traveled overland trail from Independence along the Platte River
and through the South Pass.   His defense against the accusation
fills three columns in the *Congressional Globe*,[1] and the burden of it
is that "the Department supposed Congress to be in search of a
route that could be found safe, comfortable, and certain during
every season of the year, as well for the transportation of the
mails as for the accommodation of emigrants, and the future location of a railroad to the Pacific," and that the El Paso route, in
his estimation, "filled the bill."

After a consideration of the attitude of the political parties, as set out in their platforms and resolutions, and of the
administration as set out in letters, messages and reports, the
friends of Pacific railway legislation seemed to have good reason
to expect some concrete results from the Thirty-fifth Congress,
(1857-1859) particularly as the administration party, solidified by
the opposition of Whigs and Republicans after the repeal of the
Missouri Compromise, had a majority in both Houses,[2] but it was
not to be.   The swifter the revolutions of the public will became,

[1] Report of Postmaster General, Appendix to *Congressional Globe*, Volume
40, pages 25-28, 35th Congress, 1st Session.

[2] The Senate stood,—39 Democrats, 20 Republicans, 5 Americans ; the House
of Representatives stood,—131 Democrats, 92 Republicans, 14 Americans.

the stronger the centrifugal force of sectionalism and localism was exerted.

The first session of the 35th Congress convened December 7, 1857, and soon afterwards the House of Representatives, upon the receipt of the President's message and accompanying documents, undertook to distribute the several parts of them among the standing committees. What disposition to make of the portions relating to the Pacific railway was a question that showed from the beginning the difficulties to be encountered. Cobb (Alabama) tried to have the matter referred to his committee (on Public Lands), and Jones (Tennessee) tried to have it referred to his committee (on Roads and Canals). In either case, the matter would have been pretty effectually smothered, as both Cobb and Jones and their committees were opposed to legislation on it. Among the friends of the Pacific railway measure, matters were little better. When Phelps (Missouri) moved for a Select Committee (of which, according to custom, he would have been chairman), eastern and northern friends were found opposing him. And when Bennett (New York) made a similar motion, the Saint Louis and Memphis "friends" were found in opposition. The contest for the "nursing of this particular bantling" went so far that Bennett finally offered the following resolution, showing in its every line the fatal weakness of the project:

"Resolved, that so much of said message and accompanying documents as relates to the subject of a Pacific railroad be referred to a Select Committee of thirteen, to be appointed by the Speaker. And in order to fairly represent the various sections of the Union, said Committee shall be appointed from the different States, as follows:

From the New England States, New York, Michigan, Wisconsin, Iowa and Illinois (80 members) - - - -	4
From New Jersey, Pennsylvania, Ohio and Indiana (62 members)	3
From Maryland and Virginia (19 members) - - -	1
From Delaware, Florida, North Carolina and Georgia (18 members)	1
From Tennessee, South Carolina and Arkansas (18 members) -	1
From Kentucky, Missouri and Texas (19 members) - -	1
From Alabama, Mississippi and Louisiana (16 members) -	1
From California - - - - - -	1

It was quite unnecessary for Bennett to add in explanation of his proposed resolution, " I do not want the southern route to be a foregone conclusion in the organization of the committee. For one, I shall go against any, committee, whether standing or select, unless it is understood that all the routes are to have fair play." That Bennett's sentiment was not entertained by him alone appears from the fact that his resolution was defeated only by a vote of 61 to 76. Finally on the proposition of Washburn (Maine) a Select Committee of fifteen was appointed on the 25th of January, 1858, seven weeks after the commencement of the session. On the 9th of February following, when the committee asked to be allowed a clerk, the pusillanimity of the opponents of the project was displayed by a refusal of the House to grant the request, by a vote of 87 to 42. During the session, five Pacific railway bills were introduced and referred to the committee, but it made no report.

In the Senate, in the first session, the usual Select Committee of nine members on the Pacific railway was appointed, and reported a bill on the 18th of January for a road from San Francisco to some point between the mouths of the Big Sioux and Kansas Rivers. After the usual amendments had been suggested for and in behalf of the several sections and localities from the Gulf of Mexico to the 49th parallel, and for two roads and three roads — the stock amendments, — the Senate, particularly in view of the proceedings that had already been had in the House, discreetly postponed the further consideration of the report of the Select Committee to the following December, the second session of the 35th Congress.

In the fall of 1858, in the second session of the 35th Congress, the Senate resumed the discussion of the bill reported by the Select Committee in the first session. The bill was of the distinctly " equality of opportunity," individualistic, *laissez faire* pattern, that had its spontaneous origin in the 34th Congress, and was perhaps the legitimate fruit of the fungus growth of the theory of " non-intervention " and " popular sovereignty." Its title proclaimed its import to be "to authorize the President of the United States to contract for the transportation of the mails, troops, seamen, munitions of war, army and navy supplies, and all other government service, by railroad, from the Missouri River to San Francisco, in the State of California," — a clear intimation that the only inducement to be held out by the government to the projectors of Pacific railways was that of expecting the national patronage to swell their gross earnings and perhaps make net earnings possible. If land was to be given to the builder of Pacific railways, it was to be the far-sighted gift of a "prudent proprietor" who expected his magnanimity to be rewarded by the increase in value of his other land. If money was to be advanced to ambitious "desert-spanners" to aid them in their undertaking, it was to be merely payment in advance for future services. The Pacific railway scheme had well-nigh lost its "nationality," at least in form, though in substance it was still to be one of the "strong arms" of the national strength. In some respects the bill was a peculiarly inconsistent confusion of political and industrial theories. According to its provisions, the President was to receive bids for performing the government services by railroad after public advertisement for them in two newspapers in each of the states and territories and the District of Columbia, and open them in the presence of his Cabinet and such others as might choose to attend; the bids were to provide that the entire railway to be contracted for should be completed within twelve years from the date of the contract, and to specify what extent and portion of the railway, beginning at the eastern and western termini, should be completed and put in operation during each and every year, and at what time the bidder would surrender the road, with appurtenances, to the United States for the purpose of being transferred to the states through which it should pass. The bidders were to receive a sum not in excess of $500 per mile per annum for twenty years for carrying the mails daily each way, and after the expiration of the contract the mails were to be carried and other services to be performed at reasonable rates. The President was to have authority to enter into contracts on the basis of the bids with the party "whose proposal should be by him deemed to be most advantageous to the United States," and the contractor was to deposit a guaranty of $500,000.00, or the value thereof in bonds of the states or United States, to be withdrawn by him in sums of $10,000.00 as rapidly as like sums had been applied by him to the fulfillment of the contract. The land grant was to be twenty sections per mile, together with two hundred feet for right of way, to be surveyed upon the completion of each section of twenty-five miles of the railway (one-fourth of the grant being retained on each such section until the following section should be completed). Further, upon the completion of each section of twenty-five miles, the contractor was to receive $12,500.00 in United States bonds for each mile completed, not exceeding in all $25,000,000.00, the amount thus advanced to the contractor to be repaid by him by the service and transportation provided for. Failure to fulfill the contract was to entail the forfeiture of the railway, and a forfeiture of the land grant was to be entailed by the failure to sell one-half of it within five years and the other half within ten years from the date of the patents. The eastern terminus was to be on the Missouri River, between the mouths of the Big Sioux and Kansas Rivers, and the western terminus was to be at San Francisco; in other particulars, the route was to be located by the contractor.

The restriction of the eastern terminus even within such limits was explained by Seward as follows : " I am one of the Select Committee who introduced this bill. We took this practical view. We tried to ascertain what bill we could submit to Congress that would obtain the votes of thirty-two members of the Senate and one hundred and eighteen members of the House of Representatives. In other words, what project is there, if any, upon which one hundred and fifty-one votes can be concentrated in the two Houses of Congress—for these constitute majorities in both houses. It would seem no easy undertaking to devise a plan which would secure one hundred and fifty-one votes on a question so distracting. We found it so, for our committee consisted of nine ; and if it had been an even number, we certainly should have found it impossible, for a long time, to devise any plan, or to find any route upon which we could get a majority of the committee to concur.   We succeeded in devising a system, and a route which would secure five votes in our committee out of the nine ; and we submit that as the best that could be done. We have made sacrifices to opinion ; sacrifices that seemed to us almost of principle ; sacrifices of devotion to local interests, for the purpose of being able to offer a bill to the House with reasonable expectation that a majority of each House of Congress could be induced to accept it." [1]   Such a confession from one of the most steadfast and far-sighted friends of Pacific railway legislation indicated the almost certain outcome of the work of the 35th Congress.

But there was a factor in the problem that had been up to this time below the surface—a wide and general cause of the extreme development of the evils of sectionalism and localism, that had been thoroughly appreciated and felt but not accorded outward expression.   A legislative body is in most respects only an exaggerated man ; it has its feelings, its controlling ideas, its modes of thought, its moods, its phases of disposition—its personality.   When a man has a physical or mental ill, he tries to persuade himself that he has it not, until the fact happens to receive an " outward expression " by word of mouth or pen, either from the victim or an observer.   Men as well as children " think out loud."   The fact that there was a fatal incongruity or inconsistency in the fundamental organization of the government of the United States, in that an industrial institution whose existence was incompatible with unity, had received recognition in the fundamental law, and in a certain sense had been made a part of it —that fact was thoroughly appreciated and felt for many decades; but the American people tried to persuade themselves that there was no inconsistency, no incongruity, no incompatibility—until the fact was openly declared.   The fact was the same and had been the same; it simply became objectified and active; self-

[1] *Congressional Globe*, Volume 38, page 1584, 35th Congress, 1st Session.

deception was no longer possible. This was the state of things from a political standpoint, in 1859, and it was reflected in (or reflected from) the state of industrial society. Statesmen had tried to persuade themselves that a Pacific railway, as a national project, was a possibility, had tried to persuade themselves that there was a nation, but all the time, in the undertow of thought and feeling, there was too keen an appreciation of a want of unity and nationality. The history of the Pacific railway has been marvelously woven in and out among the threads of national history. Aside from the great and overwhelming institution of slavery itself, there is nothing that has recorded so delicately and accurately the ebb and flow of the tide of nationality as the Pacific railway. Slavery had been a sectional institution ; the question for the Rebellion to decide was whether it might remain such, in a nation in which, in another section, it was not in existence, or must have a separate nation for itself. The question of a Pacific railway was much the same. Was it to be a measure for the benefit of a section or was it to be a national benefit ? The two questions were answered in much the same way. As a matter of form, each was largely handled as a matter incidental to the prosecution of the struggle of arms ; but as a matter of substance, the abolition of the one and the creation of the other were simply the means to the greater end of national unity. So much has been said at this point that the importance of the 35th Congress in the subject may be understood. It was the time of awakening—the time of conviction.

For about two weeks the " equal opportunity " bill had been under consideration, and every western interest from Minnesota and Wisconsin to Louisiana and Texas had offered amendments to the first section, providing for the eastern terminus. The claims of each had been advanced in the usual and customary manner, and each Senator had satisfactorily " explained his position " to his constituents.. Jefferson Davis, now Senator from Mississippi, had fairly earned the palm for the craftiest and shrewdest amendment, providing authority to the President " to contract for . . . . government service " by railway, and "that for . . . the advantages thus to be secured to the United States in the use of said road and further to aid in the construction of said road, $10,000,000.00 are hereby appropriated to be advanced as follows,—when one twentieth part of said road . . . is completed, . . . the President shall cause to be advanced to the contracting party the twentieth part . . of the whole sum of money . . . . appropriated and in ' like manner, when each succeeding section of equal extent is completed, . . . an equal amount shall be advanced to the contracting party until the whole road is completed . . . ." According to this amendment, which Davis announced to be an expression of the views of the minority of the Select Committee, the shorter the railway, the more money per mile could be advanced to the contractor. That would have insured the building of the road on the line of the 32d parallel — Davis' favorite route, the route recommended by him as Secretary of War,—for the shortest distance between the states was from El Paso del Norte on the western border of Texas to Fort Yuma on the eastern boundary of California.[1] A railroad was already projected and partly built from Shreveport and New Orleans across the state of Texas to El Paso del Norte, with the liberal aid from the state of Texas, of $6,000.00 in money and 10,000 acres of land per mile of road. This, with a line from San Francisco to San Diego and Fort Yuma, would have given the South a through line from the lower Mississippi and southern centers to San Francisco. But the amendment was not adopted.

The provision for giving authority to the President to make contracts with the bidder "whose proposal should be by him deemed to be the most advantageous to the United States" had been wholly unacceptable to the northern and central Senators. In the preceding Congress, one of the worst things that Benton was able to say of the Douglas bill was that it was an "administration

[1] The distance from El Paso del Norte to Fort Yuma was estimated at about six hundred miles, while the distance from points on the Missouri and Mississippi Rivers to the eastern border of California was variously estimated at from nineteen hundred to twenty-two hundred miles.

measure." It was now considered that Buchanan, in his first annual message[1] had expressed a preference for the route of the parallel of 32° north. It was bitterly charged that an act for a mail route from Saint Louis to San Francisco, passed in 1857, had been intended to provide an overland mail along the Platte valley and through the South Pass, but had been so construed by the administration, and particularly by the Postmaster General, that the route had followed the southern trail through Albuquerque; that the bids or proposals relating to the central overland route had been rejected, and an arbitrary route laid out by the department. This had led to a long explanation and defense by the Postmaster General in his first annual report,[2] though even Douglas, who was justly considered friendly to the administration, admitted that the wishes and purposes of Congress had been thwarted. The President was said to be under the "personal influence" of Slidell, of Louisiana, and the bent of his administration was conceded to be favorable to the South in its tendencies. This North vs. South feeling had found many covert means of expression, when on the 6th day of January, 1859, Iverson of Georgia refused to longer conceal the real difficulty, and gave "outward expression" to the thought and feeling that made a Pacific railway, depending on Federal initiation, an impossibility until 1862. "If one road is provided for and the route is left open to be selected by the company who shall undertake it, a northern route will be adopted, making its immediate connections with the northern and northwestern roads, and pouring all its vast travel and freight over those roads and into the northern states and cities of the Union." "Northern capitalists shun all southern investments as if the very touch was pollution. And, Sir, do you think that these feelings, these opinions, these prejudices would not operate in the selection and construction of a Pacific railroad? I believe that the time will come when the slave states will be compelled, in vindication of their rights, interests,

[1] Supra, page 73 et seq.
[2] Supra, page 76.

and honor, to separate from the free states, and erect an independent Confederacy; and I am not sure, Sir, that the time is not near at hand when that event will occur. At all events, I am satisfied that one of two things is inevitable; either that the slave states must surrender their peculiar institutions, or separate from the North. There is but one path of safety for the institution of slavery in the South when this mighty northern avalanche of fanaticism and folly shall press upon us; and that path lies through separation and a southern Confederacy. 'No Union, or no slavery' will sooner or later be forced upon the choice of the southern people. It is because I believe that separation is not far distant; because the signs of the times point too plainly to the early triumph of the Abolitionists, and their complete possession and control of every department of the Federal Government; and because I firmly believe that when such an event occurs the Union will be dissolved, that I am unwilling to vote as much land and as much money as this bill proposes to build a road to the Pacific, which, in my judgment, will be created outside of a southern Confederacy, and will belong exclusively to the North. The public lands now held by the United States, as well as the public treasury, are the joint property of all the states and the people of this Union. They belong to the South as well as to the North; we are entitled, in the Union, to our just and equal share, and if the Union is divided, then we are no less entitled to a fair proportion of the common fund. What I demand, therefore, is that the South shall be put upon an equality with the North, whether the Union lasts or not; that in appropriating the public lands and money, the joint property of all, in connecting the Atlantic and Pacific Oceans by railroad, the South shall have an equal chance to secure the road within her borders, to inure to her benefit whilst the Union lasts, and to belong to her when, if ever, that Union is dissolved. For the purpose of accomplishing my object, I move that this bill be recommitted to the special committee who had charge of the subject at the last session with instructions to bring in a bill providing for the construction of a railroad on each of two routes to the Pacific Ocean."[1] The bill was not recommitted, but futile efforts were made to perfect this bill in the Senate. The debate was transformed into a regulation pro-slavery, anti-slavery war of words, every hour of which showed more conclusively the impossibility of positive Pacific railway legislation in the 35th Congress. When Iverson's motion was, on motion of Doolittle (Wisconsin), modified to provide for the old Douglas plan of "a northern, a central, and a southern Pacific railroad," Hale, with a touch of irony, contributed the following apt description of the motion: "This, then, is a proposition to instruct the committee to bring in a bill for a northern and southern route, looking prospectively to the dissolution of the Union, so that the South and North shall each have a railroad to the Pacific. The amendment of my friend from Wisconsin, I suppose, is to put in a central route, so that if there are a few who stick to the old constitution, who do not go off with either of the extremists, . . . they may have a conservative, national road, a middle ground, what the classics would call *tutissimo medio.*"[2] The theory of union and disunion was discussed for several days, but the propriety of its application to the particular subject of the Pacific railway was never questioned.

After the debate had taken such a direction, it was useless for Green (Missouri) to try to unite the sentiment of the Senate on a modification of the original one-road bill providing for "two branches, one on the south, commencing not south of Fulton, in the state of Arkansas, the other on the north, commencing not north of the mouth of the Big Sioux, and connecting at the most practicable point not farther west than the one hundred and second degree of west longitude."

Wilson (Massachusetts) and Bigler (Pennsylvania) were

[1] *Congressional Globe*, Volume 41, pages 243-244, 35th Congress, 2d Session.

Wilson, of Massachusetts, called the route of the 32d parallel, the "desert and dis-union route." *Congressional Globe*, Volume 41, page 245, 35th Congress, 2d Session.

[2] Ibidem, page 326.

more successful (temporarily) with an amendment providing that
the entire single road should be divided into three equal grand
divisions, for each mile of which on the eastern and western divisions, twenty sections of land should be donated and $12,500.00
in bonds advanced, and for each mile of which in the middle
division, no land was to be donated, but the bonds advanced
were to be doubled in amount, $25,000.00 per mile. This was
not found in the final form of the bill, though it was temporarily
incorporated with slight modifications, in the bill under consideration. Its importance consists in its later application in the
acts of 1862 and 1864, and it is the first full recognition of the
lack of uniformity in the quality of lands and facilities for railway building between the Missouri River and Pacific Ocean.

Wilson later offered an amendment for the location and construction of a road between the 34th and 43d parallels from some
point on the Missouri River, between the mouths of the Big Sioux
and Kansas Rivers, to San Francisco, directly by the Federal
government, through the agency of a board of five commissioners to be appointed by the President, by and with the advice
and consent of the Senate, for whose use, during the first year,
$10,000.00 should be appropriated. This amendment was defeated
by a vote of 13 to 32.[1]

After the waste of almost an entire month in changing,
re-changing and transforming the original bill reported by the
Select Committee after its many concessions, it had taken a
form in which its best friend could not have recognized it, and
Gwin himself disowned it. The bill in its final form, passed
by the Senate on the 27th of January, 1859, by a vote of 31 to
20, had been proposed by Bell (Tennessee) as satisfying the
desires of the Senate elicited in the long debate, and provided
that the Secretary of the Interior should advertise for eight
months in two newspapers in each state for "separate proposals
for the construction and working of three railroads from the
valley of the Mississippi to the Pacific Ocean," a northern, a

[1] *Congressional Globe*, Volume 41, pages 577, 578 and 602, 35th Congress,
2d Session.

central, and a southern Pacific railway. The proposals should specify: first, the time within which each road would be commenced and completed; second, "the amount, or extent, and description of the aids, facilities, and privileges which will be expected or required from the government, whether consisting of land, money, or both; and, if in part of money, whether in the shape of a loan or otherwise; and, if a loan, when and how to be refunded;" third, the rates of charges for government services; fourth, at what time the road should be surrendered to the government; fifth, the guarantees proposed for the faithful fulfillment of any contract made, and the imposition of fares and charges neither excessive nor exorbitant. The proposals were to be sealed, and were to be opened by the Secretary of the Interior in the presence of the other heads of departments before the first session of the next Congress, and copies of them were then to be transmitted to each House of Congress as soon as organized.

The work on the bill in the Senate had a fit ending. When the vote on the passage of the bill had been announced, the *Congressional Globe* bears evidence of the following proceedings:

"The Presiding Officer. The title of the bill will be read.

[The reading of the original title of the bill was greeted with great laughter].

Mr. Gwin: Inasmuch as I think we have performed a great day's work, and consummated the greatest farce that ever was known in any legislation, I move that the Senate adjourn.

Several Senators: Let us change the title of the bill.

Mr. Bell: I call the Senator from California to order. He has no right to denounce any proposition adopted by the Senate, in such terms.

Mr. Gwin: What does the Senator say?

The Presiding Officer: Senators must come to order.

Mr. Gwin: I say and I repeat it, it is a farce. The Senator from Tennessee knows where to find me.

Mr. Bell: I do not mean—

The Presiding Officer: The Senator from California and the Senator from Tennessee are not in order. The question is on the motion to adjourn."[1]

[1] *Congressional Globe*, Volume 41, page 634, 35th Congress, 2d Session. It may merely be a matter of justice to add that on the following day, Senator

Then the title[1] was amended so as to read, "A bill to authorize and invite separate proposals for the construction of a railroad from the valley of the Mississippi to the Pacific Ocean, upon the separate routes."[2]

In the House of Representatives, in this second session, some Pacific railway bills were introduced, but no action was taken on them. The Select Commitee in the House, out of courtesy to Representative Curtis, of Iowa, permitted him to report a bill from it, but nothing further was done. When the "farce" passed by the Senate was sent to the House of Representatives for concurrence, that body did not even take time to laugh at it.

VIII.

The characteristic feature of Pacific railway legislation—or attempted legislation—from 1859 to 1861, was the corporation through the medium of which its objects were expected to be accomplished. There was nothing new in the scheme of land grant or other government aid, and the squabble of localities and sections for the benefits of the route and termini have a familiar ring.

In his annual message of 1859, Buchanan gave the project a kindly impetus by again expressing "a most decided opinion in favor of the construction of a Pacific railroad, for the reasons stated in my last two annual messages." The President gave no offense by seeming, as in a former message,[3] to indicate a preference for a particular route, but amplified his opinion of the means that should be employed in the undertaking. "I repeat the opinion contained in my last annual message, that it would be inexpedient for the Government to undertake this great work

Gwin offered to the Senate a quite sufficient apology for his remarks on this occasion, which by the standard acknowledged in that body were undoubtedly less elegant than true.

[1] For the original title, and a synopsis of the original bill see pages 78 to 80 supra.

[2] *Congressional Globe*, Volume 41, page 634, 35th Congress, 2d Session.

[3] Supra, page 75.

by agents of its own appointment and under its direct and exclusive control. This would increase the patronage of the executive to a dangerous extent, and would foster a system of jobbing
and corruption which no vigilance on the part of federal officials
could prevent. The construction of this road ought, therefore,
to be intrusted to incorporated companies, or other agencies,
who would exercise that active and vigilant supervision over it
which can be inspired alone by a sense of corporate and individual interest." [1]

In the House of Representatives of the 36th Congress, the
Pacific railway had at last found a champion in Samuel R. Curtis, of Iowa. In order to find an expression in positive law, an
idea must have an aggressive advocate in the turbulent Lower
House. Moreover, the Democratic majority in the 35th Congress
had been replaced by a Republican plurality [2] of aggressive, com-
bative representatives of Northern anti-slavery, anti-secession pro-
clivities, like John Sherman and " Tom " Corwin, of Ohio ; Colfax, of Indiana ; Thaddeus Stephens, of Pennsylvania ; Charles
Francis Adams, of Massachusetts ; Roscoe Conkling, of New
York ; and William Windom, of Minnesota. There was an unusual percentage of new men, and the House was a trifle gruff and
quite too intolerant in disposition. The " previous question "
was a favorite weapon in this Congress and was wielded unspar-
ingly ; personal charges and recriminations were the sauce of
debate in the House.

On the 9th of March, 1860, in accordance with a resolution
of an earlier date, a Select Committee of fifteen on the Pacific
railway was appointed by the Speaker, with Curtis as chairman.
On the 26th of the same month, Curtis introduced a bill and had
it referred to the Select Committee, which, in turn, reported a
bill on the 13th of April following. The majority report of the
Committee was signed by only nine of its members, and there

---

[1] Appendix to *Congressional Globe*, Volume 46, page 6, 36th Congress, 1st
Session.

[2] The House of Representatives stood,— 101 Democrats, 113 Republicans,
23 Independents. McKee's Platforms and Parties, page 61.

were two minority reports. The majority report provided for one central road to San Francisco, by way of Great Salt Lake, with two branches from the western boundaries of Iowa and Missouri. The minority report of Cyrus Aldrich (Oregon) favored one road on the Northern Pacific route. The minority report of Hamilton (Texas) provided for two roads, one on the route of the 32d parallel, and the other on the central route favored in the majority report. Phelps (Missouri), Taylor (Louisiana), and Smith (Virginia) concurred in none of the reports. Henry Winter Davis (Maryland) concurred in the majority report, except as to "the plan of construction."[1] The plan of construction was the only new feature in the bill. It provided for the construction by a "company" consisting of forty-five persons[2] named in the bill and of such others as they should associate with them, who should be aided in their undertaking by an issue of United States bonds to the extent of not more than $60,000,-000.00, and by a land grant of the alternate sections (odd numbers) within one (!) mile of the road. The bonds were to bear interest at five per cent, and to mature in thirty years; and until repaid to the government by the services performed by the company, the amount of them was to be secured by a first lien upon the property of the company. Whether the company was to be incorporated was open to question, under the terms of the bill. An amendment was offered by Reagan (Texas), to make the body of men named in the bill mere trustees for the formation of a company, instead of the company itself. After two days of debate and nothing accomplished, the bill was re-committed to the Select Committee. On the 14th of June, 1860, the commit-

[1] House of Representatives, Reports of Committees, 36th Congress, 1st Session, No. 428.

[2] Of the men named in the bill, seven were from New York; five from Pennsylvania; four each from Illinois, Iowa, and Missouri; three each from Maryland, Ohio, Indiana, California, and Massachusetts; two each from Michigan and Oregon; and one each from Virginia and Tennessee. It was expected by the committee that the Southern states would either not participate in the construction of the central line, or would be given charge of the southern line, if it should be provided for by amendment of the bill.

tee again reported,.and the further consideration of the bill was postponed to the following December, when the second session of the 36th Congress would begin. In the Senate, during this first session, a perfunctory notice was given by Gwin that he would call up for hearing in the early part of April, 1860, the bill that had been under consideration in the Senate and had been emasculated by amendment before its passage; but the futility of pushing the project at that time was too manifest and the measure was not called up.

Not long after the beginning of the second session, Curtis called up, on December 18, 1860, the day to which it had been postponed, the bill reported by the Select Committee, entitled "a bill to secure contracts and make provision for the safe, certain, and more speedy transportation of troops, munitions of war, military and naval stores between the Atlantic states and those of the Pacific, and for other purposes," for the purpose of having it made a special order for the consideration of the House on a future day. A vigorous parliamentary combat was caused by a point of order raised by Branch (North Carolina), and Smith (Virginia), the representatives of the extreme Southern state-rights opponents of the Pacific railway ; it was insisted by them that the rule requiring " a motion or proposition for a tax or charge upon the people " to "receive its first discussion in Committee of the Whole House," applied to this bill, because it proposed the issuance of bonds in aid of the construction of the railroad ; and the Speaker decided the point in favor of the obstructionists. This was a vital point, because the reference of the bill to the Committee of the Whole was tantamount to its defeat, as it would there be taken up only in its order on the calendar and could not be taken up as a special order in the Committee of the Whole without unanimous consent, not being a general appropriation bill. The result of this effort on the part of the minority, by technical means, to defeat the bill, which had been on ultra-sectional lines, and marked by much bitterness and personal feeling, was only to arouse a feeling of resentment in the majority. Fire was fought with fire. Two days afterwards, on the 20th day of

December, 1860, a bill "granting land in alternate sections to aid in the construction of certain railroads in the Territory of Nebraska," was reached on the calendar, and taken up by the House in Committee of the Whole. John Sherman promptly moved an amendment in the nature of a substitute, and Curtis moved to amend the amendment by the substitution of a bill almost identical with the Pacific railway bill reported by the Select Committee. Galusha Grow, of Pennsylvania, occupied the chair and was in sympathy with the Northern majority. The amendments of Curtis and Sherman were promptly adopted. Under the technical rules of the House of Representatives, after the adoption of the substitute, amendment could be only by additional sections, and each such section proposed was promptly rejected by the united majority. The Committee of the Whole reported to the House that it had " had . . . under consideration . . . the bill . . . granting land in alternate sections to aid in the construction of certain railroads in the Territory of Nebraska," and recommended "that the bill, as amended, do pass." Curtis demanded the previous question on the bill and amendment, the majority seconded the demand for the previous question, and the amendment was concurred in. After engrossment, Curtis again demanded the previous question on the passage of the bill, and the yeas and nays were called by the Clerk in the midst of such an uproar and turmoil and confusion that responses could hardly be heard. Motions to adjourn and lay on the table were thrust aside as coming too late to be entertained during the roll-call. The bill was passed by a vote of 95 to 74, and the title changed so as to be almost identical with that of the bill reported by the Select Committee. Thus the first Pacific railway bill passed by the House of Representatives was dragooned through, by a rough-shod majority, without debate and without discussion, and by the perverted use of the technical rules of parliamentary procedure. The over-ridden minority could not complain with good grace, though they wailed piteously at the disregard of their rights, and Reagan called it a "contemptible trick;"—the minority had adopted the same method in opposing the bill, and had been temporarily successful;—they had found their perversion of the rules of the House a boomerang. But the majority had overdone its work. The bill passed was crude and imperfect, well deserving the name given it by Senator Lane, a " bill of abominations."

As sent to the Senate, the bill provided for a central railway with two branches on the east from the borders of Iowa and Missouri uniting within two hundred miles west of the Missouri River, and thence proceeding west by way of Great Salt Lake to San Francisco, and for a southern railway with two branches from the western borders of Arkansas and Louisiana, uniting near the meridian of 97° west, and thence proceeding on the route of the 32d parallel to Fort Yuma and north to San Francisco. The work on the central route was to be performed by a company of fifty-three persons named in the bill, and persons associated with them, who should be incorporated under the laws of the states and territories through which the road should pass. The work on the southern line was to be done by the Southern Pacific Railroad Company, already chartered by the State of Texas for the building of the line from Shreveport to El Paso del Norte. The aid to be extended was the grant of one section of public land per mile for the central line, and of six sections per mile for the southern line (except in California, where the grant was to be of ten sections per mile), and a loan of bonds (secured by a first lien on the property) of from $12,000.00 to $46,000.00 per mile, not exceeding in all, $60,000,-000.00 for the central line and $36,000,000.00 for the southern line, to mature in thirty years, with interest at five per cent, all to be repaid to the government by services for the government. When the Senate had finished the consideration of it on the 30th day of January, 1861, it was passed by a vote of 37 to 14, with forty-five amendments. A northern line and a branch from Sacramento to Portland had been added, and the list of incorporators had been increased to more than one hundred, and their powers restricted; it had also been provided that thirty per cent of the bonds should be retained until the entire work was completed, and that the corporators should have no right or title in the bonds or land until incorporated and their charter approved by Congress. The manner of passing the bill in the House of Representatives had made its enemies in the Senate vindictive; there the South had more nearly equal representation with the North, and the advocates of the central line, in order to secure the votes of Oregon, Minnesota, and Wisconsin and other advocates of the northern line, had to submit to the burden of amendments; besides, the bill had been too hastily considered by the House, and was seriously defective in many particulars.

When it was returned to the House of Representatives for concurrence in the amendments of the Senate, Curtis and Sherman still had the solid majority with them, and were hopeful of securing the accession of the House to the demands of the Senate. But the attention of both branches of Congress was taken up with matters of greater and more vital importance, and, as the venerable Crittenden suggested in the Senate, the project of a Pacific railway had to give way to questions of national life and death. Besides, if the Senate amendments should be concurred in, it was foreseen that the bill would be too crude and unwieldy to produce practical results. Again, only eighteen days of the session remained, and the appropriation bills and other business always massed at the end of the short session, made it impossible to expect enough attention for the bill to carry it through.

As to the bill of 1860–1861, " Gwin says, in his *Memoirs*, that there was a large majority in the Senate in favor, and that ' there was an equally large majority in its favor in the House, but the majority of that body determined to defeat its passage then in order to give the credit of inaugurating this great system of transcontinental railroads to the incoming administration of Mr. Lincoln.' "[1] But such an explanation is hardly satisfactory. The truth is that the bill was simply crowded out by other business. Senator Gwin's opinion was undoubtedly colored by his Southern sympathies.

[1] Bancroft, History of California, Volume VII., page 527.

CHAPTER IV.

THE CHARTER.

I.

IN the light of the history of the Pacific railway from 1845 to 1860, one is not surprised to find in the platform of the Republican party, adopted by the national convention at Chicago in May, 1860, a plank "That a railroad to the Pacific Ocean is imperatively demanded by the interests of the whole country ; that the Federal Government ought to render immediate and efficient aid in its construction ; and as preliminary thereto, a daily overland mail should be promptly established;" and in the Charleston platform of the Democratic party adopted in April, 1860, a more cautious resolution as follows :

" Resolved, That one of the necessities of the age, in a military, commercial and postal point of view, is speedy communication between the Atlantic and Pacific states ; and the Democratic party pledges such constitutional government aid as will insure the construction of a railroad to the Pacific coast at the earliest practicable period." In the Baltimore platform of the branch of the Democratic party that had withdrawn from the Charleston convention, the resolution of the latter was duplicated (in June, 1860) almost literally as follows: " Whereas, One of the greatest necessities of the age, in a political, commercial, postal and military point of view, is a speedy communication between the Pacific and Atlantic coasts,—Therefore, be it resolved, That the Democratic party do hereby pledge themselves to use every means in their power to secure the passage of some bill, to the extent of the constitutional authority of Congress, for the construction of a Pacific railroad from the Mississippi River to the Pacific Ocean, at the earliest practicable moment."

The short session of Congress following a presidential election is almost always a "do-nothing" session, particularly when there has been a radical change in public sentiment, as expressed at the polls. The election in 1860 of a Republican President in Lincoln and a majority of substantial opponents of slavery in the Republican Representatives and Senators of the Northern constituencies was a severe rebuke to the party dominant in Washington, and left its representatives in no disposition to transact any but the most perfunctory public business in the session of 1860-1861. When the special session of the Thirty-seventh Congress, called by President Lincoln's proclamation, convened on the 4th of July, 1861, the "friends" of the Pacific railway found that the progress of events had brought to their project conditions more favorable than it had ever before enjoyed.

The secession of the eleven Southern states had taken from both Houses of Congress the most vigorous opponents of a Pacific railway to be constructed by the aid of the government. By continual self-instruction the people and their representatives had been taught to look upon its construction largely as a war measure, bound up with the great struggle for national unity. The dear financial experience of the Rebellion was to accustom the members of Congress to large expenditures of public means. The same source had yielded an intense national sentiment. Congress was soon to find itself so busy with weightier matters that peace from the clamors of California and the Mississippi valley for a transcontinental railway would be cheap at one hundred millions of national credit. All that was left of the sectionalism and localism, that were the theme of the preceding chapter, was the rivalry of the Saint Louis interest, the Eastern (or Chicago) interest, and the Northern Pacific interest, which last had developed since 1855. But Saint Louis was weak, even with the support of the Baltimore, Philadelphia and New York lines of railway, of which that city was the western terminus, and even with the influence that it acquired from the traffic of the Mississippi, Missouri, and Ohio Rivers. Missouri was a black sheep in the flock of loyal states, and the inertness and inanity of slavery

7

and Southern industrial ideas had left Saint Louis slow and backward. Chicago, with the New England and New York energy and wealth, and the traffic of the Great Lakes and of the systems of east and west trunk railways behind it, was powerful. The Chicago interest was identified with the political party of freedom in the North and received its support from the representatives of that party. There were two principal systems of east and west transportation—one, of railways between Philadelphia and New York on the east, and Saint Louis and Saint Joseph on the west; the other, of railways between New York and Boston on the east and Chicago on the west, and of lakes and canals between Canadian points, Portland, New York, Buffalo, Cleveland, and Detroit on the east, and Chicago, Milwaukee and Duluth on the west. From Saint Louis, the first named system had sought a connection with the future Pacific railway by the Missouri Pacific railway from Saint Louis to Kansas City, and by the Hannibal and Saint Joseph railway from the Mississippi due west to Saint Joseph. The Chicago system had reached Dubuque, Rock Island and Burlington, on the Mississippi, and the future Chicago and Northwestern, Rock Island, and Burlington lines were extending with all possible haste across Iowa to Sioux City, Council Bluffs and Platte City (Plattsmouth). Further north, Wisconsin, Minnesota, Oregon and the Territory of Washington had been rapidly colonized by emigrants from the Old World and settlers from the Eastern states. The superior fertility of the soil of Dakota, Montana and Washington, as compared with that of the "Great American Desert" in western Nebraska and Kansas and the Great Basin between the mountain ranges—and the consequent greater possibility of using a land grant to good purpose—united with a far greater adaptability of land surface to railway construction, gave to the extreme northern tier of rapidly growing young states and territories a substantial basis for demanding a transcontinental railway from Lake Superior or Saint Paul on the east to the Columbia River or Puget's Sound on the west. Asa Whitney's advocacy, followed by the revelations of the government surveys of 1853–1855, had given to the

Northern Pacific project substantial strength, when Josiah Perham, in 1860, originated the popular and attractive scheme embodied in his People's Pacific Railroad Company, by which the road was to be constructed with the proceeds of a grant of government land and popular subscriptions of stock without the aid of bonded indebtedness. This interest was active and aggressive in 1861.

Thus it was that when the Thirty-seventh Congress came to give serious attention to the details of a Pacific railway scheme, under the new set of conditions imposed by the attempted secession of the South from the Union, it found three contending influences, in favor, severally, of a Northern Pacific railway, a Pacific railway from the border of Iowa, and a Pacific railway from the border of Missouri.

Within a week after the opening of the special session, Curtis (Iowa) introduced, July 8, 1861, in the House of Representatives, a bill substantially similar to the bill championed by him in the preceding Congress and having the same title ; this represented the Chicago (or Eastern) interest. On this motion the bill was referred, as usually, to a Select Committee of nine members. On the 22d day of the same month, Washburne (Illinois) presented a bill for "granting public lands and a loan of the Government to the People's Pacific Railroad Company to aid in the construction of a railroad from the Mississippi River to the Pacific coast" — the Northern Pacific project — which was referred to the same committee. The Saint Louis project last received expression in a bill offered by Rollins (Missouri), on February 5, 1862, and intended "to aid in constructing a railroad and telegraph line from the Missouri River to the Pacific Ocean, and to secure to the government the use of the same for postal, military and other purposes." This was tossed into the sieve of the Select Committee along with the other bills and the sifting began. Three corresponding bills were introduced in the Senate, a Curtis bill by Latham (California), July 17 ; a People's Pacific Railroad bill by Morrill (Maine), July 25 ; and a prototype of the Rollins bill by Pomeroy, (Kansas) February 4, 1862 ; and these were likewise referred to a Select Committee, originally of five, later of nine, and finally of ten members.

Curtis had been made chairman of the Select Committee in the House, but soon afterwards resigned his seat to assume active military duties in the war, and the leadership of the "little legislature" was given over to Campbell (Pennsylvania). The committee reported to the House what its chairman described as the Curtis bill, changed in some slight particulars to avoid technical objections, but members soon discovered in it a measure quite different. The committee was timid and irresolute, inclined rather to follow than to lead, and to reflect the opinion of the House rather than to mold it. At first the Northern Pacific scheme had been included in the bill, largely because the Senate had tacked it to the Curtis bill in the last Congress, but when it was found that a bill satisfactory to the two other interests could get votes enough to pass without the assistance of the Northern Pacific interest, that part of the bill was expunged, though it was thought best to pacify Oregon with a branch line from the vicinity of Sacramento. Then the committee reported the Rollins bill as a substitute, and the efforts to perfect the substitute constituted the active work of the House for the session.

Bancroft would have it believed that the Union Pacific Railroad Company was so named, not because it was created by the national act of the Union, but because its work was to be accomplished by the *union* of several corporations.[1] Whatever be the true origin of the name, some color is given to Bancroft's explanation by the provisions of the Rollins bill. According to them, the Leavenworth, Pawnee and Western (chartered by Kansas) was to build a main line from Kansas City to the 102d meridian

[1] History of California, Volume VII., page 528. The historian does not give his authority for this statement, and its correctness is to be doubted. The managers of the company, of late years, have certainly assumed a different origin of the name, as shown by their constant use of the Union shield as an emblem, with its blue field and its thirteen red and white stripes, in every conceivable place, from the side of a freight car to the letterheads of stationery. Compare with this the name given by Senator Wilson to the projected railroad on the route of the 32d parallel—the "disunion" line. (Supra, page 86, note.)

(the western boundary of Kansas) and a branch line to it from Leavenworth. Saint Joseph was to have a branch line to be constructed by the Hannibal and Saint Joseph (chartered by Missouri). The Missouri Pacific (chartered by Missouri) might connect at Kansas City. All three were empowered to unite in constructing the branch lines. From Iowa, at points not farther west than Kansas City, were to extend two branches to unite with the main line in Kansas at not more than three hundred miles west of Kansas City, to be constructed by four companies (or any or either of them)—the (1) Dubuque and Sioux City, (2) Cedar Rapids and Missouri, (3) Mississippi and Missouri, and (4) Burlington and Missouri River (all chartered by Iowa). From the 102d meridian through Colorado and Utah, the Union Pacific Railroad Company was to build, "upon the most direct, central, and practicable route," to the Nevada border, thence the Nevada Railroad Company (chartered by the Territory of Nevada) was to pass it along to the California border, and the Central Pacific Railroad Company of California was to complete the line to Sacramento. Other companies chartered by California and Oregon might construct a branch from the Central Pacific line to the Columbia River. This was doubtless the "union" scheme to which Bancroft refers. The land grant was to be five sections per mile, and the bond subsidy was to be the same as finally provided[1], except for the Oregon branch, and for that it should not exceed $8,000.00 per mile. After this "Joseph's coat of many colors," or "crazy-quilt," as members described it, was modified by doubling the land grant, lopping off the Oregon branch, and providing that the Union Pacific company should build a branch line from Iowa to unite with the Leavenworth, Pawnee and Western on the 102d meridian, and should thence build westwardly to the California border (thus rejecting the Nevada company), the bill passed the House on the 6th of May, 1862, by a vote of 79 to 49. This left the Saint Louis party with an advantage, though their battle had been fought by the Kansas representatives,—Saint Louis was to have the direct or main line, and Chi-

[1] Infra, page 105.

cago was to have a side or branch line, and the Kansas line could by its western termination govern the course of the remainder of the line.

When the bill reached the Senate, it suffered the slovenly championship of McDougall as chairman of the Senate committee, and would probably have been lost, had Latham not come to the aid of his colleague. Practically nothing was done for six weeks, when the bill was reported back to the Senate with many amendments, most of them purely technical, but one of them substantial and radical.

On the pretext that putting the point of union of the Iowa and Missouri branches on the 102d meridian would make them too long and expensive, Harlan (Iowa), who had been added as a tenth member of the Select Committee, insisted that the junction should be at or near Kearney, Nebraska, and the matter was compromised by providing a point on the 100th meridian. But such a point of junction would cause a part of the line to be built by the national corporation within a state, as the Kansas company could not build outside of the state of Kansas. And this possible disregard of state rights encountered an old constitutional scruple in the breasts of some "War Democrats" like Lyman Trumbull, to conciliate which a further amendment was agreed upon, so that the initial point was described as "a point on the one-hundredth meridian of longitude west of Greenwich, between the south margin of the valley of the Republican River, and the north margin of the valley of the Platte River, in the Territory of Nebraska." This was the important point, and the contest in the Senate was focused on it, as its determination would settle the question whether Chicago or Saint Louis should have the main line and leave its rival the branch line. The bill, with amendments, was passed by the Senate, June 20, 1862, by a vote of 25 to 5.

If the House of Representatives should concur in the Senate amendments, Chicago would have the advantage of the trunk line, and Saint Louis (through Kansas City) and Saint Joseph would have the branch line. Remarkably enough, the proposed amendments were concurred in by the House of Representatives without a syllable of debate, by a vote of 104 to 21, on the 24th day of June, 1862. On the first of July following, the approval of Abraham Lincoln made the bill a law, and nationalism had won its first victory over sectionalism and localism.

The Act of 1862, as finally passed and approved, created a corporation to be known as "The Union Pacific Railroad Company," and to be composed of one hundred and fifty-eight persons named in the act,[1] "together with five commissioners to be appointed by the Secretary of the Interior, and all persons who shall or may be associated with them, and their successors." The capital stock was to consist of one hundred thousand shares of one thousand dollars each, of which not more than two hundred shares were to be held by any one person.[2] The one hundred and fifty-eight persons, with the five more to be appointed by the Secretary of the Interior, were constituted a " Board of Commissioners of the Union Pacific Railroad and Telegraph Company " to set the corporation in motion by opening books for the subscription of stock in the principal cities of the United States, and by calling a meeting of the stockholders for the election of directors as soon as two thousand shares of stock had been subscribed and ten dollars per share paid in ; when the directors had been elected and the property of the corporation turned over to them by the board of commissioners, the duties of the latter should cease and terminate, and thereafter the stockholders should constitute the corporation. The stockholders should have annual meetings and should make by-laws, rules and regulations touching all matters appertaining to the concerns of the company. The directors, to be elected by the stockholders, were to be not less than thirteen in number, to

[1] These persons were distributed among the states and territories as follows: New York, 24; California, 15; Pennsylvania, 13; Wisconsin, 9; Iowa, 8; Ohio, Michigan, Illinois, Indiana, Minnesota and Kansas, 7 each; Missouri, Massachusetts and Nebraska, 5 each; Rhode Island, Connecticut, Maine and Vermont, 4 each; Kentucky, Oregon and Maryland, 3 each; New Jersey, New Hampshire and Nevada, 2 each; and Colorado, 1. Total, 158.

[2] Amended by Act of 1864. Infra, page 126.

be *bona fide* owners of at least five shares of stock each, to be elected triennially, to elect a president and vice-president (from their own number), and a secretary and treasurer, and to hold office for three years; at the time of the election of the directors, the President of the United States was to appoint two additional directors, who should not be stockholders and who should hold office for three years. The directors, president and vice-president were to hold office for three years or such less time as should be prescribed by the by-laws ; the secretary and treasurer, at the will and pleasure of the directors.

The corporation thus created was "authorized and empowered to lay out, locate, construct, furnish, maintain and enjoy a continuous railroad and telegraph, with the appurtenances, from a point . . . . on the one hundredth meridian of longitude west from Greenwich, between the south margin of the valley of the Republican River and the north margin of the valley of the Platte River, in the Territory of Nebraska, ... a point to be fixed by the President of the United States, ... thence running westerly upon the most direct, central, and practicable route, through the Territories of the United States to the western boundary of the Territory of Nevada, there to meet and connect with the line of the Central Pacific Railroad Company of California." The main line and branches provided for in the act were to be " first-class railroads, the rails and all the other irons used in the construction and equipment . . . . to be American manufacture of the best quality, ... the track . . . . of uniform width, ... the grades and curves not [to] exceed the maximum grades and curves of the Baltimore and Ohio Railroad, the whole . . . . to be used for all purposes . . . . as one connected, continuous line." The line from the "initial point" to the western boundary of Nevada was required to be completed before July 1, 1874.

A right of way through the public lands of two hundred feet on each side of the track,[1] and the right to take from adjacent public land earth, stone, timber and other materials for con-

---

[1] Modified by the Act of 1864, infra, page 126.

struction[1] were granted to the company. In addition was granted a subsidy of "every alternate section of public land, designated by odd numbers, to the amount of five alternate sections per mile on each side of said railroad, on the line thereof and within the limits of ten miles on each side of said road, not sold, reserved, or otherwise disposed of by the United States, and to which a preëmption or homestead claim may not have attached, at the time the line of said road is definitely fixed ;" mineral lands were also excepted from the grant, but where such lands contained timber, the timber was granted.[2] "And all such lands, so granted, ... which shall not be sold or disposed of by said company within three years after the road shall have been completed, shall be subject to settlement and preëmption, like other lands, at a price not to exceed one dollar and twenty-five cents per acre, to be paid to said company." For further aid, the Secretary of the Treasury was to issue to the company thirty-year bonds of the United States, bearing interest at six per cent per annum, payable in United States treasury notes or any other legal tender, to the amounts of $16,000.00 for each mile of railway and telegraph east of the eastern base of the Rocky Mountains or west of the western base of the Sierra Nevada Mountains, $48,000.00 for each mile of one hundred and fifty miles west of the western base of the Rocky Mountains, and of a like distance east of the western base of the Sierra Nevada Mountains, and $32,000.00 for each mile of the distance intervening between the two mountain spaces of one hundred and fifty miles each.[3] But the amount of bonds issued for the main line should not exceed, in all, a total of $50,000,000.00. The land grant was to be set apart, and the bonds delivered, as fast as earned, upon the completion and equipment (to be certified by three commissioners appointed by the President of the United States) of sections of road and telegraph of forty miles each, where the bond subsidy was at the

[1] Limited by Act of 1864, infra, page 127.

[2] Amended by Act of 1864, infra, page 127.

[3] The eastern and western bases of the Rocky Mountains and Sierra Nevada Mountains respectively were to be fixed by the President of the United States.

rate of $16,000.00 per mile, and of twenty miles each where the rate of the bond subsidy was in excess of $16,000.00 per mile. On each installment of bonds issued on the lines east of the 100th meridian and west of the western base of the Sierra Nevada Mountains, twenty-five per cent, and of each installment of bonds earned on the remaining lines, fifteen per cent should be reserved by the Secretary of the Treasury until all the lines provided for should be completed, and if any part of the system should fail of completion within the time required by the act, all the reserve bonds should be forfeited to the United States.[1]

The grant of land and bonds was " made upon condition that said company shall pay said bonds at maturity, and shall keep said railroad and telegraph line in repair and use, and shall at all times transmit dispatches over said telegraph line, and transport mails, troops, and munitions of war, supplies and public stores upon said railroad for the government, whenever required to do so by any department thereof, and that the government shall at all times have the preference in the use of the same for all purposes aforesaid (at fair and reasonable rates of compensation, not to exceed the amounts paid by private parties for the same kind of service); and all compensation for services rendered the government shall be applied to the payment of said bonds and interest until the whole amount is fully paid, ... and after said road is completed, until said bonds and interest are paid, at least five per centum of the net earnings of said road shall also be annually applied to the payment thereof."[2]   " To secure the payment . . . . . of the amount of said bonds so issued and delivered to said company, together with all interest thereon which shall have been paid by the United States, the issue of said bonds and delivery to the company shall *ipso facto* constitute a first mortgage on the whole line of the railroad and telegraph, together with the rolling-stock, fixtures, and property of every kind and description, and in consideration of which said bonds may be issued ; and on the refusal or failure of said

[1] Repealed by Act of 1864, infra, page 128.

[2] Act of 1862, section VI.   Modified by Act of 1864, infra, page 128-129.

company to redeem said bonds, or any part of them, when required to do so by the Secretary of the Treasury, in accordance with the provisions of this act, the said road, with all the rights, functions, immunities, and appurtenances thereunto belonging, and also all lands granted to said company by the United States, which at the time of said default shall remain in the ownership of said company, may be taken possession of by the Secretary of the Treasury, for the use and benefit of the United States."

The Central Pacific Railroad Company of California (a California corporation), was authorized to construct a line "from the Pacific coast, at or near San Francisco, or the navigable waters of the Sacramento River, to the eastern boundary of California," to meet and connect with the Union Pacific, upon the same terms and conditions as the latter corporation. If either the Union Pacific or Central Pacific should reach the California boundary before the other, either might proceed to a meeting with the other, and the latter might even complete the branch lines to the Missouri River, if they should be incomplete when reached.[1]

On the east, four branches, to be constructed on the same terms as the Union Pacific and Central Pacific, were provided for. (1) The Iowa branch was to be constructed by the Union Pacific to join with the main line at the "initial point" on the 100th meridian, "from a point on the western boundary of the State of Iowa, to be fixed by the President of the United States."[2] (2) The Sioux City branch was to be built by the Union Pacific company from Sioux City (whenever there should be a line of railway completed to that point through Minnesota or Iowa), so as to connect with the Union Pacific main line or Iowa branch at some point not further west than the 100th meridian, to be fixed by the President of the United States.[3] Failure to construct and

---

[1] Infra, pages 148–149.

[2] See page 129, infra, for further information on the Iowa branch.

[3] By the Act of 1864, (Section 17) the Union Pacific was relieved of the duty of building the Sioux City branch, and the duty was shifted to such company, having completed a line to Sioux City from the east or north, as should be designated by the President of the United States, with the proviso that such company

operate the Sioux City and Iowa branches as required was to entail the forfeiture by the Union Pacific of all its rights under the act creating it. (3) The Missouri branch was to be constructed by the Leavenworth, Pawnee and Western Railroad Company (afterwards known as the Union Pacific Railway Company, Eastern Division, and even later as the Kansas Pacific Railway Company), from the mouth of the Kansas River and a connection with the Pacific Railroad of Missouri (now called the Missouri Pacific, and having its main line from Saint Louis to Kansas City) to the "initial point" of the Union Pacific on the 100th meridian in Nebraska.[1] (4) The Saint Joseph (or Atchison) branch was to be an extension of the Hannibal and Saint Joseph road from Saint Joseph via Atchison. to connect with the Kansas line, or if rendered desirable by actual survey, from Saint Joseph westward to some point on the Iowa branch or to the initial point on the 100th meridian—but the Hannibal and Saint Joseph was to receive subsidy land and bonds for only one hundred miles of road. The Central Pacific and Leavenworth, Pawnee and Western, after their lines were finished, might unite with the Union

should receive no larger sum. in subsidy bonds than the Union Pacific would have received, if it had constructed the line. The Sioux City and Pacific Railroad Company was afterward designated by the President to build this branch, and the result was the irregular line from Sioux City down the east side of the Missouri River to Missouri Valley and thence west to Fremont, Nebraska.

[1] The Leavenworth, Pawnee and Western was also authorized by the Act of 1862 to connect its Kansas line (the Missouri branch) with Leavenworth by a sub-branch. By the Act of 1864, it might either build through Leavenworth from Kansas City or connect Leavenworth by a sub-branch from that point to a point at or near Lawrence—but for the Leavenworth-Lawrence branch it should receive no subsidy bonds. The Act of 1864 provided that any company authorized . . . . to construct its road and telegraph line from the Missouri River to the "initial point " on the 100th meridian, might "connect with the Union Pacific at any point, westwardly of such initial point," but with no greater subsidy of bonds than if it had constructed to the "initial point." The Union Pacific Railway, Eastern Division (or Kansas Pacific) thereupon headed for Denver, and the Act of March 3, 1869, provided that for the purpose of the connection, the Denver Pacific Railway and Telegraph Company's line from Denver to Cheyenne might be considered an extension of the Kansas Pacific, and Cheyenne the junction point with the Union Pacific.

Pacific in building its lines, though the Iowa branch would have to be finished before subsidy bonds could be issued for building the main line. The Hannibal and Saint Joseph, Missouri Pacific, and Union Pacific or either of them, might unite with the Leavenworth, Pawnee and Western in building the Missouri branch.

All of the companies named in the act, or two or more of them, might be consolidated into one or more companies, without loss of benefits under the act. If a continuous line from the Missouri River to the navigable waters of the Sacramento River should not be ready for use July 1, 1876,[1] "the whole of said railroads . . . together with all their furniture, fixtures, rolling-stock, machine shops, lands, tenements, hereditaments, and property of every kind and character, shall be forfeited to and be taken possession of by the United States." If any of the companies should fail to comply with the terms and conditions of the act by not completing the main line and branches within a reasonable time, or by not keeping them in repair and use, but should permit them to remain unfinished or out of repair or unfit for use, Congress might pass an act to insure the speedy completion of the lines, or put them in repair and use, and direct their income to be devoted to the reimbursement of the United States for the expenditures occasioned by the neglect and default of the companies.

Instead of constructing new telegraph lines, the companies might arrange with companies having existing overland lines of telegraph to remove and transfer them along the lines of railway to be operated in connection with them.

For the protection of the public and to insure future control of the companies, it was provided, "That whenever it appears that the net earnings of the entire road and telegraph, including the amount allowed for services rendered for the United States, after deducting all expenditures, including repairs and the furnishing, running, and managing of said road, shall exceed ten per cent upon its cost (exclusive of the five per centum to be paid to the United States), Congress may reduce the rates of fare

[1] By the Act of 1864, the time was extended one year.

thereon, if unreasonable in amount, and may fix and establish the same by law. And the better to accomplish the object of this act, namely, to promote the public interest and welfare by the construction of said railroad and telegraph line, and keeping the same in working order, and to secure to the government at all times (but particularly in time of war) the use and benefit of the same for postal, military, and other purposes, Congress may at any time, having due regard for the rights of said companies named herein, add to, alter, amend, or repeal this act."

Each company was required to make an annual report to the Secretary of the Treasury, containing the names and residences of its stockholders, directors, and officers; the amount of stock subscribed, and the amount of it actually paid in; a description of the lines of road surveyed, of the lines fixed upon for the construction of the road, and the cost of the survey; the amounts of revenue from passenger and freight traffic, and the expense of the road and fixtures; and an itemized statement of the company's indebtedness.[1] By the Act of June 25, 1868, the reports were to be made to the Secretary of the Interior, and in addition to the information required by the Act of 1862, were required "all reports of engineers, superintendents and other officers who make annual reports to any of . . . [the] companies."

II.

The bait offered by the act of 1862 was thrown to the shoals of railway investors, nibbled at, and rejected. Something more seductive was necessary to induce the patriotic but wary capitalists and railway contractors to "bite." The meeting of the "Board of Commissioners"[2] was held in Chicago in September, 1862, and the advantages and disadvantages of the recent act of Congress were thoroughly considered, formally and informally, by the commissioners and prominent "railroad men," capitalists, and contractors in attendance; the conclusion was that the undertaking could not be made a success under the conditions

[1] 12 Statutes, 489.

[2] Supra, page 103.

imposed by Congress, and that " further inducements " were necessary. When, therefore, the books were opened for subscriptions of stock, it is no matter of wonder that the subscriptions
were not general, and that the few shares subscribed were not by
men having faith in the enterprise itself, but almost wholly by
men relying on further assistance from Congress, capitalists
who did not wish to prejudice future opportunities of gain by
"turning a cold shoulder" to the project in its infancy, and
patriotic men of smaller means, like Congressman Pruyn, who
subscribed for the laudable purpose of "saving the charter" by
effecting the preliminary organization required by law.

Senator McDougall was present at the meeting in Chicago,
and readily learned from the capitalists and others in attendance
that under the terms of the act of 1862 the Pacific railway could
not, or at least would not, be built. Accordingly, early in
the third (short) session of the Thirty-seventh Congress, he
took steps for additional legislation, with the view of extending
to prospective railway builders sufficient inducements to produce
a Pacific railway. On the 23d of December, 1862, he introduced in the Senate a bill to amend the Act of 1862, and it was
referred on his motion to a Select Committee, of which he was
made chairman. After two months of incubation, the committee
hatched a report, February 23, 1863, in which the passage of
McDougall's bill was recommended. The bill had few provisions. It provided, in order to make the subscription of stock
more popular and general, that the capital should be in one million shares of one hundred dollars each, instead of one hundred
thousand shares of one thousand dollars each, and that the
directors should be owners of at least fifty, instead of five, shares
of stock.[1] The right of way, instead of extending two hundred
feet on each side of the railway track, was to extend one hundred
feet on each side, with additional ground when necessary, for
depots, turnouts, and other required structures. Adequate provision for the condemnation of private land for right of way supplied the defects of the Act of 1862 in that regard. The provis-

[1] See supra, page 103; also infra, page 126.

ion for the reservation of a percentage of the bonds until the completion of the entire system of railways [1] was to be modified so that the bonds reserved should be delivered on the completion of each continuous section of one hundred miles. If the main line should not be located so as to pass through Denver, the Union Pacific was to be "authorized and empowered" to build a branch line thither from the main line, and to receive therefor the same subsidy per mile as for the main line. The assignment of the Central Pacific to the Western Pacific and San Francisco and San José companies of its line from Sacramento to San Francisco, via San José, was to be ratified and confirmed, the assignees "to enjoy the same rights, privileges and benefits as if they had been particularly named" in the Act of 1862. The modification of the "bond reservation" provision was at first resisted by Collamer (Vermont) and the conservative element in the Senate, and defeated by a vote of 24 to 12; McDougall offered a compromise amendment by which the provision should not apply to the part of the line between the eastern base of the Rocky Mountains and the western base of the Sierra Nevada, and by which the bonds reserved on the rest of the line should be delivered at the rate of one-fifth for each continuous section of two hundred miles completed on that part of the line; but even this was at first rejected by the same conservative party, though later the opposition was withdrawn and the compromise accepted. The Denver branch was effectually disposed of by an amendment that the Union Pacific should receive no subsidy of land or bonds for building it. Senator Sherman offered an innocent looking amendment that if the government saw fit, it might pay the Union Pacific money in place of delivering bonds to it, which was readily adopted. Pomeroy (Kansas), a most obsequious "friend" of Pacific railway legislation, and particularly devoted to the policy of "adequate inducements," suggested military despotism as a help-meet of the Pacific railway, in an amendment that "the said company is hereby authorized to enlist laborers for the construction of said

[1] Supra, page 106.

road under a military[1] organization, with penalties for desertion or default being stipulated in the printed articles of enlistment, and to advance thereupon the cost of transporting said laborers to the line of said railroad, which articles of enlistment and the forfeitures and penalties stipulated therein, being first approved and sanctioned as reasonable and just by the President of the United States and the Attorney General of the United States, shall be valid and binding on all parties, and shall be maintained and enforced by the military forces of the United States." This amendment, it need hardly be added, was speedily rejected. But Pomeroy deserved more credit for having suggested an amendment permitting the company to buy its rails abroad whenever the price in the American market should exceed sixty dollars per ton. But as the favor of the protectionists for the Pacific railway had been purchased by the limitation of the supply of rails to the "home market," their favor could be retained only by maintaining the limitation, while the government loaned the company money with which to buy the rails. The bill was passed by the Senate February 25, 1863.

In the House of Representatives, on the 2d of March following, Campbell tried to get it up for consideration, but Holman (Indiana) raised the point that the Sherman clause made the bill an appropriation bill, and it was, referred by the rules of the House, to the Committee of the Whole, on the 3d of March, at the close of the short session—parliamentarily throttled.

The Union Pacific has always been a source of discord and contention. No feature of it has ever been brought before Congress without precipitating a conflict of opposing interests. Even the gauge of the track could not be determined without hours of debate, persistent lobbying, and a full measure of political chicanery. The Act of 1862 provided (Section 12) that "the track upon the entire line of railroad and branches shall be of uniform width, to be determined by the President of the United States, so that, when completed, cars can be run from the Missouri River to the Pacific coast (!)" The modestly aspiring tone of the pro-

[1] The word "military" was afterwards changed to "voluntary."

vision seems to contain no element of discord. But when President Lincoln's attention was called to his duty under the law and the urgent necessity of his performing it, he intimated that he would be glad to determine the gauge, if he knew what was the best gauge; the Secretary of the Interior was called upon for information, and having collected the opinions of engineers and " railroad men " on the subject, laid them before the President for his edification.

At that time American railways did not have a uniform gauge. In England, a commission had been created by Parliament to determine and report on the best gauge for railways; after taking much testimony and giving full consideration to the question, the commission had reported in favor of a gauge of 5 feet 3 inches. After much controversy, the Grand Trunk Railway of Canada had adopted and was using a gauge of 5 feet 6 inches. The Erie, in New York, was using a gauge of 6 feet. One railway in New England had a gauge of 7 feet. In California, the law of the state had established a gauge of 5 feet. The Missouri Pacific, the western connection of Saint Louis, had a gauge of 5 feet 6 inches ; the Ohio and Mississippi, east of Saint Louis, had the broad gauge of 6 feet. But the New York Central, Michigan Central, Baltimore & Ohio, and all the Chicago and Iowa railways used the " standard " gauge of 4 feet 8½ inches.[1]

Lincoln was perplexed; Chicago wanted the standard gauge, Saint Louis wanted the broad gauge, and California wanted the gauge of 5 feet, and each interest had its representatives on the ground. A full Cabinet meeting was held and the matter was long and seriously discussed. At last, Lincoln settled on the gauge of 5 feet, the California gauge, and made an executive order accordingly. On the basis of the executive order, the Central Pacific ordered a large amount of rolling

[1] In building the Chicago & Northwestern from Chicago, William B. Ogden had built forty miles on the gauge of six feet and had then changed the gauge to the "standard," and relaid the rails. The managers of the Erie were also considering the advisability of relaying their line on the "standard " gauge.

stock and machinery, to be constructed for use on a five-foot track. But the New York-Chicago-Iowa combination was not to be outdone. Harlan (Iowa) promptly introduced in the Senate a bill "to establish the gauge of the Pacific railroad and branches," on the 24th of January, 1863 ; it was referred to the Select Committee on the Pacific Railroad, but the committee evidently could not agree; for they later asked to be relieved from further consideration of the bill, and it was taken up for general debate in the Senate. McDougall argued vigorously for the California gauge, and Harlan and Trumbull for the standard gauge, while the broad gauge had its advocate in Fessenden. It was a day's work to dispose of the bill, but on the 9th of February, 1863, a vote of 26 to 9 sent it to the House of Representatives, there to be passed without debate on the 2d of March, 1863. One of the briefest laws in the statutes of the United States is : "Be it enacted by the Senate and House of Representatives of the United States, in Congress assembled, That the gauge of the Pacific Railroad and its branches throughout their whole extent, from the Pacific coast to the Missouri River, shall be, and hereby is, established at four feet, eight and one-half inches."[1]

III.

When the third session of the Thirty-eighth Congress began in December, 1863, the subject of the Pacific railway was approached by the national law-makers with timidity and serious apprehensions. The opinion was almost universal that additional legislation was needed to make the Act of 1862 effective, but the point where the limit of aid to patriotic capitalists should be set was difficult to determine. The Act of 1862 had been carried to shore by a tidal wave of national feeling. The power of the federal government had been so long restrained by state-rights and strict construction statesmen that when secession suddenly removed the pressure, there was a veritable explosion of national power. But the feeling or consciousness of suddenly acquired national energy spent itself to some extent in about two years,

[1] 12 Statutes, 807.

and by the fall of 1863, a considerable opposition had arisen against the vigorous prosecution of the war and other manifestations of the newly appreciated national strength, including the Pacific railway. The vast expenditures of the war and the consequent drain on the resources of the people, accompanied by the odium of inquisitorial modes of taxation with which three generations of Americans had been happily unfamiliar, had given body and blood to a resistance that resulted in a serious impairment of the Republican majority in Congress. Worst of all, the shiftless management of the war and woefully misguided administration of the finances had placed the national government at the mercy of a parasitical growth of army contractors, stock jobbers and speculators. No part of the public service was touched that was not found infested with the vermin of political and financial putridity. Congress was slow to approach the carcass of the Pacific railway lest contact should reveal the odor of the general corruption. In the national convention of the Republican party in the spring of 1864, "immediate and efficient aid" for the Pacific railway was not suggested,[1] and California had to be contented with a bare "Resolved, That we are in favor of a speedy construction of the railroad to the Pacific coast," while the sprouting stump of the Democratic party found enough to do in general condemnation of the war, without risking the expression of any sentiment on the Pacific railway.

Members of Congress only shared the current public suspicion that the Pacific railway project might prove to be only another hiding place for a band of public plunderers. The election of directors and other officers of the company at New York in October, 1863, had been characterized by the reluctance and even refusal of prominent and responsible public men to be actively identified with the management of the company's affairs. Only a few of the thirty prominent men elected directors were actively interested, many were elected without their candidacy,

---

[1] Compare the attitude of the Republican party in the convention of 1864, as differing from the attitude of the party in the conventions of 1856 and 1860, described on pages 72 and 96, supra.

knowledge, or consent, and many declined to serve. General John A. Dix, elected president, had not time, opportunity, or inclination to give active personal attention to the duties of the office, and the burden was practically transferred to the vice-president, Thomas C. Durant. While no public spirited man or set of men seemed inclined to take charge of the great project, Washington was filled to overflowing with lobbyists and "interested parties," and even the gauge of the road could not be determined without an invasion of patriotic "friends," who had no apparent pecuniary interest in the matter, but chose such a convenient occasion to show their disinterested public spirit. The several really reputable men who had subscribed stock to "save the charter," respectfully declined to be identified with the corporation except as well wishers. "Everybody's dog is nobody's dog." But something had to be done. The Republican party had gone too far to be able to recede in safety. The Pacific railway had to be built, because an intense public sentiment demanded it, and it had long been promised to the people. Private parties would not build it with their own means. Moreover, if the government was to have an intimate connection with the construction of the railway, the connection must be made without delay. The tide of public opposition to immense and unusually wasteful expenditure of means, increased taxation, and incessant "looting of the Treasury," was rising higher and higher each day. The fear of a centralized government was obtaining firmer hold on the public mind, and was daily finding louder and more emphatic expression. But the Republican majority in Congress resumed the task, though in fear and trembling, lest the burden of the Pacific railway should prove as overwhelming as that of the Cumberland Road and Bank of the United States had been for its predecessor, the old Whig party. Shall we simply give more aid, in the same way in which we gave it in 1862? Shall the government not circumvent public plunderers by building the road directly, instead of trying to filter its responsibility through a corporation? Shall we obtain a little doubtful relief by postponing the whole matter to the next session of Congress? These were the three questions that were answered by the Pacific railway legislation of 1864.

On motion of Anthony (Rhode Island) the customary Select Committee was superseded in the Senate by a standing "Committee on the Pacific Railroad," December 22, 1863; and Howard (Michigan) was the first chairman of the new committee.[1] In February, 1864, Sherman introduced a bill, of which he disclaimed being the originator, and which he said others had asked him simply to present for the consideration of the Senate; in March, Conness (California) introduced a bill; and after deliberating on the two bills, the committee (to whom of course they had been referred) reported, in May, 1864, the Sherman bill with an amendment. In a later report of May 18, 1864, the committee proposed, as a substitute for the Sherman bill, a bill in which the act of 1862 was to be repealed, its main provisions retained and digested, and two important changes made. (1) Instead of loaning to the companies bonds, for the amount of which the government was to have a lien on the companies' property, they were to be allowed to issue their own bonds to the extent of $24,000.00 per mile for the lines east of the eastern base of the Rocky Mountains, $96,000.00 per mile for the lines one hundred and fifty miles westward from the eastern base of the Rocky Mountains and one hundred and fifty miles eastward from the western base of the Sierra Nevada, $48,000.00 per mile for the intervening line, and $24,000.00 per mile for the California line (except for a space of fifteen miles in the Contra Costa Mountains, where the rate was to be $48,000.00 per mile). The bonds were to mature in thirty years, bear interest at six per cent per annum, and be secured by a mortgage or a deed of trust to be approved by the Secretary of the Treasury and Attorney General. As rapidly as the lines should be completed (in sections) and the fact of completion duly certified, the holders of the bonds might present them to the Secretary of the Treasury and he would stamp upon them "The United States

---

[1] In the House of Representatives, March 2, 1865, the customary Select Committee was superseded, in a resolution to take effect at the close of the session, by a standing "Committee on the Pacific Railroad."

hereby undertake and agree with the lawful holder of the within bond to pay the first year's interest accruing thereon, as a gratuity to the Union Pacific Railroad Company, the obligor; and to pay the interest accruing thereon for the subsequent nineteen years, immediately upon default of such payment by said obligor." (2) The "initial point," instead of being "between the south margin of the valley of the Republican River and the north margin of the valley of the Platte River, in the Territory of Nebraska," was to be "between the south margin of the valley of the Smoky Hill fork of the Republican or Kansas River and the north margin of the Platte River in Nebraska."[1] This change would give the Saint Louis and Kansas party a chance to regain the ground they had lost in 1862, but on the motion of Harlan (Iowa), by a vote of 17 to 15, the innovation was rejected and the original expression of the act of 1862 was reinstated. A minor departure from the Act of 1862 was found in the anti-monopoly provision limiting individual holdings of stock to $500,000.00. The bill (being substantially identical with the Act of 1862, except as to the "guaranteed bonds" and "stock limitation" provisions) passed the Senate by a vote of 23 to 5 on the 23d of May, 1864, after five days of debate.

When the Senate bill reached the House of Representatives, it found there an independent bill already under discussion. Price (Iowa) had introduced, March 16, 1864, a bill to amend the Act of 1862; and that was made the basis of the work of the

[1] Note the interesting and important difference occasioned by the omission in the second clause of the comma found in the first clause after "Platte River." It cost the publishers of the *Congressional Globe* the expense of a column of printing to reproduce the opinions of learned Senators on the effect of the punctuation, or omission of it. Part of the valley of the Republican River is in Kansas. The presence of the comma required the initial point to be in Nebraska —a territory; the omission of the comma would permit the initial point to be in Kansas—a state; and this "point" precipitated a heated discussion of the old question of the power of the federal government to charter a corporation for internal improvements within a state. Moreover, behind the discussion of the constitutional question, the presence of the comma insured the advancement of the Chicago interest; the absence of it would permit the advancement of the Saint Louis interest. The comma was restored.

usual Select Committee of thirteen, of which Price himself was chairman. After being reported back by the committee early in May, 1864, the bill was taken up by the House for consideration at a night session on the 16th of June; the provisions of the bill were substantially those that ripened into law in the Act of 1864.

Holman (Indiana) began the opposition to the bill by proposing an amendment, " That said road shall be a public highway, and shall transport the property and troops of the United States, which transportation thereof shall be required free of toll or other charge." The debate that followed was, on the part of Holman, a bitter denunciation of railway companies in general, and of the "land grant roads," and Illinois Central and Union Pacific in particular. If the general government should succeed in getting from the Pacific railway free transportation of property and troops, that, he intimated, would be all that it would ever get in return for the immense aid to be given to it.

Two days afterwards, E. B. Washburne (Illinois) followed Holman with an amendment to strike out the since celebrated " Section X.," which provided that the government's lien for the amount of bonds advanced to the companies should be inferior and subject to the lien of holders of the companies' bonds to an equal amount.[1] Referring to Section X. in particular he proclaimed, " On my responsibility as a Representative, I pronounce this as the most monstrous and flagrant attempt to overreach the government and the people that can be found in all the legislative annals of the country." [2] With general reference to the bill, he complained "What is the present status of the company and the government under the law? The company is organized. It has its stockholders, its president, directors and officers. The question of the good faith of its organization has been raised. Has no one man more than the amount of stock limited by law, that is, two hundred shares? Are all the directors owners, *bona fide*, of the amount of stock required? On the other hand, is it

[1] Infra, page 138.

[2] *Congressional Globe*, 38th Congress, first session, page 3152.

not notorious that one single individual owns or controls a majority of the stock, and has organized the company in such a way as completely to control it ; and is it not alleged that there are directors in the board who are not *bona fide* owners of a single dollar of stock?   And it must be understood that under the existing law, parties who have subscribed for $1,001,000.00 worth of stock (the whole amount subscribed being only $2,000,-000.00) can control the whole concern.   While the government is liable for $100,000,000.00, and has donated millions upon millions of acres of public land to this great work, yet this entire organization has gone into the hands of parties who have put in but a trifle over one per cent of the whole amount that the government is liable for.   And the government is utterly without any controlling voice in the direction of this company, as it has but two directors out of the whole number.   Does it not seem, therefore, that the government is " left out in the cold " in the arrangement as it now stands?   But gentlemen point us to the long list of the present board of directors who are men of well known integrity and of capital ; but I desire to ask what number of these men of integrity and capital who appear in the list as directors are active and managing men, controlling and directing the action of the company?   Such directors as General Dix, ... have either resigned their positions or refused to take any part in the management of the affairs of the company, while the real management is in the hands of a set of Wall Street stock jobbers who are using this great engine for their own private ends, regardless of what should be the great object of the company or of the interests of the country.   Who are the men who are here to lobby this bill through?   Have the men of high character and of a national reputation, whose names were, at an earlier period, connected with this enterprise, been here, animated by a commendable public spirit and by motives of patriotism, to ask us to pass this bill?   I have not heard of such men being here for that purpose, but on the other hand the work of 'putting the bill through,' has gone into the hands of such men as Samuel Hallett and George Francis Train — *par nobile fratrum.*"[1] Washburne's arraignment could be met only, as it was met, by vigorous denials that the company was controlled by one man, that the stockholders were actuated by evil motives, or that stock-jobbers had gained an insidious influence over the course of the enterprise. The Select Committee, it was urged, was composed of honorable members (!) who had "spent six months" in perfecting their report (!).

Then Pruyn (New York) who had himself, with others, been instrumental in "saving the charter" by subscribing stock and soliciting others to subscribe stock in the Union Pacific, sounded a note of alarm from another quarter. Was it best that persons who had contributed only $2,000,000.00 to a project universally recognized and considered as a purely national project, should have the management of sixty millions of government aid and of millions of acres of public land, with almost no safeguards for their economical and prudent use? If the federal government was to provide the means for building the road, would it not be better for it to build the road than to turn the means over to be handled by possibly irresponsible and dishonest men? His amendment provided that "The President of the United States shall, by and with the advice and consent of the Senate, appoint a board of commissioners, to consist of seven persons, who shall have and possess all powers now vested in the Union Pacific Railroad Company under the act entitled 'an act . . . . approved July 1, 1862,' and that said commissioners shall proceed without delay to construct the said railroad and telegraph line as authorized by the said act. The said commissioners shall not be entitled to any compensation for their services; but their necessary expenses, to be audited by the Secretary of the Treasury, shall be paid to them respectively."[2]

The Holman amendment was defeated by a vote of 82 to 39 (61 not voting!). The Pruyn amendment received only 20 votes, while 72 votes were against it. Then Pruyn, evidently anticipating the unfavorable vote, proposed two amendments more, the

---

[1] *Congressional Globe*, 38th Congress, first session, page 3151.

[2] Ibidem, page 3150.

first providing for the appointment by the President of the United States of three disinterested engineers to approve the routes and termini selected by the companies, before they should be established—rejected ; the second provided that before subsidy bonds should be issued to the companies, all contracts made by them for work and material should be approved by the Secretary of the Treasury and Attorney General—rejected. An amendment proposed by Wilson (Iowa) and agreed to, made the superior lien of the first mortgage bondholders subject to the paramount right of the government to the use of the lines of railway and telegraph guaranteed by Section VI. of the Act of 1862.[1]

An agreeable amendment for which Dawes (Massachusetts) was responsible, allowed the pestiferous branch lines, or any of them, to connect with the Union Pacific west of the initial point (but without increase of subsidy) if " more practicable or desirable." [2] Lest the Kansas line should first reach the initial point and continue the construction westward, thus making Kansas City (or Saint Louis) the principal eastern terminus, to the detriment of Chicago (and Iowa), an amendment urged by Allison (Iowa) provided " That no bonds shall be issued or land certified by the United States to any person or company for the construction of any part of the main trunk line of said railroad west of the one hundredth meridian of longitude and east of the Rocky Mountains, until said road shall be completed from or near Omaha, on the Missouri River, to the said one hundredth meridian of longitude."

A motion by Washburne to postpone the further consideration of the bill to the next session of Congress was speedily voted down, and motions to adjourn by Holman shared the same fate. Then the bill was passed by a vote of 70 to 38 (74 not voting), Pruyn, with excessive delicacy, declining to vote because he was a stockholder in the Union Pacific !

The bill passed by the Senate had reached the House while the House bill was under consideration, and had been referred by

[1] Section VI. of the Act of 1862 is quoted in full on page 106, supra.

[2] Supra, pages 107–109

the House to the Select Committee, which, by some peculiar rule of procedure, could not, it was said, be reported back to the House because the committee would not be called again during the session ; more probably its provisions were not agreeable to. the " friends" of the Pacific railway in the House, and if reported back, it might have interfered with their plans.   When the House bill reached the Senate, and was referred, the Senate committee tartly reported it back with an amendment in the nature of a substitute, the proposed substitute being the Senate bill already passed.   Of course the House would not concur in the Senate amendment and the Senate insisted on its own measure ; the consequence was an inevitable Committee of Conference, of which Senators Harlan, Foster and Conness, and Representatives Stevens, Cole and McClurg were the members.   The report of the " Little Congress " acceded to the demands of the House on the question of bonded aid, while the only important concession to the Senate was the refusal to the Kansas branch of a bond subsidy for constructing the Leavenworth branch ; the House bill had ratified the assignment by the Central Pacific to the Western Pacific of its line from Sacramento to San José ; the Senate bill had raised a new corporation for the construction of the line ; the committee of conference struck out both provisions.[1]   The report of the committee was immediately accepted by both Houses, without being printed or read, and with only a meagre verbal description by a member of the committee in each House on the last day of the session.   The approval of Lincoln on the 2d of July, 1864, completed (with the exception of a few minor provisions afterwards added) the charter of the Union Pacific Railroad Company.

The opponents of Pacific railway legislation afterwards com-

[1] The Pacific railways have usually got what they have wanted, soon or late, and in the next session of Congress, the national legislature passed an act of which one provision was, "That the assignment made by the Central Pacific . . , to the Western Pacific . . . of the right to construct all that portion of said railroad and telegraph from the city of San José to the city of Sacramento is hereby ratified and confirmed   . . .   with all the privileges and benefits of the several acts of Congress relating thereto, and subject to all the conditions thereof."

plained bitterly of the influence exerted by the lobby on the occasion of the discussion of the bill of 1864 in the House, and of the
undue haste with which the measure was pushed through. The
night session, on the 21st of June, 1864, was afterwards described
by E. B. Washburne as follows : "The consideration of the bill
was again resumed in the evening session of June 21, and no
gentleman who was here at that time will ever forget the extraordinary scene which was presented. The lobby mustered in its
full force. I say nothing here of the shameful means which it
was alleged were used in a 'confidential way' to carry through
this bill ; but I do say that the scene was one of the most
exciting that I have ever witnessed in a service of nearly
sixteen years. The galleries were packed with people interested in the measure, by lobbyists, male and female, and by
shysters and adventurers hoping for something to 'turn up.'
Your gilded corridors were filled with lobbyists, who broke
through all rules and made their way upon the floor and into the
seats of members."[1] The same vigorous champion of the opposition has put on record a true description of the proceedings of
the House on the reception of the report of the Committee of
Conference in these words : "On the 1st of July, the committee
of conference reported, bringing in such new matter as would, in
my opinion, be a violation of every rule which governs committees of conference in legislative bodies. . . . And this
report, changing so materially the bill as acted on by the House
and Senate, was gagged through ; the opponents of the measure
were not permitted to have it printed and postponed, so that they
could see what it was. I struggled in vain for the printing
of the report and for its delay until the members of the House
could have an opportunity of reading it ; but the gentleman from
Pennsylvania (Thad Stevens) demanded the previous question,
which was seconded and the main question ordered to be put ;
and it would seem incredible that in a matter of legislation
involving interests so vast and pledging amounts of money so

[1] *Congressional Globe*, 40th Congress, 2d Session, page 2135, March 26,
1868.

enormous, even the yeas and nays were refused ; that even tellers were refused. . . . Thus ends the story of the action of the House touching this extraordinary legislation, which will go down into the history of this country."[1]

The Act of 1864 provided an adequate procedure for the condemnation of private property for right of way, the necessity of which had been entirely overlooked in the Act of 1862. But in such cases the right of way was to be only one hundred feet on each side of the track, unless more should be needed for excavations or embankments, or depots and other structures.[2]

The shares of the capital stock of the Union Pacific were reduced from one thousand dollars to one hundred dollars each, and the number of shares increased from one hundred thousand to one million ;[3] the limitation of individual holdings of stock was removed.[4] Subscription books were to be kept open until the entire capital should be subscribed, and the capital stock should not be increased "beyond the actual cost" of the road ; assessments on stockholders, payable in money only, of not less than five dollars per share, and at least as often as every six months, should be made until the par value of all shares should be fully paid. The general office of the company was fixed by implication at New York.[5] The directors elected by the stockholders should be holders of fifty, instead of five shares of stock, and were to be fifteen, instead of "not less than thirteen," in number ; their

[1] *Congressional Globe*, 40th Congress, 2d Session, pages 2136 - 2137, March 26, 1868. See infra, pages 148–149, for a statement of the serious charge made by Senator Conness that the report of the committee of conference or bill was tampered with.

[2] Compare the right of way granted through the public lands by the Act of 1862, supra, page 104.

[3] Supra, pages 103 and 111.

[4] Supra, page 103.

[5] Afterwards, by the Act of 1869, when vexatious litigation and disputes of factions in the company made New York inconvenient for the purposes of a general office, the stockholders were permitted "to establish their general office at such place in the United States as they may select." The general office has since been in Boston.

term of office was limited to one year.[1] The government directors were increased in number from two to five, of whom at least
one should be a member of each standing and special committee
of the board of directors, and who were required to. "visit all
portions of the line" "as often as may be necessary to a full
knowledge of the condition and management" of it, and to make
reports to the Secretary of the Interior, from time to time, when
called upon by him to do so.

The time for the completion of the roads was extended one
year, and the Central Pacific was limited to one hundred and fifty
miles of road east of the California border.[2] " The failure of any
one company to comply fully with the conditions and requirements [of the Acts of 1862 and 1864] shall not work a forfeiture
of the rights, privileges, or franchise of any other company . . .
that shall have complied with [them]." [3]

The land grant was increased from five to ten odd-numbered
sections on each side of the road and within twenty miles of it.[4]
Mineral lands (excepted from the grant of 1862) should not
include coal and iron lands. "Any lands granted by [the Acts of
1862 and 1864] shall not defeat or impair any preëmption, homestead, swamp land, or other lawful claim, nor include any government reservation or mineral lands, or the improvements of any
bona fide settler, or any lands returned and denominated as mineral lands, and the timber necessary to support his said improvements as a miner or agriculturist ;" "the quantity thus exempted
. . . . shall not exceed one hundred and sixty acres for each settler who claims as an agriculturist, and such quantity for each
settler who claims as a miner as the . . . . Commissioner [of the
General Land Office] may establish by general regulation." The
grant of timber on mineral lands should not extend beyond ten
miles on each side of the road.

[1] Supra, pages 103–104.
[2] See infra, pages 148–149, for a more detailed statement of the " one hundred and fifty miles " question.
[3] See page 109, supra.
[4] Compare page 105, supra.

The reservation of bonds on each completed section of road was withdrawn.[1] A proportion of the [subsidy] . . . bonds, not exceeding two-thirds of the amount . . . authorized to be issued [and not] exceeding two-thirds of the value of the work done," should be delivered to the companies upon the certified completion of "a certain proportion of the work required to prepare the road for the superstructure on any [and each] section of twenty miles" between the eastern base of the Rocky Mountains and the western base of the Sierra Nevada, "the remaining one-third to remain until [each] section is fully completed and certified by the commissioners," but no such advance of bonds should be made to the Union Pacific for work west of Salt Lake and more than three hundred miles beyond the completed continuous line from the "initial point." Again, the companies might each, "on the completion of each section of [twenty miles] of road,[2] issue their first-mortgage bonds on their respective railroad and telegraph lines to an amount not exceeding the amount of the bonds of the United States, and of even tenor and date, time of maturity, rate and character of interest with the bonds authorized to be issued to said railroad companies respectively. And the lien of the United States bonds shall be subordinate to that of the bonds of any or either of said companies hereby authorized to be issued on their respective roads, property and equipments, except as to the provision of the sixth section of the Act [of 1862] relating to the transmission of dispatches and the transportation of mails, troops, munitions of war, supplies, and public stores for the Government of the United States."[3] The government bonds were also to be delivered on the certified completion of each section of twenty instead of (in some places) forty miles.[4]

[1] See page 106, supra.

[2] Even this provision was amended by the Act of March 3, 1865, so that, instead of waiting for the completion of each section, each company might "issue . . . . bonds to the extent of one hundred miles in advance of a continuous completed line of construction."

[3] Section VI. of the Act of 1862 is quoted in full on page 106, supra. See also page 123, supra.

[4] See pages 105–106, supra.

"Only *one-half* [instead of *all*][1] the compensation for services rendered for the government by [the] companies [should] be required to be applied to the payment of the bonds issued by the government in aid of the construction of [the] roads."

The amendatory provisions of the Act of 1864, as affecting the several branches of the Pacific railway, have been considered in a more convenient place.[2] When the Union Pacific Railway, Eastern Division,[3] should reach the "initial point" on the 100th meridian, if the Union Pacific should not be "proceeding in good faith to build" its road through the territories, it might proceed westward on the same line to a connection with the Central Pacific, with the proviso, however, that it should receive no bonds or land until the Iowa (or Omaha) branch had been completed.[4] The Burlington and Missouri River Railroad Company was authorized to extend its line from its Missouri River terminus (near the mouth of the Platte River) through the territory of Nebraska to a connection with the Union Pacific at a point not west of the 100th meridian; as aid were granted the right of way and odd-numbered sections of public land (not disposed of and not mineral land) within ten miles on each side of the road, but no government bonds were granted.

Congressional control in the future was intended to be preserved by a final provision "That Congress may, at any time, alter, amend, or repeal this act."[5]

IV.

The legislation that constitutes the Union Pacific charter is readily recognized by the student as unique and significant in American history. The first and second Banks of the United States had been imposed on the people by the government; the

[1] See page 106, supra.

[2] See pages 107–109, supra.

[3] Earlier called the Leavenworth, Pawnee and Western, and later the Kansas Pacific.

[4] See page 107, supra.

[5] 13 Statutes, 356.

Union Pacific was imposed on the government by the people. The Cumberland Road brought into exercise such powers of the national government that the states were alarmed for their own powers, and the national government eventually ceded that strife-stirring highway to the separate states through which it passed ; but the argument that the Pacific railway was "a national under-taking for national purposes" has been regarded even by the Supreme Court of the United States without disapproval,[1] although the national importance of connecting the Potomac and Ohio differs from the national importance of connecting the Missouri and Pacific only in degree of intensity. In the minds of the people, the expenditure of national means on the Cumber-land Road was not justified by its necessity for postal and mili-tary purposes, but the same speculative necessity afforded a readily accepted excuse for an unprecedented loan of national means to the Pacific railway and its branches. Monroe labored acutely in his celebrated message vetoing an appropriation for the Cumberland Road to demonstrate the unconstitutionality of the expenditure of national revenue within the limits of the states, even with their consent ; Jackson held that the national government might expend its means on roads within the several states when they were of national importance, and the Maysville Road bill met his veto because he did not consider a road through a part of Kentucky a national necessity ; but Lincoln was one of the most ardent promoters of legislation to grant land and loan bonds to Pacific railway companies in Kansas and California. Lewis Cass and his "old school" of Democrats denounced, in 1850, the creation of federal corporations for internal improvements within the states, but the Republican statesmen of the sixth decade did not hesitate to endow the Union Pacific with corporate power to extend its lines through Kansas and California. When DeWitt Clinton wanted federal aid in the construction of the Erie Canal, his presumption was derided. When Huntington and Durant wanted the credit of the federal government as a basis for the construction of the

---

[1] United States *vs.* The Union Pacific Railroad Company, 91 U. S. R. 79.

Pacific railway, the only serious question was as to the extent of the assistance to be given.

The steps in the constitutional advance are not difficult to trace. In the first place, the people wanted roads, canals, and railways, as their industrial growth made them necessary. How was the want to be supplied? The national government attempted to supply the want by directly building the roads or some of them, but the political mind of the people had not been "educated up" to the level of such an exercise of national powers, and as yet the people had not acquired the strength of conscious united industrial effort, now exerted through corporations and associations that threaten to absorb the individual and destroy his autonomy; the united effort had to be put forth through some agency, and the states were the only agencies that the people had learned to regard as embodying their collective energy. The state was near to the individual, and the nation was far from him; the nation was regarded by the states as a creature composed of the contributions by them of slices of their sovereign powers, and if the nation was possessed of an immense public domain, it was considered as holding it largely as a trustee for the separate states for whom it was at least inconvenient to hold property in common. Individual men, in casting about for a convenient instrument with which to exercise collective industrial effort in creating means of intercommunication among the people, found in existence and fully organized, the instrument through which they exercised their collective political power, the state. Nothing, therefore, was more natural for the man of 1825-1840 than to expect New York to dig the Erie Canal, Michigan to build the Michigan Central railway, or Pennsylvania to build the Pennsylvania railway. But the states were not always in possession of the means with which to satisfy the desires of the people to exert for them their collective industrial efforts; they had, however, as they considered, a deposit of public domain in the hands of their trustee, the nation; accordingly, when the people of Illinois wanted a railway, the state of Illinois drew on its national deposit of public land and turned the proceeds over to the people to be used in satisfying their desire. If, for a time, the people used their political instrument for industrial purposes, they soon found that it was unwieldy and that it was lacking in sufficiently direct responsibility for results and practically uncontrollable ; the corporation grew into use as a more handy and effective industrial implement, to which the state—the people politically organized —very willingly delegated most of the active industrial attributes which the people in their rapid growth and development of new social wants had temporarily attached to it. The next step, then, was for New York to donate the Erie Canal to the people, and for Michigan and Pennsylvania to sell their lines of railway to corporations,[1] as being more fit instruments for the accomplishment by the people of their industrial purposes. The man that has a check cashed at a bank holds the banker in higher relative estimation than he holds the man who gave him the check ; likewise the industrial corporation which received a grant of land to aid in building a railway learned to elevate the nation that held the deposit of land above the state through which the corporation received the benefit of the deposit ; as a consequence, the corporation aspired to more intimate relations with the banker nation. Next the corporation—the people in industrial collectivity—made bold to ask aid of the nation directly, without the intermediation of the state,—the day of the lobby had come. It was only a short step from asking a grant of public land to asking for a public loan of credit. The final step was taken when the nation itself (not the state) created a corporation, and not only endowed it with the land grant that it had become accustomed to give to the states whenever they had applied for it, but even essayed to reach beyond its final step and loaned its credit to its creature for the accomplishment of the purpose of its creation ; at the same time, the nation granted land and loaned credit to

[1] It is considered significant that the Erie Canal was completed, while the railways were incomplete ; it is not so difficult for the state to manage and control an industrial mechanism after it is constructed, but in undertaking its construction, the state has always encountered serious trouble ; if the Erie Canal had been only partly constructed, the state of New York might have been expected to turn it over to a corporation.

corporations created by the states, and even gave power to its own created corporation to exercise its energies within the limits of the states. The most remarkable feature of the history of the United States is the growth of a nation from a loose combination of states. Between the nether millstone of the nation and the upper millstone of the municipalities, the states are being ground "exceeding small." The significance of the Pacific railway legislation is that it marks the high-water level of the flood of national power; it is part of the drift, along with high protection, reconstruction, river and harbor bills, and oleomargarine inspection laws, that was left at the highest point on the shore, when the flood of nationality receded.

If the charter of the Union Pacific and the bonds in aid of it and the other parts of the Pacific railway had not been granted at the particular time of the Rebellion, it is safe to say that they never would have been granted at all. Yet the acts of 1862 and 1864 were not "war measures," unless the expression be used with material qualifications. All the systems of transcontinental railways, of which there are now several, had their origin, first, in an economic need of communication between western Europe and eastern Asia; then, of communication between the Mississippi valley and the Pacific coast; and finally, of communication as a means of developing the intervening country and its resources. All railways and nearly all other instruments of industry are of undoubted value to a nation in time of war; the Pacific railway was expected to be valuable to the United States in controlling the western Indians and possibly in defending California against the attacks of foreign sympathizers with the South, but the inspiration of the Acts of 1862 and 1864 was rather in the general industrial need of communication, the incessant demands of California for it (because the people of that state wanted to be a part of the nation in fact as well as in name), and in the desire of national unity, itself deeper than the causes of the Rebellion, and the essence of all that is valuable in the federal constitution. The Pacific railway, in the nature of existing industrial conditions, one would have expected to be built by individuals, either alone or in some form of association or incorporation; but railways had come to be regarded as exceptions to the general rule, and instead of being built in response to the demand of a developed community, were built to create the demand and in anticipation of it ; the exaggeration of the public function of railways and their intimate association with the settlement of the public domain had made land grants to railways common, and apparently very proper. In the case of the Pacific railway the situation was peculiar, in that widely separated communities were already sufficiently developed to create the demand for railways, while the intervening public domain was considered as of no value, and presented apparently unsurmountable obstacles to railway construction ; moreover, the railway would be almost entirely in the territories of the United States, and could not be constructed under the patronage and control of states, as had been the case with most prior land grant railways.   Financial aid would have been extended to a Pacific railway project long before 1862, if it had not been for local and sectional prejudices and jealousies ; the Rebellion (and consequent resignation by Southern members of their seats in Congress) simply removed the pressure to some extent, though enough of it was left to provide for the miserable Missouri River branches and to give a charter to the Northern Pacific Railroad Company on the same day in 1864 on which the Union Pacific charter was perfected.   As soon as the war was over, and even before reconstruction had been perfected, Congress was deluged with applications for aid in government bonds or guaranties of interest on railway bonds for the construction of a Pacific railway on the 32d parallel, an international line from Cairo to Mexico, a Southern branch of the Pacific railway from Kansas to the Gulf of Mexico, and a flood of other like projects, but such of the applications as received serious attention were honored only by grants of public land.   Congress insisted that the granting of aid in bonds and financial credit had not become the settled policy of the government, and that the case of the Union Central Pacific railway had been made an exception to the general rule. The very desire of national unity that gave strength to the purpose of putting down the Rebellion gave body to the purpose of securing a Pacific railway—the source of one was the source of the other. The Pacific railway was not built (under a "war measure") for the purpose of assisting to put down the Rebellion ; the conditions brought into being by the Rebellion simply permitted what had been long desired and often essayed—government aid for the Pacific railway.

CHAPTER V.

DONE !

WRITERS and public speakers of every class have well-nigh exhausted their resources of expression in detailing the attributes of the Pacific railway project, its promotion, accomplishment and effects. The modest writer of the *Emigrant* article was content with describing it as "one of those great projects which none but a great nation could effect," and its consequence to make the United States "the first nation in the world." Asa Whitney, more enthusiastic, assured his readers in 1845, "You will see that it will change the whole world . . . [and] bring [it] together as one nation, allow us to traverse the globe in thirty days, civilize and christianize mankind, and place us in the center of the world, compelling Europe on one side and Asia and Africa on the other to pass through us." When John A. Dey left the position of chief engineer of the Union Pacific, he regretted that he was resigning "the best position in [his] profession this country has offered to any man." Thomas H. Benton passionately pleaded that the great line "be adorned with its crowning honor, the colossal statue of the great Columbus, whose design it accomplishes, hewn from the granite mass of a peak of the Rocky Mountains, overlooking the road, the mountain itself the pedestal, and the statue a part of the mountain, pointing with outstretched arm to the western horizon, and saying to the flying passenger, 'There is the East! There is India!'" [1] The congressional orator has not considered himself justified in addressing his fellow members (or his constituents) on the subject of a Pacific railway without crowning his effort with a fulsome pero-

[1] Speech in Saint Louis, October, 1849, before a National Pacific Railroad Convention.

ration on the greatness and grandeur of the project. Senator Butler (South Carolina) once complained, " It was said of the Nile that it was a god. I think that this Pacific railroad project comes nearer being the subject of deification than anything else I have ever heard of in the Senate. Every one is trying to show his zeal in worshiping this great road." [1] Charles Sumner, greatest scholar of them all, when invited in 1853 to attend the celebration of Independence-day in Boston, profusely apologized in a letter to the mayor of the city for his inability to attend, and added, " The day itself comes full of quickening suggestions, which can need no prompting from me. And yet, with your permission, I would gladly endeavor to associate at this time one special aspiration with the general gladness. Allow me to propose the following toast : ' The railroad from the Atlantic to the Pacific—traversing a whole continent and binding together two oceans, this mighty thoroughfare, when completed, will mark an epoch of human progress second only to that of our Declaration of Independence. May the day soon come!' " [2] The favorite rhetorical figure of the Pacific railway orator was a comparison of his theme with the Seven Wonders of the ancient world, and a declaration, not admitting of contradiction, that they "dwindled into insignificance" in the comparison. [3]

The project was thoroughly saturated and fairly dripping with the elements of adventure and romance. Before the building of the Pacific railway, most of the wide expanse of territory west of the Missouri was *terra incognita* to the mass of Americans. The interest of Thomas Jefferson in the new national purchase of Louisiana had inspired the " novel and arduous undertaking" of Lewis and Clarke in 1804, 1805 and 1806, and the tales of

[1] *Congressional Globe*, 33d Congress, 2d Session, page 351.

[2] Letter to Hon. Benjamin Seaver, Mayor, etc. Works of Charles Sumner, Vol. III., page 228.

[3] Senator Rusk (Texas) in a letter to the Philadelphia Railroad Convention, in 1850, referred to the Pacific railway as the " Colossus of *Rhodes*," and another dignified Senator, with less originality, afterwards referred to it in debate as the "Colossus of *Rail-Rhodes*."

bears, snakes and buffaloes, and descriptions of weird Indian customs compiled in their reports had excited the curiosity of many readers. The trappers and fur traders of the Northwest had brought back from the wilderness, at long intervals, a mass of astonishing information of the fierce savages, strange animals and peculiar vegetation of Oregon and the mountains. The widely circulated reports of Fremont's three explorations, and of the dangers and perils of the mountains and desert West, had made the Pathfinder a hero and a presidential candidate. The "Pacific Railroad Surveys" from 1853 to 1855[1] added to the fund of popular information, and as each succeeding volume left the hands of the public printer, with its wealth of illustration and description, the naturally keen Anglo-Saxon appetite for adventure and acquisition was only whetted the sharper. Stansbury, Bonneville, Pike, and Long came later, with more particular information of the central West. The acquisition of California and Texas served only to heighten the ardor of the people to explore the "Great West." The discovery of the precious yellow dust in California hung up before the imagination of the "Argonauts of '49" a golden fleece that stimulated thousands of them to the privations of "prairie schooner" voyages. And the later discovery of the baser but equally valuable metals in Nevada and Colorado, in 1860 and 1861, swelled the ranks of the wealth Crusaders. The "Mormon Rebellion," and the periodical outbreaks of the western Indians, followed by the Civil War and the impending loss to the Union of the Pacific coast territory, made the Pacific railway, in the minds of most men, a national military necessity, and made its projectors and builders heroes of the first order.

The inducements offered by the act of 1862 were insufficient to attract to the Union Pacific individual capitalists anxious to display industrial heroism and save the nation (!), but doubling the amount of the prizes by the amendments of 1864 had the desired effect, and a beginning was made by the completion of eleven miles of the Union Pacific by the 25th of September,

[1] Supra, pages 59-60.

1865, and of forty miles by the end of the year 1865. On October 5, 1866, the mileage had increased to two hundred and forty-seven miles. By January 1, 1867, the road was finished and operated to a point three hundred and five miles west from Omaha. In 1867, two hundred and forty miles were built. The year 1868 produced four hundred and twenty-five miles; and the first four months of 1869 added the one hundred and twenty-five miles necessary to complete the road to its junction with the Central Pacific at Promontory Point. Work on the Central Pacific had been commenced at Sacramento more than a year before work had been begun on the Union Pacific at Omaha, and by the time the first eleven miles of the latter had been completed, the former had attained a length of fifty-six miles, increased by January 1, 1867, to ninety-four miles. In 1867, forty-six miles were built; in 1868, three hundred and sixty-three miles were added ; in 1869, the remaining one hundred and eighty-six miles were covered, and Promontory Point was reached. The Union Pacific had built one thousand and eighty-six miles from Omaha ; the Central Pacific had built six hundred and eighty-nine miles from Sacramento.

The natural obstacles presented by the mountains and desert land, the absence of timber on the prairies, of water in the mountains, and of both in the alkali desert, had made the work exceptionally difficult and expensive. The Central Pacific, though under the necessity of getting its iron, finished supplies, and machinery by sea, via Cape Horn or Panama, had the advantage of Chinese coolie labor and the unified management of its construction company ; while the Union Pacific, having no railway connection until January, 1867, was subjected to the hardship of getting its supplies overland from the termini of the Iowa railways or by Missouri River boats, and had to depend on intractable Irish labor and the warring factions of the Credit Mobilier. The Sierra Nevada furnished the Central Pacific all the timber needed for ties, trestle-work, and snow-sheds, but the Union Pacific had little or no timber along its line, except the unserviceable cottonwood of the Platte valley, and many boats were kept busy for a hundred miles above and below Omaha on the Missouri River in furnishing ties and heavy timbers. Both roads were being built through a new, uninhabited, and uncultivated country, where there were no foundries, machine shops, or any of the other conveniences of a settled country. The large engine used in the Union Pacific railway shops was dragged across the country to Omaha from Des Moines. As to labor, twenty-five thousand men, about equally divided between the two companies, are said to have been employed during the closing months of the great work. Several thousand Chinamen had been imported to California for the express purpose of building the Central Pacific. On the Union Pacific, European emigrant labor, principally Irish, was mostly employed.[1] At the close of the Rebellion, many of the soldiers, laborers, teamsters, and camp-followers drifted west to gather the aftermath of the war in the similar work of railway construction,

The work was military in character, and one is not surprised to find among the superintendents and managers a liberal sprinkling of military titles. The work was in many respects only an after-chapter of the Rebellion, added by Columbia "to bring her work down to date." The surveying parties were always accompanied by a detachment of soldiery as a protection against interference by Indians. The construction trains were amply supplied with rifles and other arms, and it was boasted that a gang of track-layers could be transmuted at any moment into a battalion of infantry. And assaults on the trains by the Indians were not infrequent. "There was nothing we could ask them [the United State army] for that they did not give, even when regulations did not authorize it, and it took a long stretch of authority to satisfy all our demands. The commissary department was open to us. Their troops guarded us, and we reconnoitered, surveyed,

---

[1] In his annual report for 1863, J. P. Usher, Secretary of the Interior, reported that out of fifteen hundred laborers employed on the Pacific railway, three hundred were negroes and "performed their duty faithfully and well." He seriously recommended legislation with the view of aiding the early employment of more of the surplus "freedmen" on the same work.

located and built inside of their picket line. We marched to work to the tap of the drum with our men armed. They stacked their arms on the dump and were ready at a moment's warning to fall in and fight for their territory. General Casement's track-train could arm a thousand men at a word; and from him, as a head, down to his chief spiker, it could be commanded by experienced officers of every rank, from general to a captain. They had served five years at the front, and over half of the men had shouldered a musket in many battles. An illustration of this came to me after our track had passed Plum Creek, 200 miles west of the Missouri River. The Indians had captured a freight train and were in possession of it and its crews. It so happened that I was coming down from the front with my car, which was a traveling arsenal. At Plum Creek station word came of this capture and stopped us. On my train were perhaps twenty men, some a portion of the crew, some who had been discharged and sought passage to the rear. Nearly all were strangers to me. The excitement of the capture and the reports coming by telegraph of the burning train brought all men to the platform, and when I called upon them to fall in to go forward and retake the train, every man on the train went into line, and by his position showed that he was a soldier. We ran down slowly until we came in sight of the train. I gave the order to deploy as skirmishers and at the command they went forward as steadily and in as good order as we had seen the old soldiers climb the face of Kenesaw under fire." Such is the testimony of General G. M. Dodge, chief engineer of the Union Pacific during its construction.[1]

[1] See Paper on Transcontinental Railways, read before the Society of the Army of the Tennessee, at Toledo, Ohio, September 15, 1888.

Students of folk-lore will doubtless discover some substantial historical material in the refrain of a song that the author has often heard sung by an old Irish friend — evidently having seen service in more than one campaign :

"Then drill, my paddies, drill,
Drill, my heroes, drill,
Drill all day,
No sugar in your tay,
Workin' on the U. P. Railway."

The military coloring of the work of building the Union Pacific is well described in the following quotation from a newspaper of the day:

"One can see all along the line of the now completed road the evidences of ingenious self protection and defense which our men learned during the war. The same curious huts and underground dwellings, which were a common sight along our army lines then, may now be seen burrowed into the sides of the hills or built up with ready adaptability in sheltered spots. The whole organization of the force engaged in the construction of the road is, in fact, semi-military. The men who go ahead, locating the road, are the advance guard. Following them is the second line, cutting through the gorges, grading the road and building bridges. Then comes the main line of the army, placing the sleepers, laying the track, spiking down the rails, perfecting the alignment, ballasting the rails, and dressing up and completing the road for immediate use. This army of workers has its base, to continue the figure, at Omaha, Chicago, and still further eastward, from whose markets are collected the materials for constructing the road. Along the line of the completed road are construction trains constantly pushing forward 'to the front' with supplies. The company's grounds and work shops at Omaha are the arsenal, where these purchases, amounting now to millions of dollars in value, are collected and held ready to be sent forward. The advanced limit of the rail is occupied by a train of long boxcars, with hammocks swung under them, beds spread on top of them, bunks built within them, in which the sturdy, broad-shouldered pioneers of the great iron highway sleep at night and take their meals. Close behind this train come loads of ties and rails and spikes, etc., which are being thundered off upon the roadside to be ready for the track-layers. The road is graded a hundred miles in advance. The ties are laid roughly in place, then adjusted, gauged, and leveled. Then the track is laid.

"Track-laying on the Union Pacific is a science, and we, pundits of the far East, stood upon that embankment, only about a thousand miles this side of sunset, and backed westward before that hurrying corps of sturdy operators with a mingled feeling of amusement, curiosity, and profound respect. On they came. A light car, drawn by a single horse, gallops up to the front with its load of rails. Two men seize the end of a rail and start forward, the rest of the gang taking hold by twos, until it is clear of the car. They come forward at a run. At the word of command the rail is dropped in its place, right side up with care, while the same process goes on at the other side of the car. Less than thirty seconds to a rail for each gang, and so four rails go down to the minute! Quick work, you say, but the fellows on the Union Pacific are tremendously in earnest. The moment the car is empty it is tipped over on the side of the track to let the next loaded car pass it, and then it is tipped back again, and it is a sight to see it go flying back for another load, propelled by a horse at full gallop at the end of sixty or eighty feet of rope, ridden by a young Jehu, who drives furiously. Close behind the first gang come the gaugers, spikers, and bolters, and a lively time they make of it. It is a grand Anvil Chorus that those sturdy sledges are playing across the plains. It is in triple time, three strokes to the spike. There are ten spikes to a rail, four hundred rails to a mile, eighteen hundred miles to San Francisco. . . . Twenty-one million times are those sledges to be swung—twenty-one million times are they to come down with their sharp punctuation, before the great work of modern America is complete!"[1]

It must be remembered that the only settlements between Omaha and Sacramento in 1862 were those of the Mormons in Utah, and Denver and a few mining camps in Colorado and Nevada. Colorado was given over to the Kansas Pacific,[2] and Salt Lake City was left for a branch line; Ogden, a Mormon town of a few hundred inhabitants, was the only station between the termini of the Union-Central Pacific. The necessities of the work of con-

[1] It is regretted that direct credit can not be given for these paragraphs. They are quoted in an article on "Pacific Railroads," by W. A. Bell, on pages 572 and 573 of the *Fortnightly Review* for May, 1869.

[2] See page 108, supra.

struction created new settlements and stations as it progressed, and as fast as the road was completed to each convenient point, it was operated to it, while the work went on from the terminus-town as a headquarters or base of operations ; thus, when the entire line was put in operation, July 15, 1869, such places as North Platte, Kearney, and Cheyenne, had " got a start," while other towns, being made the termini of branch lines, secured the additional impulse due in general to junction towns. Some of the " headquarters towns," like Benton, enjoyed only a temporary, Jonah's-gourd existence, and nothing is now left to mark their former location. The life in them was rough and profligate in the extreme. A few paragraphs from the journal of a few days' sojourn in Benton in August, 1868, are instructive :

" Westward the grassy plain yields rapidly to a desert ; at Medicine Bow we took final leave of the last trace of fertility, and traversed a region of alkali flats and red ridges for fifty miles. In the worst part of this desert, just west of the last crossing of the Platte, we found Benton, the great terminus town, six hundred and ninety-eight miles from Omaha. Far as [we] could see around the town, not a green tree, shrub, or spear of grass was to be seen ; the red hills, scorched and bare as if blasted by the lightnings of an angry God, bounded the white basin on the north and east, while to the south and west spread the gray desert till it was interrupted by another range of red and yellow hills. All seemed sacred to the genius of drouth and desolation. The whole basin looked as if it might originally have been filled with lye and sand, then dried to the consistency of hard soap, with glistening surface tormenting alike to eye and sense.

" Yet here had sprung up in two weeks, as if by the touch of Aladdin's lamp, a city of three thousand people ; there were regular squares arranged into five wards, a city government of mayor and aldermen, a daily paper, and a volume of ordinances for the public health. It was the end of the freight and passenger, and beginning of the construction, division ; twice every day immense trains arrived and departed, and stages left for Utah, Montana, and Idaho ; all the goods formerly hauled across the

plains came here by rail and were reshipped, and for ten hours
daily the streets were thronged with motley crowds of railroad
men, Mexicans and Indians, gamblers, 'cappers,' and saloon-
keepers, merchants, miners, and mule-whackers. The streets
were eight inches deep in white dust as I entered the city
of canvas tents and pole houses ; the suburbs appeared as
banks of dirty white lime, and a new arrival with black clothes
looked like nothing so much as a cockroach struggling through
a flour barrel. . . . . .

" It was sundown, and the lively notes of the violin and guitar
were calling the citizens to evening diversions. Twenty-three
saloons paid license to the evanescent corporation, and five dance-
houses amused our elegant leisure.

" The regular routine of business, dances, drunks and fist-
fights met with a sudden interruption. . . . Sitting in a tent
door, . . . I noticed an altercation across the street, and saw
a man draw a pistol and fire, and another stagger and catch hold
of a post for support. The first was about to shoot again when
he was struck from behind and the pistol wrenched from his hand.
The wounded man was taken into a tent near by and treated with
the greatest kindness by the women, but died the next day. It
was universally admitted that there had been no provocation for
the shooting, and the general voice was, ' Hang him !'

" Next day I observed a great rush and cry on the street, and
looking out, saw them dragging the murderer along towards the
tent where the dead man lay. The entire population were out at
once, plainsmen, miners and women mingled in a wild throng,
all insisting on immediate hanging. Pale as a sheet and hardly able
to stand, the murderer, in the grasp of two stalwart vigilantes,
was dragged through the excited crowd, and into the tent where
the dead man lay, and forced to witness the laying out and
depositing in the coffin.

" What was the object of this movement nobody knew, but
the delay was fatal to the hanging project. Benton had lately been
decided to be in the military reservation of Fort Steele, and that

10

day the general commanding, thought fit to send a provost guard
into the city. They arrived just in time, rescued the prisoner
and took him to the guard house, whence, a week after, he
escaped.

"But the excitement thus aroused seemed to create a thirst
for blood. I had just retired to the tent when I heard a series of
fearful screams, and running to the door, saw the proprietor of a
saloon opposite beating his 'woman.' He was a leading ruffian
of the city, and of a hundred men looking on not one felt called
upon to interfere. At length he released his hold, and struck her a
final blow on the nose which completely flattened that feature
and sent her into the middle of the street, where she lay with the
blood gushing in torrents from her face, mingling with the white
dust and streaking her clothing with gore. The provost guard
arrived again, after it was all over, and took the woman away, but
paid no attention to the man. Four days after, I saw them
together again, having apparently made it up and living on the
same free and easy terms of illegal conjugality. Two more rows
wound up the evening, the last ending up with a perfect fusilade
of pistol shots, by which only two or three persons were 'scratched'
and nobody 'pinked.' For a quiet railroad town I thought this
would do, and began to think of moving on.

"The great institution of Benton was the 'Big Tent,' sometimes, with equal truth, but less politeness, called the 'Gamblers'
Tent.' This structure was a nice frame, a hundred feet long and
forty feet wide, covered with canvas and conveniently floored
for dancing, to which and gambling it was entirely devoted. It
was moved successively to all the mushroom terminus 'cities,'
and during my stay was the great public resort of Benton. A
description of one of these towns is a description of all; so let
us spend one evening in the 'Big Tent,' and see how men amuse
their leisure when home life and society are lacking.

"As we enter, we note that the right side is lined with a
splendid bar, supplied with every variety of liquors and cigars,
with cut-glass goblets, ice-pitchers, splendid mirrors, and
pictures rivaling those of our eastern cities. At the back end a

space large enough for one cotillon is left open for dancing; on a raised platform a full band is in attendance day and night, while all the rest of the room is filled with tables devoted to monte, faro, rondo coolo, fortune wheels, and every other species of gambling known.

. . . .

"During the day the 'Big Tent' is rather quiet, but at night, after a few inspiring tunes at the door by the band, the long hall is soon crowded with a motley throng of three or four hundred miners, ranchmen, clerks, 'bull-whackers,' gamblers, and 'cappers.' The brass instruments are laid aside, the string music begins, the cotillons succeed each other rapidly, each ending with a drink, while those not so employed crowd around the tables and enjoy each his favorite game. To-night is one of unusual interest, and the tent is full, while from every table is heard the musical rattle of the dice, the hum of the wheel, or the eloquent voice of the dealer.

. . . .

"The evening wears along, many visitors beginning to leave, the games languish, and a diversion is needed. The band gives a few lively touches, and a young man with a capacious chest and a great deal of openness to his face, mounts the stand and sings a variety of sentimental and popular songs, ending with a regular.rouser, in the chorus of which he constantly reiterates— in other words, however—that he is a bovine youth with a vitreous optic 'which nobody can deny.' As he wears a revolver and a bowie-knife in plain view, nobody seems inclined to deny it. A lively dance follows, the crowd is enlivened, and gambling goes on with renewed vigor.

. . . .

"Transactions in real estate in all these towns were, of course, most uncertain; and everything that looked solid was a sham. Red-brick fronts, brown-stone fronts, and stuccoed walls, were found to have been made to order in Chicago and shipped in (pine) sections. Ready made houses were finally sent out in lots, boxed, marked, and numbered; half a dozen men could erect a block in a day, and two boys with screw-drivers put up a 'habitable dwelling' in three hours. A very good gray-stone stucco front, with plain sides, twenty by forty tent, could be had for $300.00; and if your business happened to desert you, or the town moved on, you only had to take your store to pieces, ship it on a platform car to the next city, and set up again. There was a pleasing versatility of talent in the population of such towns.

. . . .

"Ten months afterwards I revisited the site. There was not a house or tent to be seen; a few rock piles and half destroyed chimneys barely sufficed to mark the ruins; the white dust had covered everything else, and desolation reigned supreme."[1]

It had been expected that the Central Pacific, chartered by the state of California, would build east to the Nevada boundary, and that the Union Pacific, chartered by the national government, would build westward from Omaha through the territories to a meeting at the California boundary. But the object of the Pacific railway charter was to secure a railway from the Missouri to the Pacific, by whomsoever constructed, and its terms (section 10 of the act of 1862) had provided that "in case said first named [Union Pacific] company shall complete their line to the eastern boundary of California before it is completed across said state by the Central Pacific Railroad Company of California, said first-named company is hereby authorized to continue in constructing the same through California . . . . until said roads shall meet and connect, ... and the Central Pacific Railroad Company of California, after completing its road across said state, is authorized to continue the construction of said railroad and telegraph through the territories of the United States to the Missouri river, including the branch lines specified, ... until said roads shall meet and connect." This provision was changed in the Act of 1864 (section 16) to one that the Central Pacific might "extend their line of road eastward one hundred and fifty miles on the established route, so as to meet and con-

[1] The Undeveloped West, or Five Years in the Territories, by J. H. Beadle, pages 87 to 99, passim.

nect with the line of the Union Pacific road." Of which change Huntington, of the Central Pacific, has said, "One hundred and fifty miles ought not to have gone into the bill ; but I said to Mr. Union Pacific, when I saw it, I would take that out as soon as I wanted it out. In 1866 I went to Washington. I got a large majority of them without the use of a dollar." [1] Accordingly, the Act of 1866 renewed the original provision of the Act of 1862, and provided (section II) that "the Central Pacific Railroad Company of California, with the consent and approval of the Secretary of the Interior, are hereby authorized to locate, construct, and continue their road eastward, in a continuous completed line, until they shall meet and connect with the Union Pacific Railroad." [2]

The renewed provision resulted in the greatest race on record. The Central Pacific had to surmount the Sierra Nevada

[1] See Bancroft's History of California, Volume VII., page 551, note.

[2] When the act of 1866 was under consideration in the Senate, Conness (California) charged that the act of 1864 had been tampered with. "In 1864 the Senate passed a Pacific railroad bill ; I had a copy of it before me this morning. The House of Representatives passed another. The Senate refused to pass the House bill, and the House refused to pass the Senate bill ; and the matter was referred to a committee of conference upon the questions of disagreement. In neither of those bills did this arbitrary condition that I have named, confining one of these great companies to one hundred and fifty miles east of the California line, occur. It was not in either bill ; there was not a word or a tittle of it in either. I was a member of the conference committee. . . . . . Point by point the differences between the two Houses were arranged and agreed upon, and I undertake to say that that arbitrary condition now in the law, and in the law when it was printed, never was considered in that conference. It was stolen in through the corruption of some parties and the clerk who eventually made up the report. The report of the conference committee was presented here on the last day of the session and compelled to be adopted without examination. What I state cannot be contradicted, and the Senate and Congress ought to justify itself by a close inquiry as to who dared to make laws for the Congress of the United States." *Congressional Globe*, 39th Congress, 1st session, page 3261, June 19, 1866. When Conness' charge was afterwards read in the House, by a California representative, in the course of debate on the same measure, Thad Stevens, who had been a member of the committee of conference, said, "Although my recollection is precisely that of the Senator, . . . yet I shall make no charges against anybody." Ibidem, page 3422, June 26, 1866.

range at the beginning of its course, but the "Big Four," under the legal disguise of Charles Crocker and Company, were plucky, and the rise of 7012 feet above the sea level in the one hundred and five miles east of Sacramento to Summit was accomplished by the autumn of 1867. The Central Pacific did not wait for the completion of its fourteen tunnels, and especially its longest one of more than 1600 feet, at Summit, but hauled iron and supplies, and even locomotives, over the Sierra Nevada beyond the completed track, and went ahead with track laying, to be connected later with the track through the tunnels. The Union Pacific had comparatively easy work from Omaha along the Platte valley and up the slope to the summit of the Rocky Mountains, and boasted that their line would reach the eastern side of the Sierra Nevada before the Central Pacific had surmounted it.[1] But the boast was not justified.

In the autumn of 1867, the invading army of Mongolians emerged from the mountains on the west, while the rival army of Celts had reached the summit of the Black Hills, and were beginning their descent into the Great Basin on the east. Every mile now meant a prize of from $64,000.00 to $96,000.00 for the contending giants, with the commercial advantage of the control of the traffic of the Salt Lake valley in addition. The construction of road went on at the rate of from four to ten miles a day. Each of the two companies had more than ten thousand men at work.

"For the purpose of facilitating the work," the amendatory

[1] In maps published by the Union Pacific in pamphlets in the summer of 1867, the light line west of the eastern boundary of California is marked "Central Pacific," and the heavy line from the California boundary to Omaha is marked "Union Pacific;" and the line from Fort Bridger to Humboldt Wells is drawn south of Great Salt Lake, through Salt Lake City. In a map published by the Central Pacific in the same year, the red line of the Central Pacific meets the blue line of the Union Pacific between Fort Bridger and the Utah-Wyoming boundary, and the line sweeps north of Great Salt Lake. See also map published in *Harpers' Monthly*, June, 1867, page 3, and a map in Dilke's *Greater Britain*, Volume I., page 95 (written in 1867 or 1868); in the two latter maps, the line of railway passes through Salt Lake City and along the south shore of the lake to the later route in the vicinity of Humboldt Wells.

Act of 1864 had permitted, on the certificate of the chief engineer
and government commissioners that a portion of the work
required to prepare the road for the superstructure was done,
that a proportion of the bonds to be fully earned on the final
completion of the work, not exceeding two-thirds of the value of
the portion of the work done, and not exceeding two-thirds of
the whole amount of bonds to be earned, should be delivered to
each company ; the full benefit of this inducement was sought
by each of the contestants.   The Union Pacific company had its
parties of graders working two hundred miles in advance of its
completed line in places as far west as Humboldt Wells, but
financial difficulties prevented its following up this advantage.
The Central Pacific Company, on the other hand, had its grading
parties one hundred miles ahead of its completed line and thirty
miles east of Ogden.   When the two roads met at Promontory
Point, it was found that the Central Pacific had graded eighty
miles to the east that it would never cover and the Union Pacific
had wasted a million dollars on grading west of the meeting
place that it could not use.   The Central Pacific had craftily
obtained from the Secretary of the Treasury an advance of two-
thirds of the bond subsidy on its graded line to Echo Summit,
about forty miles east of Ogden, before its completed line had
reached Promontory Point ; while the Union Pacific had actually
laid its track to and westward from Ogden, and appeared thus to
have gained the advantage of controlling the Salt Lake valley
traffic from Ogden as a base.   The Union Pacific was pushing
westward from Ogden with its completed line about a mile distant from and parallel with the surveyed and graded line of the
Central Pacific, and the two companies were each claiming the
right to build the line between Ogden and Promontory Point on
their separate surveys.   The completed lines were threatening to
lap as the graded lines already lapped, when Congress interfered
and tried to clear the muddle by statute.   Before Congress could
reach a conclusion, the companies compromised their differences,
and Congress then approved the settlement by a joint resolution,
April 10, 1869, "That the common terminus of the Union Pacific

and the Central Pacific Railroads shall be at or near Ogden ; and the Union Pacific Railroad Company shall build and the Central Pacific Railroad Company pay for and own the railroad from the terminus aforesaid to Promontory Summit, at which point the rails shall meet and connect and form one continuous line." In the following year, Congress, by further enactment, fixed " the common terminus and point of junction" at a particular point about five miles " northwest of the station at Ogden;" later the Union Pacific leased to the Central Pacific the five miles of track between the station at Ogden and the point fixed by Congress ; thus Ogden became the actual point of junction of the two links of the completed Pacific railway.

It had at first been generally assumed that the transcontinental railway would pass through Salt Lake City and south of Great Salt Lake,[1] and the Mormons had used their influence to obtain such a route ; but before the final surveys were made, the north line was found by the Union Pacific to be more acceptable and was approved by the government. Brigham Young thereupon called a meeting of the dignitaries of the Mormon Church, and an order was issued that no Mormon should make further grading contracts with the Union Pacific. As the Mormon traffic was one of the prizes of the railway race, and the assistance of Mormon contractors was highly needful, the Union Pacific management awaited with some apprehension the action of the Central Pacific, but the latter also decided in favor of the route along the north shore, and Zion had to be content with the prospect of a future branch line. The Mormons then resumed their old relations with the eastern company, and many miles of well graded road-bed bear witness of their participation in the great enterprise.

The disputed question of the point of junction did not interfere with a due celebration of the meeting and joining of the two " ends of track " at Promontory Point on the 10th of May, 1869 A space of about one hundred feet was left between the ends of the lines. Early in the day, Leland Stanford, Governor of Cal-

[1] Supra, page 150, note.

ifornia and President of the Central Pacific, arrived with his
party from the west ; during the forenoon, Vice-President Durant and Directors Duff and Dillon, of the Union Pacific, with
other prominent men, including a delegation of Mormon saints
from Salt Lake City, came in on a train from the east. The
national government was represented by a detachment of "regu-
lars" from Fort Douglas, with the opportune accessories of orna-
mental officers and a military band. Curious Mexicans, Indians,
and half-breeds, with the Chinese, negro, and Irish laborers, lent
to the auspicious little gathering a suggestive air of cosmopoli-
tanism. The ties were laid for the rails in the open space, and
while the coolies from the west laid the rails at one end, the paddies from the east laid them at the other end, until they met and
joined. The "last spike" remained to be driven. Telegraphic
wires were so connected that each blow of the descending sledge
could be reported instantly on the telegraphic instruments in
most of the large cities from the Atlantic to the Pacific ; corresponding blows were struck on the bell of the City Hall in San
Francisco, and with the last blow of the sledge a cannon was
fired at Fort Point. General Safford presented a spike of gold,
silver and iron as the offering of the Territory of Arizona ; Tut-
tle, of Nevada, performed with a spike of silver a like office for
his state. The tie of California laurel was put in place, and
Doctor Harkness, of California, presented the "last spike" of
gold in behalf of his state. A silver sledge had also been presented for the occasion. The driving of the spike by President
Stanford and Vice-President Durant was greeted with lusty cheers
by the onlookers, and the hurrahs and shouts of the little crowd
of six hundred persons, to the accompaniment of the screams of
the locomotives' whistles and the blare of the military band, in the
midst of the desert, found hearty and enthusiastic echoes in the
great cities east and west. After the last spike had been driven,
the Central Pacific train was backed up, and the Union Pacific
locomotive, with its train, passed slowly over the point of junction and back again ; then the Central Pacific locomotive, with

its train, went through the same ceremony, and the two engines stood where they inspired Bret Harte to write

WHAT THE ENGINES SAID.

What was it the Engines said,
Pilots touching,—head to head,
Facing on the single track,
Half a world behind each back?
This is what the Engines said,
Unreported and unread.

With a prefatory screech,
In a florid western speech,
Said the Engine from the West,
"I am from Sierra's crest;
And, if altitude's a test,
Why, I reckon, it's confessed,
That I've done my level best."

Said the Engine from the East,
"They who work best talk the least,
S'pose you whistle down your brakes;
What you've done is no great shakes,
Pretty fair,—but let our meeting
Be a different kind of greeting.
Let these folks with champagne stuffing,
Not their Engines, do the puffing.

"Listen! Where Atlantic beats
Shores of snow and summer heats;
Where the Indian autumn skies
Paint the woods with wampum dyes,
I have chased the flying sun,
Seeing all he looked upon,
Blessing all that he has blest,
Nursing in my iron breast
All his vivifying heat,
All his clouds about my crest;
And before my flying feet
Every shadow must retreat."

Said the Western Engine, "Phew!"
And a long, low whistle blew.

"Come now, really that's the oddest
Talk for one so very modest.
You brag of your East! You do?
Why, I bring the East to you!
All the Orient, all Cathay,
Find through me the shortest way;
And the sun you follow here
Rises in my hemisphere.
Really,—if one must be rude,—
Length, my friend, ain't longitude."

Said the Union, "Don't reflect, or
I'll run over some Director."
Said the Central, "I'm Pacific,
But, when riled, I'm quite terrific.
Yet to-day we shall not quarrel,
Just to show these folks this moral,
How two Engines—in their vision—
Once have met without collision."
That is what the Engines said,
Unreported and unread;
Spoken slightly through the nose,
With a whistle at the close.

The "driving of the last spike" was simultaneously announced
by telegraph in all the large cities of the Union. Telegraphic
inquiries at the Omaha office, from which the circuit was to be
started, were answered: "To everybody. Keep quiet. When
the last spike is driven at Promontory Point, we will say 'Done.'
Don't break the circuit, but watch for the signals of the blows of
the hammer." Soon followed the message from Promontory
Point, "Almost ready. Hats off; prayer is being offered;" then,
"We have got done praying. The spike is about to be presented," and—"All ready now. The spike will soon be driven.
The signal will be three dots for the commencement of the
blows." The magnet tapped—One—Two—Three—then paused
—"Done!" Wires in every direction were "hot" with con-
gratulatory telegrams. President Grant and Vice-President Colfax were the recipients of especially felicitous messages. In San
Francisco it had been announced on the evening of the 8th of

May from the stages of the theaters and other public places that the two roads had met and were to be wedded on the morrow. The city could not wait; the celebration began at once and practically continued through the 10th. The booming of cannon and the ringing of bells were united with the other species of noise-making in which jubilant humanity finds expression for its feelings on such an occasion. The buildings in the city and the shipping in the harbor were gay with flags and bunting. Business was suspended, and the longest procession that San Francisco had ever seen attested the enthusiasm of the people. At night the city was brilliant with illuminations. Free railway trains filled Sacramento with an unwonted crowd, and the din of cannon, steam whistles and bells followed the final message. At the eastern terminus in Omaha, the firing of a hundred guns on Capitol Hill, more bells and steam whistles, and a grand procession of fire companies, civic societies, fraternities, citizens and visiting delegations from surrounding places, echoed the sentiments of the Californians. In Chicago a procession of four miles in length, a lavish display of decorations in the city and on the vessels in the river, and an address by Vice-President Colfax in the evening, were the evidences of the city's feeling. In New York, by order of the mayor, a salute of a hundred guns announced the culmination of the great undertaking. In Trinity church the Te Deum was chanted and prayers were offered, and when the services were over the chimes rung out "Old Hundred," the "Ascension Carol" and national airs. The ringing of bells on Independence Hall and the fire stations in Philadelphia produced an unusual concourse of citizens to celebrate the national event. In the other large cities of the country the expressions of public gratification were hardly less hearty and demonstrative.

But when were the Central Pacific and Union Pacific completed? The Act of 1862 provided (section vi) that "after said road is completed, until said [government subsidy] bonds and interest are paid, at least five per centum of the net earnings of said road shall also be annually applied to the payment thereof."

Though the entire line, in sections of twenty and forty miles, had been inspected and approved by government commissioners as often as reported under oath by the presidents of the companies to be complete, so that they might obtain their government bonds and issue their own bonds in an equal sum, Congress, to "make sure," resolved (April 10, 1869) "that to ascertain the condition of the Union Pacific Railroad and the Central Pacific Railroad, the President of the United States is authorized to appoint a board of eminent citizens, not exceeding five in number, and who shall not be interested in either road, to examine and report on the condition of, and what sum or sums, if any, will be required to complete, each of said roads, for the entire length thereof to the [common] terminus as a first class railroad, in compliance with the several acts relating to said roads." The "five eminent citizens" appointed on the board were Hiram Walbridge, S. M. Fenton, C. B. Comstock, E. F. Winslow, and J. F. Boyd. In October, 1869, they filed an oracular report with the Secretary of the Interior that, "in the opinion of the commission, the requirements of the law will be satisfied, and the designs of Congress carried out, if the roads be properly located, with judicious grades; have substantial roadbeds of good width; ballasting which with proper care, shall be able to keep the track in good condition throughout the year; permanent structures for crossing streams, good cross-ties, iron and joint fastenings; sufficient sidings, water tanks, buildings, machinery and adequate rolling-stock, the more important machine shops and engine houses being of masonry; and the commission is glad to be able to say that, in its opinion, while some expenditures still need to be made, these two roads are substantially such roads to-day. The expenditures needed for completion, will be given in detail for each road." The report was closed with a detailed estimate of $576,650.00 and $1,586,100.00 as the amounts of the expenditures needed on the Central Pacific and Union Pacific respectively. In accordance with the joint resolution of April 10, 1869, the Secretary of the Treasury withheld $1,000,000.00 of bonds claimed to be due the companies and exacted from them undertakings and collateral security for the completion of each road according to law; and the Secretary of the Interior issued no more patents for the land grant, until the "five eminent citizens" might prophecy.

In November, 1869, after the rendition of the Janus-headed report of the "eminent citizens" in the preceding month, the Secretary of the Treasury seemed to have gleaned from it that the roads were "completed," and released to the company the bonds withheld from them and the collateral security deposited by them, the companies undertaking that the requirements of the commission should be complied with. But the Secretary of the Interior was only half convinced, as evidenced by his order of November 3, 1869, to the Commissioner of the General Land Office:—

"Sir : . . . . . [the commissioners'] report being accepted and made the basis of an adjustment of the accounts between the United States and said railroad companies, you are hereby authorized to commence the patenting of lands to said companies, ... as follows : In addition to the bonds retained by the United States as security for the completion of said roads in the matters reported deficient, ... one-half of the lands ready for patenting to the Union Pacific Company will have patents suspended until further directions from this department. The other half may be patented to said company. . . . . . Patents to the Central Pacific may in like manner . . . . . issue."

For nearly five years the Secretary of the Interior declined to give "further directions," and the companies applied in vain for patents for the balance of their land grant. In May, 1874, on application of the Union Pacific, the Acting Secretary of the Interior appointed another commission of three sagacious citizens (James Moore, Ira L. Merriam, and J. S. Delano), whom he instructed :

"SIRS : On the 30th of October, 1869, 'five eminent citizens,' who were appointed commissioners by the President, under joint resolution of 10th April, 1869, reported certain deficiencies in the construction of the Union Pacific railroad.

" The president of the company that constructed said road applied, on the 8th instant, for its examination, to determine whether it has been completed as required by law and the report of said commissioners.

" You are hereby appointed commissioners to make such examination and report to this department.

" It will be your duty to examine said road with special reference to the deficiencies above referred to, and to report whether they have been supplied. If they have been, and the road is completed as required by law and departmental instructions, you will ascertain as near as possible, and report the date of such completion.

" You will report whether the company has shown a disposition to act in good faith in supplying such deficiencies ; give full and exact information as to the present condition of the road ; and, if it be not yet completed, state what is, in your judgment, necessary to such completion."

The verdict of this inquest was, " This commission has . . decided that the road was completed as required by law, by the report of the former commission, and to comply with the instructions of the Interior Department, October 1, 1874, at a total cost of $115,214,587.79, as shown by the books of the company."

When the Secretary of the Treasury (Bristow), as directed by the Act of 1874, demanded of the Union Pacific Company the payment of the five per centum of the net earnings applicable " after said road is *completed*,"[1] his demand extended back to " the 6th day of November, 1869, the day of completion of said Union Pacific Railroad ;" in the case of the Central Pacific, the demand extended back to " the 16th day of July, 1869, the day of the completion of said Central Pacific Railroad." In opposition to this view the companies naturally enough insisted, in and out of court, that the day reported by the commission of three (October 1, 1874) was the date of completion,— a view readily endorsed, of course, by the obsequious government directors.[2]

[1] See page 106, supra.

[2] See Report of Government Directors for the year 1875.

When a suit, brought by the United States against the Union Pacific to recover the five per cent of net earnings, reached the Supreme Court for decision in the fall of 1878, Justice Bradley, delivering the opinion of the court, was not willing to say when the Union Pacific was completed (if, indeed, a railroad could ever, in one sense, be completed) but held simply that by the attitude assumed by the company for the purpose of obtaining its subsidy bonds, it was estopped to deny that at the time the last bonds were delivered, November 6, 1869, the road was completed, even though required at the same time to give security that it should be made more complete.[1]

The question of the eastern terminus of the Union Pacific was involved for a long time in as much doubt and obscurity as the questions of western terminus and time of completion. Where is the eastern terminus ? The Act of 1862 seemed to intend it to be at a point on the 100th meridian on the edge of the desert in Nebraska ; the amendment of 1866 permitted the construction of the line " from Omaha . . . westward . . . without reference to the initial point on the 100th-meridian ; " according to the Act of 1862 — an act " to aid in the construction of a railroad . . . from the Missouri River to the Pacific Ocean, [etc.]," the Union Pacific was required to construct its Iowa (or Omaha) branch from a point on the western boundary of the State of Iowa, to be fixed by the President of the United States." Abraham Lincoln had first fixed the point " within the limits of the township, in Iowa, opposite the town of Omaha, in Nebraska," and later more particularly as "east of, and opposite to, the east line of Section Ten . . . " — a section bounded on the east by the Missouri River.[2] Finally, the Bridge Act (approved February 24, 1871) gave to the Union Pacific authority " to issue such bonds and secure the same by mortgage on the

---

[1] United States vs. Union Pacific Railroad Company, 99 U. S. R., 402.

[2] As a matter of fact, the Union Pacific did not locate its Council Bluffs station or end of line opposite Section Ten, but a considerable distance south of it; as noted in the decision of the case of Union Pacific Railroad Company vs. Hall, et al., cited on page 161, infra.

bridge [between Omaha and Council Bluffs] and approaches and appurtenances, as it may deem needful to construct and maintain its bridge over said [Missouri] river, and the tracks and depots required to perfect the same, as now authorized by law. . . . Provided, that nothing in this act shall be so construed as to change the eastern terminus of the Union Pacific railroad from the place where it is now fixed under existing laws, nor to release said . . . company . . . from its obligations as established by existing laws." The Union Pacific persisted in regarding Omaha as the terminus, made up all its trains there, and operated the bridge and approaches as a stub-line with Council Bluffs at the end of the stub. Citizens of Council Bluffs applied to the United States courts for a writ of mandamus to compel the Union Pacific to operate its line from their city as the true terminus of the line, required by its charter to be operated as "a continuous line." The snarl was left for the Supreme Court to untangle. "From Omaha westward" probably did not mean "from Council Bluffs westward." "From the Missouri River" might mean "from either the east or west side of the Missouri River." "The western boundary of the State of Iowa" was the middle of the Missouri River, and probably the point had in mind by Lincoln was not strictly on that boundary line. It required much acute reasoning and legal hairsplitting for the Supreme Court to decide that "the legal terminus of the railroad is fixed by law on the Iowa shore of the river" and to sustain the lower court in ordering that the writ of mandamus issue, though even then Justice Bradley dissented from the opinion of the court on the ground that the whole river was the boundary and "from the river or boundary of Iowa westward" meant "from the western shore of the river westward," an interpretation that he considered to be approved by Congress in the Bridge Act.[1]

Whatever may be the technical termini of the Union Pacific or the date of its completion, the past or present relations of the corporation to the government or people, or the industrial and

[1] Union Pacific Railroad Company *vs.* Hall et al., 91 U. S. R., 343.

11

political forces that created the company and the railway, the fact remains that the building of the Pacific railway marks an epoch in the history of railways. The great length of the line, the rapidity with which it was constructed and equipped, the extreme natural difficulties presented by the country it traversed, and the important industrial and political results that have followed its completion afford ample justification for the erection at Sherman, on the Union Pacific—for many years the highest railway station in the world,—of a massive granite monument in memory of the Ames brothers (Oakes Ames and Oliver Ames), to whose energy and ability the successful completion of the Union Pacific is most justly ascribed. But with all honor to the men whose individual efforts have contributed most to the accomplishment of a great national purpose, the Pacific railway itself is a greater monument to the irrepressible and progressive energy of the people of the United States.

CHAPTER VI.

CREDIT MOBILIER.

I.

THE instrumentality through which the Union Pacific railway was built is one of the most interesting and instructive features of its development. It was quite typical of railway construction from 1855 to 1880, and holds up before the mind of the student one of the darkest phases of the railway problem.

The Board of Commissioners met at Chicago in September, 1862, and was organized by the election of officers. Books were then opened in the large cities of the country for subscriptions of stock, and by October, 1863, 2180 shares had been subscribed and $218,000.00 had been paid in. The first meeting of stockholders was held in New York, October 29 and 30, 1863, and directors and other officers were elected. The directors were thirty in number ; the other officers were John A. Dix, president ; Thomas C. Durant, vice-president ; Henry V. Poor, secretary ; John J. Cisco, treasurer.

Durant was the active man in the management of the company's business. In August, 1864, he had one H. M. Hoxie, an irresponsible man (an employé in charge of the ferry at Omaha), offer to take a contract for the construction of the line one hundred miles westward from Omaha at $50,000.00 per mile, to be paid in securities of the company ; this proposition was signed " H. M. Hoxie, by H. C. Crane, attorney," and Crane was the "confidential man" in Durant's office. October 3, 1864, " H. M. Hoxie, by H. C. Crane, attorney," proposed to the company that if his contract be made to extend from one hundred miles so as to cover the distance from Omaha to the one hundredth meridian, he would subscribe or cause to be subscribed $500,-

ooo.oo of stock in the Union Pacific Railroad Company; the proposition was accepted by the company. On the 7th of the same month, Hoxie agreed to assign his contract to Durant or any person he (Durant) might designate ; on the same day, the assignment was made to a company (simple partnership—not a corporation or company of limited liability) composed of Durant, McComb and a few others, all stockholders in the Union Pacific. The scheme is plain enough. Durant's theory was that all the money made out of the Union Pacific project would be made in the construction of the road, and that the road itself would never, as a legitimate business enterprise, yield a profit. The government had offered an immense bonus to any set of men that would build the road, and in order to get the benefit of the bonus, the persons controlling the company had to control the construction contracts and share in their profits.

The construction company formed by Durant subscribed $1,600,000.00 to carry out the Hoxie contract and paid in twenty-five per cent of the amount subscribed. By the time the second assessment was made, the immense responsibility and unlimited liability had frightened the members of the company and they failed to respond with further payments. At this point the since famous Credit Mobilier was brought into service.

From 1850 to 1860, before general incorporation laws were common, when each corporation was the creation of a special legislative enactment, what might be called " charter shops" came to be among the established industries of the country. Charters were obtained from state legislatures, principally by persons of past political influence and usefulness, not for the purpose of using them but of selling them to others to use. Such charters, of course, contained as broad and elastic provisions as could be obtained by the applicants for them ; they were thus more serviceable and salable as stock in trade. Duff Green had been an editor and politician of some importance during Jackson's administration, but in 1859 he had become dusty on the back shelf of politics ; and when, in that year, he applied to the legislature of Pennsylvania for a charter fit to be used for a stock brokerage company, investment company, railroad company, or almost any kind of company, the childish old man was tolerated and his whim satisfied with little hesitation ; the result was the legal entity known by the innocent corporate name of the " Pennsylvania Fiscal Agency," possessed of conveniently elastic powers and a limitation of liability of its shareholders to the amount of stock subscribed.

Durant had evidently anticipated the difficulties to be encountered in the unlimited individual liability of the contractors for the construction of the Union Pacific, and as early as March, 1864, through the mediation of irrepressible George Francis Train, had purchased the charter of the Pennsylvania Fiscal Agency for future use. Soon after the purchase, the name of the corporation was changed by legislative enactment to " The Credit Mobilier of America."[1] Under the liberal provisions of the charter, an agency or branch was established in New York, with a railroad bureau under five (afterward seven) managers, elected from among the directors and stockholders. After the members of Durant's construction company had made their first payments, their attention was turned to the Credit Mobilier, and they were given stock in it for the amounts they had paid in on the capital of the construction company. Holders of the $2,180,000.00 of Union Pacific stock were then permitted either to receive Credit

---

[1] The change of name is said to have been inspired by George Francis Train, who had spent much time in France and, while there, had been much impressed by the operations of the famous Credit Mobilier of France. The latter had been chartered in France in 1853, under the influence of the brothers Isaac and Émile Péreire, for the development of railways, public works, and other internal improvements and for general banking and stock brokerage operations. The company accomplished by its aid the establishment of the Paris Gas Company, the Paris Omnibus Company, and the Grand Hôtel du Louvre, and promoted railway enterprises in France, Switzerland, Spain, Austria and Russia. Excessive dividends in 1855 were followed by decreasing profits until 1867, when the company went into liquidation and bequeathed to its managers (who had accumulated from its gambling schemes great private fortunes) a crushing burden of litigation and public condemnation. The change in name of the Pennsylvania corporation was unfortunate. (See Rowland Hazard's "Credit Mobilier of America," pages 15-17.)

Mobilier stock for the amounts they had paid in or to sell it to the Credit Mobilier or back to the Union Pacific for what they had paid in on it. Thus the stockholders in the Union Pacific and Credit Mobilier became identical, as persons, though their holdings of stock in the two corporations were not in the same proportion.

The Hoxie contract (covering the line from Omaha to the 100th meridian, two hundred and forty-seven miles) was assigned to the Credit Mobilier, and by that corporation performed, the work being finished on the 5th of October, 1866.

Next a mysterious contract was made by Durant and a man suggestively named Boomer (afterward declared to have enjoyed existence only in Durant's fertile imagination) for the construction of one hundred and fifty-three miles westward from the 100th meridian, at the rate of $19,500.00 per mile east, and $20,000.00 per mile west, of the crossing of the Platte River, bridges, station houses, and equipments to be paid for in addition. The work of construction proceeded, however, without particular reference to any contract, being actually done by the Credit Mobilier, until fifty-eight miles were completed. January 5, 1867, the board of directors of the Union Pacific resolved, "That the Union Pacific Railroad Company will, and do, hereby consider the Hoxie contract extended to the point already completed, namely, three hundred and five miles west from Omaha, and that the officers of this company are hereby authorized to settle with the Credit Mobilier at $50,000.00 per mile for the additional fifty-eight miles." The resolution was not enforced, because of a written protest filed by Durant with the board of directors, and of a more efficacious writ of injunction sued out against them by him before Judge Barnard in New York. With the same object in view, in June, 1867, the board of directors of the Union Pacific contracted with J. M. S. Williams (with the provision that, when made, the contract should be assigned to the Credit Mobilier), for the building of two hundred and sixty-eight miles westward from the 100th meridian to the base of the Rocky Mountains, at the rate of $50,000.00

per mile, including the portion of the line already completed west of the 100th meridian, and now increased from fifty-eight to ninety-eight miles. But another protest from Durant, and another writ of injunction from a New York court, effectually restrained the performance of the Williams contract on the part of the company.

The quarrel of the factions in the Union Pacific and Credit Mobilier was the outgrowth of a deep seated disagreement between Durant and his friends on one side, and the New England stockholders, the Ameses, Hazards, Alley, and their friends on the other side. Durant and his party were wasteful and extravagant, and favored the subordination of the whole project to the purpose of profits from construction, even at the expense of a cheaply built railway ; the more conservative New England party, on the other hand, while not averse to large profits from construction, held in view as an object the ultimate success of the Union Pacific as an investment, and favored the construction of a substantial and well equipped railway. The latter party, being uppermost in the Credit Mobilier, ousted Durant from the directory, and elected Sidney Dillon in his stead as president; in the Union Pacific, however, Durant's party had more relative strength, and he remained vice-president and a director, though Oliver Ames was elected president.

Durant declared, when the Union Pacific had reached the 100th meridian, that the Credit Mobilier, as a corporation, should never have another construction contract, and he had the power, in the peculiar relations of the two companies, to maintain his position. But while Durant had aggressiveness, the New Englanders had money, and peace was welcome to both parties. In the summer of 1867 the factions reconciled their differences, and from the compromise resulted the Oakes Ames contract and the anomalous Seven Trustees.

In August, 1867, the Union Pacific voted to Oakes Ames a contract for constructing and equipping six hundred and sixty-seven miles of road west of the 100th meridian at rates varying from $42,000.00 to $96,000.00 per mile and aggregating about

$47,000,000.00. Thereupon, in pursuance of the compromise made by the factions, a tri-partite agreement was entered into by Oakes Ames, party of the first part; Seven Trustees (Thomas C. Durant, Oakes Ames, John B. Alley, Sidney Dillon, Cornelius S. Bushnell, Henry S. McComb, and Benjamin E. Bates, all stockholders in both corporations), parties of the second part; and the Credit Mobilier, party of the third part; by the terms of which the three parties assumed the following obligations.: (1) Oakes Ames assigned and transferred his contract to the Seven Trustees. (2) The Credit Mobilier was to advance to the Seven Trustees the means to perform the contract at seven per cent interest, guaranteed the performance of the contract, and was to hold Oakes Ames and the Seven Trustees harmless from loss under the contract for a commission of two and one-half per cent on the money advanced. (3) The Seven Trustees were to carry out all the provisions of the Oakes Ames contract, to reimburse the Credit Mobilier and themselves all money advanced, to pay over in June and December of each year "his just share and proportion . . . of the . . . net profit on said contract . . . to each shareholder in said Credit Mobilier of America, who, being a stockholder in the Union Pacific Railroad, shall have made and executed his power of attorney or proxy, irrevocable to said [Trustees] empowering them . . . to vote upon at least six-tenths of all the shares of stock owned [or to be owned] by said shareholders of the Credit Mobilier of America in the capital stock of the Union Pacific Railroad Company," and "this trust . . . shall not inure in any manner or degree to the use or benefit of any stockholder of the Credit Mobilier of America, who shall neglect or refuse to execute and deliver [to the Trustees] his proxy or power of attorney . . . or who shall in any way . . . . interfere with the execution or performance of the trust; and finally the Seven Trustees were to pay to the Credit Mobilier the net profits of the construction of the fifty-eight miles completed prior to January 1, 1867. The resort to the compromise Trust was made subject to the written consent of every stockholder of the Union Pacific, which was obtained by October, 1867. As soon as the Seven Trustees began the performance of their duties, they entered into an agreement among themselves to cast their own votes and the votes controlled by their proxies, for such directors of the Union Pacific as the existing board of directors should nominate, or to reëlect the existing board if they should fail to nominate another; any Trustee failing to keep his agreement was to forfeit all the benefits of the Trust. The management of the Trust was further "boiled down" by the appointment of an "executive committee" of three (John B. Alley, Rowland Hazard, and Sidney Dillon) who should wield its entire power, subject only to such regulations as should be made at periodical meetings of the Seven Trustees.

Under the Trustees the construction of the Union Pacific was pushed until the track reached a point nine hundred and fourteen miles from Omaha ; then a contract similar to the Ames contract was made with one J. W. Davis for the construction of the remaining one hundred and twenty-five miles at an expense of about $23,400,000.00, was assigned to the same Trustees, and was performed by them in the same manner as the Ames contract. The Union Pacific had no money and paid the Seven Trustees for the work, as fast as completed, in government subsidy bonds, first mortgage bonds, land grant bonds, income bonds and stock.[1] The Trustees sold some of the securities and used the proceeds in meeting the expenses of construction ; the surplus of securities and money they distributed among the Credit Mobilier stockholders entitled, by the terms of the trust, to participate in them.

The entire ingenious system was simply the machinery by which the owners of the Union Pacific insured to themselves the profits of constructing and equipping the road. The use of the Credit Mobilier charter was intended to relieve the constructors of

---

[1] As to the Union Pacific stock, which the law provided (supra, page 126) should be paid for in cash at not less than par, the Union Pacific would give the Trustees its check to apply on construction account, and the Trustees would then deliver the check back to the Union Pacific in payment of stock. This was called a cash transaction, and was thus entered on the books of account of the parties.

individual liability in a doubtful enterprise; the resort to the
Trust (made necessary by the Durant quarrel) was not considered
as destroying the advantage of the corporate organization; as a
matter of law, however, the Seven Trustees made themselves
personally liable, by the tri-partite agreement, for the expense of
constructing the Union Pacific.

II.

The machinery of the Credit Mobilier and Seven Trustees is
generally considered to have given to the Credit Mobilier stockholders abnormal profits, at the expense of the bounty of the
government, often called a "trust fund" for the building of the
Union Pacific, and to have burdened the railway with a load of
debts that makes it scant security for the repayment of the means
advanced by the United States in aid of its construction.

What were the profits, as compared with the outlay? The
Wilson Committee[1] arrived at $23,366,319.81 as the "total cash
profit" on an expenditure of $50,720,958.94.[2] J. B. Crawford, in
his "Credit Mobilier of America" (pages 71 and 72), finds the
net profits to have been $8,141,903.70, on an expenditure of
about $70,000,000.00. Rowland Hazard, one of the "executive
committee of the Seven Trustees," has said, "After nearly four
years of investment, [the stockholders of the Credit Mobilier]
received sixty per cent in cash, eighty per cent in first mortgage
bonds, and seventy-five per cent in income bonds. Taking these
securities at their current prices, by their sale, and the cash dividends, each stockholder would receive his money back, and nine-
tenths as much more; that is, ninety per cent paid for four years
investment at the end of the time. Add the bonus bonds, and it
will be a little less than one hundred and twenty per cent. Besides
this, [they] received by the purchase at four dollars and a half
. . . . . and by dividend, six hundred and fifteen per cent in
stock of the Union Pacific Railroad. This, at the time, had little

[1] Infra, pages 178–179.

[2] Affairs of Union Pacific Railroad Company, House of Representatives
Reports, No. 78 (page 15), 42d Congress, 3d Session.

or no market value . . . . On [the] basis of [fifty cents on the dollar in 1881 for the Union Pacific stock], the total profit received by the stockholders of the Credit Mobilier was about $15,000,000.00 on an expenditure of about $70,000,000.00, or a little over twenty per cent. This is a high estimate, and is probably more than was realized by the great majority of stockholders. . . . On [the] basis of [the value of the stock as estimated at the time], the total profit would be about $6,000,000, or less than nine per cent. on the expenditure.[1]

The testimony of the bookkeepers of the Credit Mobilier, Ham and Crane, before the Wilson Committee, was to the effect that the profit of constructing the Union Pacific was as follows:

	COST TO UNION PACIFIC.	COST TO CONTRACTORS.	PROFIT.
Hoxie Contract -	$12,974,416.24	$7,806,183.33	$5,168,232.91
Ames Contract -	57,140,102.94	27,285,141.99	29,854,960.95
Davis Contract -	23,431,768.10	15,629,633.62	7,802,134.48
Total,	$93,546,287.28	$50,720,958.94	$42,825,328.34

But the profit ascertained by their computation consisted largely of bonds and stock, included at par, but actually depreciated in value and disposed of at a discount ; when the allowance is made for the depreciation in value, the apparent total profit of $42,825,328.34 shrinks to $23,366,319.81.

Again, by computing the profits on another basis, the dividends declared were as follows :

	DATE.	CHARACTER.	FACE VALUE.	CASH VALUE.
1	Dec. 12, 1867	First-mortgage bonds	$2,543,208.00	$2,161,726.80
2	Dec. 12, 1867	Union Pacific stock	2,543,408.00	726,962.40
3	Jan. 3, 1868	First-mortgage bonds	748,000.00	635,800.00
4	June 17, 1868	Cash	2,201,204.00	2,201,204.00
5	July 18, 1868	Cash	1,112,768.00	1,112,768.00
6	July 3, 1868	First-mortgage bonds	2,804,050.00	2,383,442.50
7	Dec. 29, 1868	Union Pacific stock	7,500,000.00	2,250,000.00
8	Dec. 1868	{ Credit Mobilier dividend of 12% on 58 miles }	420,000.00	420,000.00
		Total,	$19,872,438.00	$11,891.903.70

[1] See the "Credit Mobilier of America," a paper read by Rowland Hazard, before the Rhode Island Historical Society, February 22, 1881, pages 27–29.

By still another method of computation, the government subsidy bonds and the Union Pacific first-mortgage bonds would
appear to have paid for the construction of the railway, leaving
the income bonds, land grant bonds, and Union Pacific stock as
profit, as follows :

	FACE VALUE.	CASH VALUE.
Government bonds - - -	$27,236,512.00	$27,145,163.28
First-mortgage bonds - - -	27,213,000.00	23,718,008.77
Total, - - - - - -		$50,863,172.05
Total cost of road to contractors - - -		50,720,958.94
		142,213.11
Income bonds - - - - -		9,355,000.00
Land grant bonds - - - -		9,224,000.00
Union Pacific stock - - -	$36,000,000.00,	10,800,000.00
Total profit - - - - -		$29,521,213.11

From this "total profit" the capital of the Credit Mobilier,
$3,750,000.00 (which was entirely consumed) ought probably
to be deducted, leaving the profit, on that basis, $25,771,213.11.

While the results of different computations by different persons are at great variance, and the books of the companies themselves do not afford exact information of the profit made in the
construction of the Union Pacific, it is safe to say that it was
in excess of $20,000,000.00. Both Mr. Hazard and Mr. Craw-
ford, in their publications, convey a wrong impression by computing the entire amount expended on the Union Pacific as a
basis for the percentage of profit earned. The truth is that
although from $50,000,000.00 to $70,000,000.00 were actually
expended in the construction of the railway and its equipment,
no such sum was invested by the Credit Mobilier and Trustees at
any one time. The capital of the Credit Mobilier was at first
$2,500,000.00, and after being increased was only $3,750,000.00 ;
and a large part of the capital invested was replaced on the completion of each section of twenty miles by the proceeds of the
government bonds and railway bonds and stock received. It is
hardly probable that more than $10,000,000.00 was actually
invested in the construction of the Union Pacific at any one time ;

in that case, if the profit of $20,000,000.00 were earned in four years, the profit for each year would be $5,000,000.00, or fifty per cent on the capital actually invested.

The amount of land granted to the Union Pacific under its charter was 11,309,844 acres ; the amount of money realized by the company from its sales of land to December 31, 1886, was $19,090,672.42, and the value at that time of the unsold lands was estimated at $2,395,507.00.[1]

The haste in which the Union Pacific was built, at a time when the price of labor and material was extremely high, government bonds at a discount, gold at a premium, and the national currency inflated, and before the road (until January, 1867) had any other road within a hundred miles of a connection with it, increased the cost of it enormously. If the road had been built at an ordinary time, in an ordinary manner, and under ordinary conditions, the bonus of government bonds and land grant would have been nearly, if not quite, sufficient to build and equip the railway. As the matter stood when the work was completed, the earning power of the Union Pacific had to be exerted to pay interest on $27,000,000.00 of first-mortgage bonds, $27,000,000.00 of government bonds, $10,000,000.00 of income bonds, $10,000,000.00 of land grant bonds, and if anything should be left, to pay dividends on $36,000,000.00 of stock—in round numbers, a total of

[1] See Reports of the United States Pacific Railway Commission, Senate Executive Documents No. 51, 50th Congress, 1st Session. The status of the land grant of all parts of the Pacific railway, as contemplated by the Act of 1864, was, in 1887, as follows :

	Acres granted.	Amount realized to Dec. 31, 1886.	Value of lands unsold Dec. 31, 1886.
Union Pacific	11,309,844	$19,909,672.42	$2,395,507.00
Central Pacific	8,000,000	7,332,581.34	12,500,000.00
Western Pacific	453,794	....	....
Kansas Pacific	6,000,000	11,816,695.35	11,608,763.00
Central Branch Union Pacific	222,560	1,000,000.00	....
Sioux City & Pacific	43,336	239,364.60	....
Total	26,029,534	$39,479,213.71	$26,504,270.00

Compare the number of acres granted with the areas of the following states : Kentucky, 24,115,200 acres ; Virginia, 24,542,720 acres ; Ohio, 25,576,-960 acres ; Louisiana, 26,461,440 acres.

$110,000,000.00, or about four times what the railway ought to have cost.

III.

In another rôle, the Union Pacific and the Credit Mobilier, its *alter ego*, had a historic part to play.

Before 1867 it was extremely difficult to secure capitalists to invest in either Union Pacific or Credit Mobilier stocks. Even at that late day most capitalists regarded the Pacific Railway as destined to failure, and the reluctance to put money into the hazardous venture was increased by the fact that speculators and visionaries of the type of Durant, Hallett, and George Francis Train seemed to be in control of it, with a dead weight of stock jobbers and public plunderers hanging at their heels. But Oakes Ames was a man of exceptional energy and business ability, blunt, honest and successful, above all, a man of ample personal means and the influence to command the means of others. Though he had been a member of the House Committee on the Pacific Railroad in 1864, when the charter was completed, and had supported the bill that ripened into the Act of 1864, he had looked on the project only in the patriotic light in which most other public men had regarded it. He was first identified with the active management of the enterprise in the fall of 1865, but through the year 1866 the dissensions of the factions prevented progress. When, however, in 1867, he "put his shoulder to the wheel" in the "Ames contract," developed the mechanism of the Seven Trustees, reconciled the differences of the factions, and personally solicited the assistance of wealthy and influential men (to some of whom he gave his own guaranty against loss by the investment), success was assured. The capital stock of the Credit Mobilier, $2,500,000.00, had been exhausted in construction expenditures, and no dividends had been paid. In February, 1867, the capital stock was increased fifty per cent, to $3,750,000.00, and the original stockholders were encouraged to increase their original holdings one-half by offering to each one of them subscribing for the increase a Union Pacific first mortgage bond of $1,000.00 as a bonus for each subscription of a thousand dollars in the increased stock. Six hundred and fifty shares of the increase remained undisposed of and were sold to Oakes Ames and Durant (two hundred and eighty to the former and three hundred and seventy to the latter) with which to fulfill promises to purchasers that they claimed to have made. Of those sold to Oakes Ames, some appeared afterwards to have been distributed by him among members of Congress in December, 1867, and January, 1868.

A misunderstanding had arisen through a claim made by Henry S. McComb to three hundred and seventy-five shares of stock,—two hundred and fifty of original and one hundred and twenty-five of increase stock. In 1866, H. G. Fant, a friend of McComb, had subscribed, through him, for two hundred and fifty shares of stock, but had failed to honor a draft made by McComb on him in payment of the subscription. The weight of the evidence afterwards taken by the Poland Committee shows that the transaction was cancelled, but when Credit Mobilier stock suddenly became valuable in December, 1867, McComb made claim for the stock subscribed by Fant and the increase of fifty per cent that would have gone with it, insisting that he had had to make good his agreement with Fant out of his own stock. None of the other stockholders supported McComb in his position and he had consented in writing to the apportionment of the last stock to Ames and Durant. But he evidently expected to be able at least to coerce a settlement from the other stockholders and accordingly begun a suit against them in Pennsylvania in September, 1868, to get the stock claimed, with the dividends declared on it, or the value of them — $300,000.00 or $400,000.00. The suit dragged on until 1872, some testimony having been taken in the meantime before a master in chancery. McComb placed much reliance on three letters that Ames had written to him from Washington, letters that did not make his case stronger, but gave him an apparent leverage for a favorable settlement in that they seemed to implicate Ames in securing or attempting to secure favorable legislation for, or lack of interference with, the affairs of the Union Pacific, by presents or sales at less than market value of Credit Mobilier stock to members of Congress.

In the letter of January 25, 1868, Ames wrote : " Yours of 23d is at hand, in which you say Senators Bayard and Fowler have written you in relation to their stock. I have spoken to Fowler but not to Bayard ; I have never been introduced to Bayard, but will see him soon. You say I must not put too much in one locality. I have assigned as far as I have gone to, 4 from Mass., 1 from N. H., 1 Delaware, 1 Tenn., 1 Ohio, 2 Penn., 1 Ind., 1 Maine, and I have three to place where they will do most good to us. I am here on the spot, and can better judge where they should go." In the second letter, on the 30th of the same month, he wrote : " I don't fear any investigation here. What some of Durant's friends may do in N. Y. courts can't be counted upon with any certainty. You do not understand, by your letter, what I have done, and am to do with my sales of stock. You say none to N. Y. I have placed some with N. Y. or have agreed to. You must remember it was nearly all placed as you saw on the list in N. Y., and there was but 6 or 8 m for me to place. I could not give all the world all they might want out of that. You would not want me to offer less than one m to any one. We allow Durant to place 58,000 to some 3 or 4 of his friends, or keep it himself. I have used this where it will produce most good to us, I think. In view of King's letter and Washburne's move here, I go for making our bond dividend in full." In the third letter, February 22, 1868, Ames wrote : " I think Grimes will sell a part of his [Credit Mobilier stock] at $350. I want that 14,000 increase of the Credit Mobilier to sell here. We want more friends in this Congress, and if a man will look into the law (and it is difficult for them to do it unless they have an interest to do so) he can not help being convinced that we should not be interfered with." On the back of the second letter was a memorandum list claimed by McComb to have been made by him at the dictation of Ames in New York, and indicating what disposition had been made of stock in Washington. The memorandum was as follows :

" Oakes Ames' list of names as showed to-day to me for C. M.: Blaine of Maine, 3,000. Patterson, N. Hamp., 3,000. Wilson, Mass., 2. Painter, Rep. for In., 3. S. Colfax, Speaker, 2. Elliott, Mass., 3. Dawes [Mass.] 2. Boutwell [Mass.] 2. Bingham and Garfield, Ohio. Schofield & Kelley, Penn. Fowler, Tenn. Feb. 1, 1868."

Offers of compromise, one on the basis of $100,000.00, were made to Ames, with significant reference to the three letters, before they were introduced in evidence, but Ames refused to settle, and the letters were put in evidence before the master in chancery. The evidence was kept out of sight for a while, but by some means was finally revealed to a newspaper correspondent; on September 4, 1872, the New York *Sun* published a sensational synopsis of the evidence, including the letters, under the headlines, " The King of Frauds. How the Credit Mobilier Bought its way through Congress." In the midst of a presidential campaign, and when most of the men named in McComb's memorandum were candidates for public offices, the article in the *Sun*, followed by columns of matter in other papers, created a profound sensation. Liberal Republicans and Democrats were bitterly denouncing the abuses of public office and the political corruption that had followed in the wake of the Rebellion ; the Credit Mobilier exposé was eagerly taken up and used by them as a political weapon. Such of the men in the list as were likely to be affected by the reports rushed before the public with absolute denials of all connection with the Credit Mobilier or Union Pacific and with all too ready declarations that the reports were only " campaign slanders."

When Congress began its session in the following December, Speaker Blaine called S. S. Cox to the chair, and offered from the floor a resolution (which was readily agreed to by the House) as follows :

" Whereas, accusations have been made in the public press, founded on the alleged letters of Oakes Ames, a representative from Massachusetts, and upon the alleged affidavit of Henry S. McComb, a citizen of Wilmington, in the State of

12

Delaware, to the effect that members of this House were bribed by Oakes Ames to perform certain legislative acts for the benefit of the Union Pacific Railway Company, by presents of stock in the Credit Mobilier of America, or by presents of a valuable character derived therefrom ; Therefore,

" Resolved, That a special committee of five members be appointed by the Speaker *pro tempore*, whose duty it shall be to investigate and ascertain whether any member of this House was bribed by Oakes Ames, or any other person or corporation, in any manner touching his legislative duty.

" Resolved further, That the committee have the right to employ a stenographer, and that they be empowered to send for persons and papers."

Accordingly, Luke P. Poland (Vermont), Nathaniel P. Banks (Massachusetts), James B. Beck (Kentucky), William E. Niblack (Indiana), and George W. McCreary (Iowa) were named as the Special Committee.

On the 6th of the following month (January, 1873), Wilson, (Indiana) presented a resolution for another committee of investigation as follows :

Resolved, That a select committee of five members of this House be appointed by the Speaker, and such committee be, and is hereby, instructed to enquire whether or not any person connected with the organization or association commonly known as the " Credit Mobilier," now holds any of the bonds of the Union Pacific Railroad Company, for the payment of which, or the interest thereon, the United States is in any way liable ; and whether or not such holders if any, or their assignees, of such bonds, are holders in good faith, and for value, or procured the same illegally or by fraud, and whether or not the United States may properly refuse to pay interest thereon, or the principal thereof, when the same shall become due, and whether or not any relinquishment of first mortgage lien that may heretofore have been made by the United States with reference to the bonds of said Railroad Company may be set aside, and to enquire into the character and purpose of such organization, and what officers of

the United States or members of Congress have at any time been
connected therewith, what connection it had with the contracts
for the construction of said Union Pacific Railroad Company,
and to report the facts to this House, together with such bill
as may be necessary to protect the interests of the United States
on account of any of the bonds of the class hereinbefore referred
to; and said committee is authorized to send for persons and
papers, and to report any time."

The committee appointed under this resolution consisted of
J. M. Wilson (Indiana), Samuel Shellabarger (Ohio), George F.
Hoar (Massachusetts), Thomas Swann (Maryland), and H. W.
Slocum (New York).

The two committees were intended to cover, in their investigations all the matters of interest involving the Union Pacific, the
Credit Mobilier, Congress, and the Government. The Poland
Committee began its sessions with closed doors, but the public
could not wait for information, and suspicions of "whitewashing"
intentions were freely entertained and expressed; by resolution
the House promptly opened the doors, and the national appetite
for sensational news was regaled through the newspapers with
daily reports of the evidence taken; the Wilson Committee took
the hint and applied the "no secrecy" resolution of the House to
its sessions. After six weeks of almost daily sessions, the two
committees reported their findings and recommendations and
the evidence taken in full.

The testimony taken by the Poland Committee was referred
to the Committee on the Judiciary under a resolution of the
House, "That the testimony taken by the committee of this
House of which Mr. Poland, of Vermont, is Chairman, be referred
to the Committee on the Judiciary, with instructions to enquire
whether anything in such testimony warrants articles of impeachment of any officer of the United States not a member of this
House, or makes it proper that further investigation should be
ordered in this case."

The Committee on the Judiciary reported, of course, that
impeachment could not be resorted to, because none of the acts

complained of had been done by a person who was an officer at the time of their commission or an officer at the time of investigation as well as when the acts were committed. The committee exceeded its instructions (though that seemed to be the rule of the day) by discussing and condemning the remedy by expulsion of members from Congress for acts committed before their term in Congress in which they should be expelled.

The evidence reported by the Poland Committee showed that all the transactions of Oakes Ames and members of Congress had been in the long session of the 40th Congress, and principally in December, 1867, and January, 1868. The members and ex-members implicated, with their positions at the times of the transactions complained of and of the investigation of them, were as follows:

		1867–1868.	1872–1873.
1	*Oakes Ames, Mass.,	Representative,	Representative.
2	James G. Blaine, Me.,	Representative,	Representative (Speaker),
3	Henry L. Dawes, Mass.,	Representative,	Representative.
4	Glenni W. Schofield, Penn.,	Representative,	Representative.
5	John A. Bingham, Ohio,	Representative,	Representative.
6	William D. Kelley, Penn.	Representative,	Representative.
7	James A. Garfield, Ohio,	Representative,	Representative.
8	James Brooks, N. Y.,	Representative,	Representative.
9	Schuyler Colfax, Ind.,	Representative, (Speaker),	Vice President.
10	James W. Patterson, N. H.	Senator,	Senator.
11	Roscoe Conkling, N. Y.,	Senator,	Senator.
12	Henry Wilson, Mass.,	Senator,	Vice President elect.
13	B. F. Boyer, Penn.,	Representative,	(Out of Office).
14	John A. Logan, Ill.,	Representative,	Senator.
15	Samuel Hooper, Mass.,	Representative,	Representative.
16	James F. Wilson, Iowa,	Representative,	(Out of Office).
17	J. W. Grimes, Iowa,	Senator,	(Out of Office).
18	George S. Boutwell, Mass.,	Representative,	Secretary of the Treasury.
19	James F. Bayard, Del.,	Senator,	(Out of Office).
20	William B. Allison, Iowa,	Representative,	(Out of Office).
21	John B. Alley, Mass.,	Representative,	(Out of Office).
22	Thomas D. Eliot, Mass.,	Representative,	(Deceased).

The report of the Poland Committee concerned only the first

eight, as they were the only ones at that time members of the House; and as to them the findings were as follows:

1. Oakes Ames, for the purpose of creating in members of Congress a feeling favorable to the Union Pacific (and Credit Mobilier) had sold or agreed to sell to them stock in the Credit Mobilier at par when it was worth much more, but instead of having the stock transferred to the purchasers on the books of the company, had kept it in his own name as "trustee," had received the dividends and accounted for them to the purchasers. His purpose was not to secure positive beneficial legislation, but to prevent possible detrimental legislation, particularly legislative regulation of freight and passenger rates on the Union Pacific, as advocated by C. C. Washburn (Wisconsin) and E. B. Washburne (Illinois). His acts were tantamount to bribery—in the opinion of the committee.

2. Blaine had considered the advisability of purchasing shares of Credit Mobilier stock, recommended by Ames, but had declined to take them.

3. Dawes had purchased from Ames and paid for ten shares of Credit Mobilier stock in January, 1868 (the latter guaranteeing a profit of at least ten per cent), but became alarmed by litigation in December, 1868, returned the stock and dividends ($400.00) to Ames, and received from him the amount paid for the stock with interest at ten per cent.

4. Schofield had purchased from Ames ten shares of Credit Mobilier stock at par in December, 1867, and received two dividends (one of eighty per cent. in Union Pacific bonds and one of sixty per cent. in cash), and then in June, 1868, exchanged his Credit Mobilier stock with Ames for a Union Pacific bond of $1,000.00 and ten shares of Union Pacific stock.

5. Bingham had bargained with Ames for twenty shares of Credit Mobilier stock in December, 1867, and received part of the dividends; in February, 1872, he had settled with Ames, the latter keeping the stock and accounting to him (Bingham) for all dividends.

6. Kelley had agreed with Ames in December, 1867, to take

ten shares of Credit Mobilier stock, but had not the money to pay for it ; Ames agreed to carry it for him until he could pay for it. By June, 1868, the dividends on the stock amounted to $329.00 more than the par value of the stock with interest. Ames paid to Kelly the $329.00, as well as $750.00 later, in September, 1868, as part of further dividends. (Kelley had testified that he understood the payments were loans to him from Ames, and the evidence of the two men was at complete variance).

7. Garfield's case was exactly the same as that of Kelley up to the point of the receipt of $329.00 ; after that there were no dealings between him and Ames. (Like Kelley, Garfield had also testified he understood the payment of the $329.00 to be a loan).

As to all of the members (except Ames and Brooks) reported on, the committee made the following childish findings :

" The committee do not find that Mr. Ames, in his negotiations with the persons above named, entered into any detail of the relations between the Credit Mobilier Company and the Union Pacific Company or gave them any specific information as to the amount of dividends they would be likely to receive further than [that the stock was good and would pay at least ten per cent]. They all knew from him, or otherwise, that the Credit Mobilier was a contracting company to build the Union Pacific road, but it does not appear that any of them knew that the profits and dividends were to be in stock and bonds of that company.

"The Credit Mobilier Company was a state corporation, not subject to Congressional legislation, and the fact that its profits were expected to be derived from building the Union Pacific road did not, apparently, create such an interest in that company as to disqualify the holder of Credit Mobilier stock from participating in any legislation affecting the railroad company. In his negotiations with these members of Congress, Mr. Ames made no suggestion that he desired to secure their influence in Congress in favor of the railroad company, and whenever the question was raised as to whether the ownership of the stock would in any way interfere with or embarrass them in their action as members of Congress, he assured them it would not.

"The committee, therefore, do not find, as to the members of the present house above named, that they were aware of the object of Mr. Ames, or that they had any other purpose in taking this stock than to make a profitable investment. It is apparent that those who advanced their money to pay for their stock present more the appearance of ordinary investors than those who did not, but the committee do not feel at liberty to find any corrupt purpose or knowledge founded upon the non-payment alone.

"It ought also to be observed that those who surrendered their stock to Mr. Ames before there was any public excitement upon the subject, do not profess to have done so upon any idea of impropriety in holding it, but for reasons affecting the value and security of the investment. But the committee believe that they must have felt that there was something so out of the ordinary course of business in the extraordinary dividends they were receiving as to render the investment itself suspicious, and that this was one of the motives of their action.

"The committee have not been able to find that any of these members of Congress have been affected in their official action in consequence of their interest in Credit Mobilier stock.

"It has been suggested that the fact that none of this stock was transferred to those with whom Mr. Ames contracted was a circumstance from which a sense of impropriety, if not corruption, was to be inferred. The committee believe this is capable of explanation without such inference. The profits of building the road under the Ames contract were only to be divided among such holders of Credit Mobilier stock as should come in and become parties to certain conditions set out in the contract of transfer to the trustees, so that a transfer from Mr. Ames to new holders would cut off the right to dividends from trustees, unless they also became parties to the agreement; and this the committee believe to be the true reason why no transfers were made.

"The committee are also of opinion that there was a satisfactory reason for delay on Mr. Ames' part to close settlements with some of these gentlemen for stock and bonds he had received as dividends upon the stock contracted to them.

"In the fall of 1868, Mr. McComb commenced a suit against the Credit Mobilier Company and Mr. Ames and others, claiming to be entitled to two hundred and fifty shares of the Credit Mobilier stock upon the subscription for stock to that amount. The suit is still pending. If Mr. McComb prevailed in that suit, Mr. Ames might be compelled to surrender so much of the stock assigned to him as trustee, and he was not therefore anxious to have the stock go out of his hands until that suit was terminated. It ought also to be stated that no one of the present members of the House above named appeared to have any knowledge of the dealings of Mr. Ames with other members.

" The committee do not find that either of the above named gentlemen, in contracting with Mr. Ames, had any corrupt motive or purpose himself, or was aware that Mr. Ames had any, nor did either of them suppose he was guilty of any impropriety or even indelicacy in becoming a purchaser of this stock. Had it appeared that these gentlemen were aware of the enormous dividends upon this stock, and how they were to be earned, we could not thus acquit them. And here as well as anywhere, the committee may allude to that subject. Congress had chartered the Union Pacific road, given to it a liberal grant of lands, and promised a liberal loan of government bonds, to be delivered as fast as sections of the road were completed. As these alone might not be sufficient to complete the road, Congress authorized the company to issue their own bonds for the deficit, and secured them by a mortgage upon the road, which should be a lien prior to that of the Government. Congress never intended that the owners of the road should execute a mortgage on the road prior to that of the Government to raise money to put into their own pockets, but only to build the road.

" The men who controlled the Union Pacific seem to have adopted as the basis for their action the right to encumber the road by a mortgage prior to that of the Government to the full extent, whether the money was needed for the construction of the road or not.

" It was clear enough they could not do this directly and in terms, and therefore they resorted to the device of contracting with themselves to build the road, and fix a price high enough to require the issue of bonds to the full extent, and then divide the bonds or proceeds of them under the name of profits on the contract. All those acting in the matter seem to have been fully aware of this, and that this was to be the effect of the transaction. The sudden rise in value of Credit Mobilier stock was the result of the adoption of this scheme. Any undue and unreasonable profits thus made by themselves were as much a fraud upon the government as if they had sold their bonds and divided the money without going through the form of denominating them profits on building the road.

" Now had these facts been known to these gentlemen, and had they understood that they were to share in the proceeds of the scheme, they would have deserved the severest censure."

8. As to Brooks, the committee reported that through his ability and promise to "take care of the Democratic side of the House," and through his appointment as government director of the Union Pacific, he had obtained, in January or February, 1868, fifty shares of Credit Mobilier stock at par, and $5,000.00 of Union Pacific bonds, from the Credit Mobilier trustees, though he had had them entered on the records of the companies in the name of one Neilson, his son-in-law; and that by reason of his former intimate connection with the affairs of the two companies, he had full and complete knowledge, at all times, of their inter-relations and their relations with the government.

As to the other men mentioned in connection with the all-absorbing scandal, the evidence taken by the Poland and Wilson Committees made the following revelations :

9. Colfax had purchased twenty shares of Credit Mobilier stock at par from Ames in December, 1867, and had paid $534.72 on the purchase in March, 1868; at this point Colfax insisted that he had rescinded the contract of purchase and donated the $534.72 to millionaire Ames on account of the latter's recent financial embarrassments ; Ames, however, testified that Colfax had received dividends amounting to about $700.00 over and

above the par value of the stock; the weight of evidence supported Ames in his statement.

10. Patterson had purchased thirty shares of Credit Mobilier stock from Ames in August, 1867, and had afterwards received $6,685.24 in cash, one hundred shares of Union Pacific stock and $2,000.00 in Union Pacific income bonds as dividends,—though he testified that he had given $3,000.00 to Ames to invest for him and supposed he had invested it for him in Union Pacific stocks and bonds and not in Credit Mobilier stock.

11. Conkling, (18) Boutwell, and (22) Eliot had never had anything to do with either the Credit Mobilier or the Union Pacific.

12. Henry Wilson in December, 1867, had contracted for twenty shares of Credit Mobilier stock for his wife (who had received a gift of $3,800.00 from friends on the twenty-fifth anniversary of their marriage), but, becoming dissatisfied, had rescinded the contract, had returned $814.00 of dividends paid to him, and received back from Ames the purchase money.

13. Boyer and his wife had together held one hundred shares of Credit Mobilier stock. He insisted that it was a legitimate and honorable transaction, and had not affected him in the discharge of his public duties. He regretted, "as the investment turned out to be profitable," "that it was no larger in amount."

14. Logan, in December, 1867, agreed to purchase at par ten shares of Credit Mobilier stock, but did not pay for it. Two dividends in 1868 amounted to more than the par value of the stock and interest, and in June, 1868, he received from Ames the surplus of $329.00. In the following month he became apprehensive of trouble and returned the money.

15. Hooper (as head of the Boston house of Samuel Hooper and Company), (17) Grimes, and (21) Alley had become the owners of Union Pacific stock and Credit Mobilier stock as early as 1866, and had continued to be such up to the time of the investigation.

16. James F. Wilson had held fifty shares of Credit Mobilier

stock from the summer of 1868 to some time in 1869, and had then disposed of it.

19. Bayard had been written to by McComb to take some Credit Mobilier stock, about January, 1868, but had referred the matter to his son, and afterwards had refused to have anything to do with the stock.

20. Allison had held ten shares of Credit Mobilier stock (purchased from Ames) from the winter of 1867-1868 or spring of 1868, and had received dividends of more than the par value of the stock. He had not paid for the stock, but the par value had been deducted from the dividends and he had received the surplus. Ames testified that after the beginning of the investigation Allison had arranged with him to consider the deal canceled until after the trouble should have "blown over."

The Poland committee, in the resolution creating it, had been instructed simply to "investigate and ascertain whether any member of [the] House was bribed by Oakes Ames, or any other person or corporation, in any manner touching his legislative duty," [1] but exceeded its instructions, to act as a jury and return a special verdict, and after finding Ames and Brooks guilty, took the liberty to recommend a punishment for them, and after recommending the punishment fit for their crime, acted on the floor of the House as prosecuting attorneys to have the punishment inflicted.[2] The committee offered and vigorously urged the passage of two resolutions of expulsion :

" 1. Whereas, Mr. Oakes Ames, a Representative in this House from the State of Massachusetts, has been guilty of selling to members of Congress shares of stock in the Credit Mobilier of America, for prices much below the true value of such stock, with intent thereby to influence the votes and decisions of such members in matters to be brought before Congress for action; Therefore,

[1] See pages 177-178, supra.

[2] Compare with this the more honorable attitude of Morrill in the Senate in presenting the resolution for the expulsion of Senator Patterson. Infra, pages 190-191.

"Resolved, That Mr. Oakes Ames be, and he is hereby, expelled from his seat as a member of this House."

"2. Whereas, Mr. James Brooks, a Representative in this House from the State of New York, did procure the Credit Mobilier Company to issue and deliver to Charles H. Neilson, for the use and benefit of said Brooks, fifty shares of the stock of said company, at a price much below its real value, well knowing that the same was so issued and delivered with intent to influence the votes and decisions of said Brooks as a member of the House in matters to be brought before Congress for action, and also to influence the votes and decisions of said Brooks as a government director in the Union Pacific Railroad Company; Therefore,

"Resolved, That Mr. James Brooks be, and he is hereby, expelled from his seat as a member of this House."[1]

Butler (Massachusetts), who had reported in behalf of the Committee on the Judiciary adversely to impeachment and had interjected an opinion adverse to expulsion,[2] offered as a substitute for the resolution of the Poland Committee :

"Whereas, A Select Committee of this House has, after investigation, reported to the House testimony which is deemed by them sufficient to show criminal action in one or more members of this House ; and, whereas, the testimony shows that similar acts have been done by other persons not now members of this House ; and, whereas, it clearly appears, whatever acts were done or offenses committed by members of this House, or by any civil officer of the United States now in office, or others, were done and committed more than five years ago, within the jurisdiction of the Supreme Court of the District of Columbia ; and, whereas, in the judgment of this House, the House of Representatives has no legal or constitutional right to use its power of expulsion of its members as punishments for crimes done and committed by a member before his election thereto, and that the

[1] See Report of Poland Committee on Credit Mobilier Investigation, House of Representatives Reports, 42d Congress, 3d Session, No. 77.

[2] See pages 179–180, supra.

punishment of all crimes and offenses against the laws should be after trial by jury and judgment of a court of competent jurisdiction ; Therefore,

"Resolved, That in the judgment of the House, as it appears there is probable cause to believe, from the report of the testimony submitted by the Select Committee of investigation of the matter of the Credit Mobilier, that grave offenses, punishable by the statutes of the United States, as well as at common law, such as giving or receiving bribes, or false swearing, may have been committed, as shown in said testimony, within the District of Columbia, that, therefore, the Clerk of the House be, and is hereby, ordered to cause a copy of the testimony so taken to be forwarded to the District Attorney, the prosecuting officer of the United States for said district, with the recommendation of this House that the same and other testimony which he may deem material he shall cause to be presented to the grand jury sitting in and for said district at the next session thereof ; that he may take such action in the premises as to law and justice shall appertain."

The debate on the Poland resolution began on the 25th of February, 1873, and occupied the major part of three days. As it progressed, it became plain that the Butler view had many supporters, and that the required two-thirds of the House could not be induced to vote for expulsion. Thereupon Sargent (California) offered a resolution that was substituted for the Poland resolution by a test vote of 115 to 110 (15 not voting); it was as follows :

"Whereas, by the report of the Special Committee herein, it appears that the acts charged against members of this House in connection with the Credit Mobilier of America, occurred more than five years ago, and long before the election of such persons to this Congress, two elections by the people having intervened ; and, whereas, grave doubts exist as to the rightful exercise by this House of its power to expel a member for offenses committed by such member long before his election thereto, and not connected with such election ; Therefore,

" Resolved, That the Special Committee be discharged from the further consideration of the subject.

" Resolved, That the House absolutely condemns the conduct of Oakes Ames, a member of this House from Massachusetts, in seeking to procure Congressional attention to the affairs of a corporation in which he was interested, and whose interest directly depended upon the legislation of Congress, by inducing members of Congress to invest in the stocks of said corporation.

" Resolved, That this House absolutely condemns the conduct of James Brooks, a member of this House from New York, for the use of his position as government director of the Union Pacific Railroad, and a member of this House, to procure the assignment to himself or family, of stock in the Credit Mobilier of America, a corporation having a contract with the Union Pacific Railroad, and whose interest depended directly upon the legislation of Congress."

On separate votes, February 27, 1873, the resolution in condemnation of Ames was agreed to by a vote of 182 to 36 (22 not voting); of Brooks, by a vote of 174 to 32 (34 not voting). The preamble was rejected by a vote of 113 to 98 (29 not voting). After the voting was over, it is said that "men who had just joined in the vote of condemnation against Mr. Ames, gathered around him to ask his pardon for having done so. They said to him ' We know that you are innocent; but we had to do it in order to satisfy our constituents.' " [1]

Resolutions of condemnation of Kelley and Hooper were laid on the table.

In the Senate, a Select Committee, consisting of Morrill, Scott, Wright, Stockton and Stevenson, was appointed to consider the evidence taken by the House committees, and reported February 27, 1873, a resolution " That James W. Patterson be, and he is hereby, expelled from his seat as a member of the Senate." On the 1st of March, 1873, Morrill, as chairman of the committee, called the attention of the Senate to the resolution, but expressly disclaimed, that he intended to act as prosecu-

[1] Crawford's Credit Mobilier of America, page 216.

tor in urging an agreement to it ; he simply left it for the independent action of the Senate. Senators demanded for the consideration of the resolution, before acting upon it, more time than the pressure of public business (only two week-days of the session remaining) would afford ; it was left over for consideration at the next session ; Patterson's term expired on the 4th of March, and the resolution was not again heard of !

On the 8th of May, 1873, exactly ten weeks from his public condemnation, the death of Oakes Ames resulted from the immense exertions of building the Union Pacific and the excitement and disgrace of the Credit Mobilier scandal ; the death of Brooks followed soon afterwards.

The Wilson committee [1] reported a bill having for its object the recovery of the excessive profits of the Credit Mobilier for the benefit of the United States.[2] The bill reported was not acted on, but when the legislative appropriation bill was reached at the end of the session, a section [3] was added to give effect to the recommendations of the committee. It provided for a suit in equity by the United States against (1) the Union Pacific Railroad Company, and "all persons (2) who may . . . have subscribed for or received capital stock in said road, which stock has not been paid for in full in money, or (3) who may have received, as dividends or otherwise, portions of the capital stock of said road, or the proceeds or avails thereof, or other property thereof, or other property of said road, unlawfully and contrary to equity, or (4) who may have received as profits or proceeds of contracts for construction, or equipments of said road, or other contracts therewith, money or other property which ought, in equity, to belong to said railroad corporation, or (5) who may, under pretense of having complied with [the Pacific railway] acts . . . have wrongfully and unlawfully received from the United States bonds, moneys, or lands which ought, in equity, to be accounted

---

[1] See pages 178–179, supra.

[2] See Report of Wilson Committee on Affairs of Union Pacific Railroad Company, House of Representatives Reports, 42d Congress, 3d Session, No. 78.

[3] Section IV., Act of March 3, 1873, 17 Statutes, 508.

for and paid to said railroad company or to the United States,
and to compel payment for said stock, and the collection and
payment of such moneys, and the restoration of such property,
or its value, either to said railroad corporation or to the United
States, whichever shall in equity be held entitled thereto." To
make the suit fully effective, the section further provided that it
"may be brought in the circuit court of any circuit, and all
. . . parties may be made defendants in one suit;" (!)
"decrees may be entered and enforced against any one or more
parties defendant without awaiting the final determination of the
cause against other parties;" (!) "the court . . . may make
such orders and decrees and issue such process as it shall deem
necessary to bring in new parties or the representatives of parties deceased, or to carry into effect the purposes of [the] act;"
"writs of subpœna may be issued by [the] court against any parties defendant, which . . . shall run into any district;" (!)
and the laws of the United States providing for proceedings in
bankruptcy shall not be held to apply to said corporation."
Future difficulties were anticipated by provisions that (1) "No
dividend shall hereafter be made by [the Union Pacific] company but from the actual net earnings thereof; (2) . . . no
new stock shall be issued, or mortgages or pledges made on the
property or future earnings of the company without leave of
Congress, except for the purpose of funding and securing debt
now existing or the renewals thereof;" (3) "no director or
officer of said road shall hereafter be interested . . . in any
contract therewith except for his lawful compensation as such
officer ; (4) any director or officer who shall pay or declare, or
aid in paying or declaring any dividend, or creating any mortgage or pledge prohibited by this act, shall be punished by
imprisonment not exceeding two years, and by fine not exceeding five thousand dollars; (5) the proper circuit court of the
United States shall have jurisdiction to hear and determine all
cases of mandamus to compel said Union Pacific Railroad Company to operate its road as required by law." Such another
example of special legislation, or edict, cannot be found in

the statute books of the United States—to such an extremity did the members of Congress conceive the nation to have been driven in its efforts to control its corporate creature. The whole trouble was in the puerile and improvident legislation of 1862 and 1864.

Under the statute, suit was brought by the Attorney General against one hundred and seventy defendants in the Circuit Court for the District of Connecticut, but a demurrer to the complaint of the United States was sustained and the case went the way of all Pacific railway litigation, to the Supreme Court. Again the demurrer was sustained, and the United States subjected to the humiliation of being instructed that they had no cause of action against the defendants; the extraordinary provisions (some of them undoubtedly unconstitutional) of the act of 1873 had been imposed upon the Federal courts to no purpose.

The Circuit Court (Justice Hunt on the bench) held that the United States could not maintain an action for the recovery from the Union Pacific of money or other property even fraudulently or unlawfully taken from the corporation, as long as the security of the United States for its loan of bonds and land should not be impaired, and as long as the corporation should perform the public functions imposed upon it by its charter; improvident and fraudulent contracts by the Union Pacific were of no concern to the United States, unless they should result in the impairment of the government's security for its debt, or the non-performance of its public functions; in such event, the remedy would be by a proper proceeding for the forfeiture of the corporation's charter. In securing the benefits expected from a Pacific railway, the government had given no more than it agreed to give, and the corporation had done and was doing all that the law required. If anyone had a right to complain that the Credit Mobilier, by fraudulent manipulations, had robbed its other self, the Union Pacific, it was only a stockholder of the Union Pacific (!) or a creditor whose security was directly affected by the fraudulent manipulations. (!) "If any person has subscribed for capital stock, or received capital stock or shares in the Union Pacific

Railroad Company which have not been paid for, the action to recover the money payable by the terms of the subscription must be in the name of the corporation. The contract was made with the corporation, as an existing person ; the money, if due at all, is, in terms, payable to the corporation as such. In law it must be recovered by the corporation, to be applied by it to the legal necessities of the railroad company. In substance and in form the money must go through and to the corporation, and no creditor, legal or equitable, can maintain an action for its money. In certain cases, if the corporation refuses to do its duty, such action may be maintained by the shareholders of the corporation, the corporation being made a party defendant. There may also be a case in which a judgment creditor can maintain an action against his judgment debtor and his creditor, to collect his debt after his legal remedies are exhausted. . . . That, however, is not the present case. The debt of the United States has not yet matured. Its bonds, issued to the railroad company, have not become payable, and their payment, when they mature, is secured by a specific lien upon the road and its franchises." The Union Pacific was not a trustee for the expenditure of public means in public improvements and accountable to the government as such, but was merely a debtor of the government bound only to the performance of such public duties as its charter imposed. The Union Pacific " is chartered for private benefit as well as for public advantage, and is legally bound to administer its affairs for the public advantage only to the extent that it does not violate the provisions of its charter or the law of the land. With this limitation such corporations are authorized to manage their own affairs for their own benefit, and such is the understanding of the government which grants such charter, and of the individuals who accept it. If, in this respect, a corporation should fail in its duty, the remedy is not by an attempt to enforce its supposed duties to the public as a trust, but to punish its illegal acts by a forfeiture of its charter. . . . No trust is declared in [the] title [of the Act of 1862] or in the sections of the act in which [the] aid is extended. . . . Not only is no trust expressed, but an idea thereof is excluded by taking a mortgage upon the road, the telegraph, its property, franchises, and all its granted lands remaining unsold. The government does not rely upon the security of an uncertain and undefined trust, but takes an express mortgage, where it intends to secure to itself the performance of conditions by the company. . . . It is apparent to the most superficial reader of the statutes that the great object of Congress was to bestow advantages, and from time to time to increase gratuities, to a corporation which should undertake the completion of a railroad to the Pacific. Conditions, restraints, or trust were but little thought of. . . . The grants of land and the issuance of bonds are to be considered as gifts, gratuities, voluntary contributions to aid in the construction of works which it is supposed would develop the resources of the country, advance its civilization and improvement, and upon which the mails and munitions of war could be transported. When given and accepted, the power of the donor is at an end, and the absolute ownership is in the corporations. The position of the government is that of a donor and not of a creditor or a *cestui que trust*, except where such position is directly specified. Voluntary conveyance creates no presumption of a trust. . . . The rights of the government are those which are expressly reserved, and do not arise from an implied trust."

In affirming the decision of the lower court in October, 1878, the Supreme Court (Justice Miller delivering the opinion) said : "It is difficult to see any right which as a creditor the government has to interfere between the corporation and those with whom it deals. It has been careful to protect its interests in making the contract, and it has the right which that control gives. What more does it ask?" . . . . "A court of justice is called on to inquire not into the balance of benefits and favors on each side of this controversy, but into the rights of the parties as established by law, as found in their contracts, as recognized by the settled principles of equity, and to decide accordingly."[1]

[1] United States *vs*. Union Pacific Railroad Company et al., 98 U. S. R. 569. Justices Swayne and Harlan dissented, except as to the question of the constitutionality of section IV. of the Act of March 3, 1873.

Such was the inglorious ending of the Credit Mobilier sensation, an object lesson of the abuses in the building of railways in the United States in the fourth and fifth decades of their development, of the imperfections of the methods of Congress in performing its public duties, and worst of all, of the weakness of a republican form of government.

IV.

The ordinary observer saw in the peculiar operations of the Credit Mobilier only a fraudulent scheme by a corrupt ring for private enrichment at the expense of the public. He saw only the quivering leaf,—he saw neither the roots of the tree nor the wind that agitated the leaf; the first were concealed from him, the latter was too subtle for him to perceive.

The Credit Mobilier scheme, though peculiar, was neither new nor uncommon ; instead of standing alone as an example of the perfidy of particular men, it was only a type of the railway construction company of the period from 1860 to 1880. Oakes Ames was not the shrewd swindler that he is often depicted. He was blunt, honest, and straightforward, did not create conditions, but took them as he found them and made his actions fit them. All the parts of the Pacific railway were built under the Acts of 1862 and 1864 in the same manner as the Union Pacific, by construction companies, controlled by the stockholders of the railway companies, through which, by hiring themselves at exorbitant rates to build their own lines, they enriched themselves at the expense of the railways and the public taxed to support them. And of the Union Pacific and Central Pacific it must in justice be said, that of all the parts of the contemplated system, the Union Pacific Company, though most villified, has come nearest to the fulfillment of the purposes of its charter, with the least abuse of the mechanism of its construction company. Most of the trunk lines of the United States have been built in the same way, and if the Credit Mobilier was a most iniquitous instrument of industrial development, it simply means that the system of railway building from 1860 to 1880 was iniquitous, and not that Oakes Ames was an arch villain among men.

Such an exaggerated estimation was put on railway bonds in the period during and following the Rebellion that it was no difficult matter to bond a railway for more than it was worth. A large part of the insane confidence that was reposed in the unimproved public land of the United States in Jackson's administration after 1830 and resulted in the panic of 1837, was bestowed on railways after 1860 and intensified the panic of 1873. The value of railways as property for present use and management was not highly regarded, but their value as future investments, after they had developed a tributary territory, made their bonds readily salable abroad as well as in the United States. In the east, railways had become valuable property, paying dividends and interest on bonds with agreeable regularity. In the west, they were expected to soon become remunerative. The railway bonds and the interest on them were payable before dividends on stock, and were usually secured by a mortgage on a land grant donated by the government as well as on the income and fixed property of the corporation; it is no wonder that they found ready sale as investments. Moreover, they had much resemblance to government securities; the railways did not appear, at first blush, to be dependent on the efforts of individuals, but rather on the condition of the tributary country, and their income was quite similar to the taxes paid to the government. The investor in railway bonds seemed to be putting his faith not in a Vanderbilt or Gould, but in the manufacturers, farmers, producers and consumers of the tributary territory upon which the roads depended for their success. The autocratic influence of "railroad managers" had not been appreciably exerted. The disastrous results of competition and "rate wars" had not yet been felt. If a railway could not pay the interest on its bonds, rates could be increased, and if it could pay the interest on its bonds, it could by a little more pressure on the tributary territory be made to pay some interest even on stock or more bonds. Thus the value of railways came to be determined not by the expense of building them, but by the amount of bonds and stock that their tributary territory could carry; if bonds were at a high premium and stock

should be paying a high rate of dividends, enough water was put
into the capital of the company to make returns normal, by building branch lines and over-capitalizing them, by issuing stock dividends, or by some of the many other methods of stock-watering.
The railway builder, urged on by the people whose towns, factories
and farms would be benefited by increased facilities of transportation, soon found, shrewdly enough, that he could usually build
his road from the bonuses of the future patrons of the road, and
the proceeds of the bonds that eastern investors, encouraged by
glittering reports of the communities through which it was to
pass, would invest in ; then he would have the stock of the road
and the privilege of operating it for the profit of his venture ; if
the road should be prosperous, his stock would be valuable ; if
not, he could at least contrive by some means to declare a dividend or two and unload his stock.   The easiest and neatest
method by which the railway projector could put water into the
capitalization of his road was by hiring himself to build it ; the
road would then appear to have really cost the amount at which
it might be capitalized, and the bondholder would have a plausible
reason to believe that his security was of actual value.   Such a
system of deriving profit from railways was regarded, with some
degree of justice, as being fully as defensible as getting a government contract at as high rates as possible and then performing
it as cheaply as possible, or as buying a stock of clothing as
cheaply as possible and selling it as dearly as possible. The only
safeguard the political economist and legislator of 1870 could
find was in the principle of competition, by which, if one railway
taxed its tributary community too heavily to pay interest and dividends on excessive issues of bonds and stock, another railway
would compete with it for its traffic ; hence, it was assumed, railway builders would, from prudential motives, refrain from excessive issues of bonds and stock. The railways in the United States
have been making economic history so fast that the political economist has hardly had time to discover a principle at the basis of
one phase of their development, before another phase of development has shattered the already "established" principle and given

the aching brain of the economist another set of effects for which to discover causes. Nothing is so little understood, even to-day, as the economic development of railways in the United States. When Congress attempted to encourage the construction of the Pacific railway in 1862 and 1864, it blundered and groped about until it enacted laws that were fundamentally out of harmony with economic conditions. It expected a large body of patriotic citizens to buy shares in the Union Pacific, and to the money derived from the sale of stock the government would add a liberal bonus of land and bonds ; then if such amount should not be sufficient to build the road, the company might issue enough first-mortgage bonds (not exceeding in amount the bonus of the government) to complete the project. A philanthropic scheme, indeed, by which patriotic capitalists and shareholders might provide their country with a Pacific railway and then wait for dividends on their stock as a reward for their patriotism ! That may be the principle on which Congress makes laws, but it is not the principle on which, since 1860, capitalists have built railways, contractors have erected buildings, and clothing merchants have dealt in coats and socks in this *laissez faire*, competitive period of economic refinement. The question that Oakes Ames and his associates put to themselves was, Will the proceeds of the sale of first-mortgage bonds and government bonds build the Union Pacific, and leave a possible surplus and stock to distribute as our profits? Indeed, that was the question that any railway projector would have asked himself between 1860 and 1870, and even to-day the question would be modified but little. The answer was finally in the affirmative, and the ordinary machinery of a construction company was put into operation, as might have been expected anywhere outside of Washington. Indeed, Congress, state legislatures, and the people did not count the cost of a Pacific railway ; the railway was what they wanted, no matter what the cost might be. Congress thought, until otherwise instructed by the Supreme Court, that the Union Pacific promoters were the agents and trustees of the government, inspired by the highest motives of patriotism to build the national highway,—they were only men of the nineteenth century, building a railway just as other men built railways, and making all the profit they could from the venture. If the Pacific railway had not been thus built, it probably would not have been built at all under the Acts of 1862 and 1864 ; the system was iniquitous, and the business communities of to-day are paying excessive taxes in fares and freights for the industrial follies of the preceding generation ; the system will pass away, just as the private banking system has passed away, and just as protection and stock gambling boards of trade will pass away as mists before the rays of economic enlightenment.   Oakes Ames did not create the Credit Mobilier, or Nicholas Biddle the Bank of the United States ; industrial society created them both, and Ames and Biddle simply fitted their engines to the groove that society made for them.   The scheme contemplated by the Acts of 1862 and 1864 was as much out of harmony with the economic conditions of its day as the system of the London goldsmiths of the sixteenth century would be out of harmony with the conditions of the present financial world.

Congress legislates least on national subjects.   The several parts of the country are so different that laws suited to one are seldom suited to all the others.   Senators and representatives represent their constituencies and business interests and not the nation.   The only constituency without representation in Washington is the United States.   It is of minor practical importance whether protection is a national benefit ; it is of the greatest moment that the agriculturists of the South and West do not favor it, while the manufacturers of New England and the Middle States insist that it is the blood of their industrial body.   What a member of Congress may consider the best kind of money for his country depends on the location of his constituency, whether it is full of importers and the creditor class, of Western farm-mortgage debtors, or of silver miners.   Legislation on banks is left largely to the bankers and capitalists in Congress ; the erection of a public building in Chicago, Philadelphia, or Kokomo will be left in the care of the congressmen and senators interested in those cities, the national necessity of the building is, within limits, a matter of secondary consideration. Pacific railway legislation was nearly always in charge of California and Nevada members, and the Central Pacific had no lack of "friends;" the senators and representatives from California had long been elected with special reference to securing government aid for a Pacific railway. With the Union Pacific the case was somewhat different; it had not the crystallized sentiment of a district behind it, and the Kansas Pacific developed into a competitor. Oakes Ames had learned from congressional experience that even proper legislation for banks, factories, sheep raising and agricultural pursuits, could only be obtained by the active advocacy of bankers, manufacturers, sheep raisers, and farmers in Congress. The Union Pacific was assailed by enemies without and enemies within; blackmailing government commissioners, stock jobbers, and shareholders were pouncing on the Union Pacific and Central Pacific at every turn; the stock market was continually agitated by threats of hostile legislation or litigation. Truly the Union Pacific was in need of "friends." Oakes Ames again took conditions as he found them, and made his actions accord with them; he sold Credit Mobilier stock to members of Congress, so that they would take an interest in the project of the Union Pacific, just as members from Pennsylvania took an interest in the protection of the iron industry, bankers from New York and Boston, in banking laws and bond-interest laws, and members from California and Nevada, in the Central Pacific. "We want more friends in this Congress, and if a man will look into the law (and it is difficult for them to do it unless they have an interest to do so), he cannot help being convinced that we should not be interfered with." [1] The condemnation of Ames in Congress was the echo of the condemnation by a thoughtless, inconsistent democracy, of the principle of divided responsibility, of checks and balances, of the principles of a republican form of government, in which the parts have interests distinct from and paramount to the interest of the whole, and in which the interests of the parts and of the whole

[1] Third letter from Oakes Ames to H. S. McComb, page 176, supra.

are less often in harmony than in opposition. The result of the Credit Mobilier investigation is degrading. The evidence taken by Poland and his committee did not convict Ames of bribing, or Brooks of being bribed. The report had found that Ames had been guilty of bribery, but that no one had been bribed. Members, it seemed, had been bribed without knowing it, and Ames had bribed them without telling them what he expected them to do in return for their bribes. It was a most miserable effort to appease public clamor by offering up to it the two most convenient victims. Ames and Brooks were both old men (both died within a few months after the end of the session), practically out of politics, and were not reëlected to serve after the term of Congress at the end of which the Credit Mobilier investigation culminated. One was a Democrat, the other was a Republican. They were simply made scapegoats for the congressional application of the logic of a republican form of government. The "friends" of the Central Pacific, of class legislation for the benefit of bankers and iron and woolen manufacturers, and of a Salary Grab Act for their own benefit,[1] sitting in condemnation of Ames and Brooks, afford an interesting spectacle of "Satan rebuking sin."

[1] The so-called "Salary Grab Act" was passed within ten days after the condemnation of Ames and Brooks.

CHAPTER VII.

THE THURMAN ACT.

I.

THE Union Pacific was born under an evil star. Internal dissensions made it an outcast in the financial world until the fall of 1867. As soon as it was generally known that it was to be a success and that its builders were to derive large profits from its construction and future operation, blackmailers, stock jobbers, and plunderers pounced upon it at every turn. One Cornelius Wendell, a government commissioner for the examination of completed sections of road, set the pace by refusing to approve a section of forty miles of road unless he should be paid $25,000.00 ; as the delivery of government subsidy bonds depended upon the approval of the completed section and delay would be ruinous to the company, the ransom was paid. McComb's exploit has already been detailed. James Fisk, in the fall of 1867, gained the control of some Union Pacific stock and was threatening the company with destruction unless he should be financially induced to restrain himself. In spite of the treaty made between the Durant and Ames factions, hostilities had been renewed, and the attempt of the latter to gain control of the directory of the Union Pacific at the annual election in October, resulted in injunctions that prevented an election. Fisk had the notorious Judge Barnard ready in New York at any time to make judicial orders to his liking, and the Ames faction wanted the office of the company removed from New York. A joint resolution introduced by Dawes in the House in December, 1867, provided that the time of the annual meeting of stockholders and election of directors should be changed from October to March, and that at each meeting the place of the next annual meeting and election should be designated.[1] But when an attempt was made to hold a meeting and elect directors in March, 1868, proceedings were stopped by an injunction, and the directors elected in 1866 continued to hold over. Then the company appealed to Congress again for protection from Fisk and his New York judges. An act fathered by Bingham (Ohio), aiming to remove the general office of the company from New York and to deprive the state courts of New York of jurisdiction over the company, passed the House without debate in March, 1869, after another attempted meeting and flourish of injunctions;[2] but when it reached the Senate, a vigorous attack was made on it by Stewart in the interest of the Central Pacific, whose Nevada " rotten borough " he represented. The two roads were so nearly completed, that only about one hundred miles intervened. The Central Pacific had not reached Promontory Point from the west; the Union Pacific, however, had passed Ogden from the east, though the Central Pacific had filed its map, graded its roadbed to a point several miles east of Ogden, and received two-thirds of its subsidy bonds from the government. The Central Pacific wanted the junction point at Ogden, so as to be able to participate in the Salt Lake valley traffic and reach a supply of coal ; the Union Pacific wanted to control both, and keep the Central Pacific out. The purpose of Stewart's attack on Bingham's very reasonable resolution was to coerce the designation of Ogden as the junction point. In the course of debate Stewart roundly denounced the Credit Mobilier and Seven Trustees, and asserted that the Union Pacific road had not been built according to law. As a result of this attack, the Senate tried to perform the duties of a court by settling the rights

[1] The joint resolution required that the place should be one of the cities of New York, Washington, Boston, Baltimore, Philadelphia, Cincinnati, Chicago and St. Louis.

[2] At this time, under an order of court, the offices and vault of the Union Pacific in New York were broken open by force, and an effort made to obtain possession of the books and records and other property of the company ; a large number of bonds were lost in the excitement of the occasion, it is said, and could never afterwards be located ; the books and records were taken by stealth across the Hudson into New Jersey.

of the two corporations as to junction point, and Garrett Davis (Kentucky) proposed an amendment for an investigation of the Union Pacific that the Senate could not refuse to adopt, though it did not reflect the matured intention of the body. Then it was stated on the floor that the two companies had compromised their differences, and the three-headed resolution was passed. The House promptly concurred in the amendment of the Senate. In its final form, the resolution provided, (1) that the stockholders of the Union Pacific might elect a board of directors at a meeting to be held on the 22d day of April, 1869, and establish their general office at any place in the United States to be designated at that meeting,[1] (2) that " the common terminus of the Union Pacific and Central Pacific Roads should be at or near Ogden ; and the Union Pacific Railroad Company shall build, and the Central Pacific Railroad Company pay for and own the road from the terminus aforesaid to Promontory Summit, at which point the rails shall meet and connect and form one continuous line,[2] (3) that the President of the United States should appoint a commission of not more than five disinterested "eminent citizens " to examine and report the condition of the two roads and what sums should be necessary to complete them as " first class roads,"[3] (4) that the President should withhold from the two companies enough bonds to insure the "full completion " of the roads, and if the amounts still to be issued to them should not be sufficient for that purpose, that " he should 'make requisition' upon them for the deficiency, and in default of obtaining such security as [is] in this section provided, the President may authorize and direct the Attorney General to institute such suits and proceedings on behalf and in the name of the United States,

[1] Under this section, the general office was removed, in 1869, from New York to Boston, at which latter place it has since remained.

[2] By the Act of May 6, 1870, (16 Statutes, 121 - 122) the terminus was more definitely ascertained by the designation of particular sections (about five miles northwest of the station at Ogden) within the limits of which the terminus should be. (Supra, page 152).

[3] For proceedings under this section, see pages 156–158, supra.

in any court of the United States having jurisdiction, as shall be necessary or proper to compel the giving of such security, and thereby or in any manner otherwise, to protect the interests of the United States in said road, and to insure the full completion thereof as a first class road, as required by law and the statutes in that case made,"[1] and (5) "that the Attorney General . . . . investigate whether or not the charter and and all the franchises of the Union Pacific Railroad Company and of the Central Pacific Railroad Company have not been forfeited, and institute all necessary and proper legal proceedings ; whether or not the said companies have or have not made any illegal dividends upon their stock, and, if so, [that he] institute the necessary proceedings to have the same re-imbursed, and . . . . . whether any of the directors, or any other agents or employés of said companies, have or have not violated any penal law, and, if so, [that he] institute the proper criminal proceedings against all persons who have violated such laws."[2]

The joint resolution, as originally introduced by Bingham, and passed by the House, had aimed to deprive the state courts of the powers over the Union Pacific that had been so effectively brought into action by Fisk, but that feature had been expunged by the Senate ; the purpose was accomplished later, however, by an anomalous section tacked to " An Act supplementary to an Act entitled ' An Act to allow the United States to prosecute Appeals without giving security ' and for other purposes," which provided "that any corporation . . . . . . other than a banking corporation, organized under a law of the United States, and against which a suit at law or in equity has been, or may be, commenced in any court other than a Circuit or District Court of the United States, for . . . . . alleged liability of such corporation, ... may have such suit removed from the court in which it may be pending, to the proper Circuit or

---

[1] For proceedings under this section, see pages 157–159, supra.

[2] This provision (5) was a nullity as to practical results ; indeed, it was never intended to be enforced ; it is one of the many examples showing the peculiar "fault finding " spirit Congress displayed towards the Pacific railway.

District Court of the United States."[1] Though this remarkable provision is general in its terms, the Union Pacific is almost the only corporation in the United States to which its description applies ; it was enacted for the express benefit of that corporation. Thus ended the " Fisk raid."

Even before the Union Pacific had completed its line to Ogden, it began to have trouble with the public over the question of rates. Passengers were charged ten cents a mile, and freight rates were so high that the people of Fremont declared they could get goods to and from Omaha (forty miles) cheaper by wagon road than by rail. Complaints reached Washington, Nebraska newspapers clamored, and eventually Congress interfered. In December, 1867, C. C. Washburn (Wisconsin) introduced in the House a bill for the regulation of rates, but it was referred to the Committee on the Pacific Railroad and appeared likely to remain in its hands ;[2] appreciating the situation, he then attempted to introduce a joint resolution for the same purpose in January, 1868,[3] but by a technicality in the rules, he could not introduce it himself,[4] Dodge (Iowa)[5] objecting, and had Windom (Minnesota) introduce it for him ; then its course was further obstructed by the demand of Higby (California) for an opportunity to debate it. February 17, 1868, another effort was made, and the same joint resolution was again introduced by Washburn ; it provided that the Secretary of War, the Secretary of the Interior, and the Attorney General . . . . are hereby constituted a Board of Commissioners, whose duty it shall be, on the first of July in each and

[1] 14 Statutes, 226.

[2] Oakes Ames was the principal member of the Committee on the Pacific Railroad.

[3] One of these is supposed to be the "Washburne's move," referred to by Ames in one of his letters to McComb, page 176, supra.

[4] According to the rule, he could introduce only one resolution when his state was called, and he had already introduced one on another subject.

[5] Granville M. Dodge was chief engineer of the Union Pacific, and a member of the House from Iowa, while his wife was a stockholder in the Union Pacific and Credit Mobilier.

every year, to fix and establish a tariff for freight and passengers over the Union Pacific and Central Pacific railroads and their branches, which tariff shall be equitable and just, and shall not exceed double the average rates charged on the lines of railroad between the Mississippi River and the Atlantic Ocean on parallels of latitude north of Saint Louis, Missouri ; and the said railroad companies shall not charge a sum in excess of the rates fixed by said board, nor . . . . . make any contract to give terms and privileges to any express company which are denied to any other express company." Dilatory tactics were again resorted to, and though the resolution was reached twice in March, 1868, it was finally referred to the Committee on the Pacific Railroad (!) on March 26, where the bill first introduced had been reposing since the beginning of the session. However, the resolution was reported back in a few days with a proviso that it should not take effect *until the road should be completed.*[1] The proviso was rejected by a vote of 75 to 48 (66 not voting) and the resolution was finally passed May 12. When it reached the Senate, it went, by reference, to the Committee on the Pacific Railroad, and never emerged. After the line was completed, the companies voluntarily reduced their rates, and further trouble was avoided.

II.

In 1870 arose the so-called "interest question." As to the repayment to the United States of the amount of subsidy bonds advanced to the Pacific railroads, the Act of 1862 (Section 5) provided, "To secure the repayment to the United States . . . of the amount of said bonds so issued and delivered to said company, together with all interest thereon, which shall have been paid by the United States, the issue of said bonds and delivery to the company shall *ipso facto* constitute a first mortgage,"[2] etc.

---

[1] See pages 156–160, supra, as to question of the time of completion. See also provision of Act of 1862 as to regulation of rates after the completion of the road, page 106, supra.

[2] Supra, page 106.

The act further (Section VI.) provided, "The grants [of bonds and land] are made upon condition that said company shall pay said bonds at maturity . . . . . and all compensation for services rendered for the government shall be applied to the payment of said bonds and interest until the amount is fully paid . . . . . and after said road is completed, until said bonds and interest are paid, at least five per centum of the net earnings of said road shall also be annually applied to the payment thereof." The Act of 1864 (Section V.) provided that "only one-half of the compensation for services rendered for the government by said companies shall be required to be applied to the payment of the bonds issued by the government." The interest on the bonds was paid regularly by the United States, of course, but no percentage of the net earnings was paid by the companies[1] and the "half compensation" amounted to less than the interest on the bonds ;[2] thus the amount of the indebtedness of the railway companies was increasing each year, and as the Indian problem was practically solved, and the consequent expenses of army transportation decreased, the annual increment of debt was likely to be greater. What was to be done?

A joint resolution, offered May 2, 1870, by Representative Van Trump (Ohio), and instructing the Secretary of the Treasury to retain all the compensation for services for the government to apply on account of the interest paid on the government bonds, was referred to the Committee on the Pacific Railroad with the usual result that it appeared likely to remain in their hands indefinitely. A demand on each company for its deficit of interest was met in each case by the answer that the interest was not payable (except by half compensation and percentage of net earnings) before the maturity of the bonds. The Secretary of the

[1] Infra, pages 212–214.

[2] Up to July, 1870, the excess of accumulated interest over payments of half compensation by the several companies was as follows : Union Pacific, $2,543,-987.81; Central Pacific, $3,326,834.45; Western Pacific, $137,798.97 ; Sioux City and Pacific, $203,470.14; Kansas Pacific, $569,261.65; Central Branch Union Pacific, $320,210.84; total, $7,101,563.26.

14

Treasury (George S. Boutwell) did not wait for instructions from Congress but acted on his own responsibility ; he obtained an opinion from Attorney General Akerman in December, 1870, "that the government may lawfully claim from the company the amount of the interest in question as soon as such interest is paid by the government," and accordingly withheld from the companies all compensation for services for the government, to apply on the reimbursement of interest. Then the Senate Committee on the Judiciary, having been instructed to inquire and report, (1) whether the companies were bound to reimburse interest paid by the government on its bonds before the maturity of the principal,[1] and (2) whether the Treasury Department had the right to retain all the compensation for services for the government to apply on said interest,[2] reported in the negative on each point (except as to half compensation and percentage of net earnings).[3] On the strength of the report, Congress tacked to the Army Appropriation bill of March, 1871, an instruction to the Secretary of the Treasury to pay over to the companies the half compensation withheld, with a proviso, however, that the payments should not affect the legal rights of the government or the obligations of the companies.

In the Legislative Appropriation Bill of March, 1873, however, the wave of hostility occasioned by the investigations of the Wilson committee into the relations of the Union Pacific and Credit Mobilier[4] was responsible for a provision directing the Secretary of the Treasury to retain all compensation for services for the Government up to an amount such as, in addition to the five per cent of net earnings, would liquidate the balance of interest not reimbursed ; but the same provision permitted the companies to bring suits against the government for their withheld

[1] Resolution by Edmunds (Vermont).

[2] Resolution by Thayer (Nebraska).

[3] The committee was composed of five members, of whom three (particularly Carpenter, who presented the report) favored the report, and two (particularly Edmunds) were opposed to it.

[4] Supra, pages 177–196.

half compensation in the Court of Claims, with a right in either party to appeal to the Supreme Court, and precedence of hearing in both courts over all other business. Suit was brought by the Union Pacific in the Court of Claims and the position of the companies was upheld. An appeal by the government to the Supreme Court resulted in an affirmance of the decision of the Court of Claims in the fall of 1875.

In delivering the decision of the Supreme Court, Justice Davis reviewed exhaustively the history of the Acts of 1862 and 1864 in order to ascertain their "reason and meaning," and the obligation created by them as to the payment by the companies of the current interest. "This enterprise was viewed as a national undertaking for national purposes, and the public mind was directed to the end to be accomplished rather than the particular means employed for the purpose. Although this road was a military necessity, there were other reasons active at the time in producing an opinion for its completion besides the protection of an exposed frontier. There was a vast unpeopled territory lying between the Missouri and Sacramento Rivers which was practically worthless without the facilities afforded by a railroad for the transportation of persons and property. With its construction the agricultural and mineral resources of this territory could be developed, settlements made where settlements were possible, and thereby the wealth and power of the United States essentially increased. And there was also the pressing want, in times of peace even, of an improved and cheaper method for the transportation of the mails and supplies for the army and the Indians.

"It was in the presence of these facts that Congress undertook to deal with the subject of this railroad. . . . . .

. "It was a national work, originating in national necessities, and requiring national assistance. . . . . .

"The policy of the country, to say nothing of the supposed want of power, stood in the way of the United States taking the work into its own hands. Even if this were not so, reasons of economy suggested that it were better to enlist private capital and individual enterprise in the project. This Congress undertook to do, and the inducements held out were such as it was believed would procure the requisite capital and enterprise. But the purpose in presenting these inducements was to promote the construction and operation of a work deemed essential to the security of great public interests. . . . . .

"[Congress] well knew that the undertaking of the government bound it to pay to the holder of any bond, interest every six months, and the principal at the time the bond matured. With this knowledge, dealing as it did with the relations the company were to bear to the government on the receipt of these bonds, had it intended to exact of the company the payment of interest before the maturity of the bonds, it would have declared its purpose in language about which there could be no misunderstanding. . . . . The provisions [of the acts] created no obligation to keep down the interest, nor were they so intended. . . . . It was in the discretion of Congress to make this requirement. . . . . This Congress did not choose to do, but rested satisfied with the entire property of the company as security for the ultimate payment of the principal and interest of the bonds delivered to it, and in the meantime, with special provisions looking to the reinbursement of the government for interest paid by it, and the application of the surplus, if any remained, to discharge the principal. . . . . Besides, it is fair to infer that Congress supposed that the services to be rendered by the road to the government would equal the interest to be paid ; and that this was not an unreasonable expectation, the published statistics of the vast cost of transporting military and naval stores and the mails to the Pacific coast, by the ancient methods, abundantly show. . . . .

"There is enough in the scheme of the act, and in the purposes contemplated by it, to show that Congress never intended to impose on the corporation the obligation to pay current interest."[1]

III.

While the "interest question" was in the courts, the companion question of the payment of the five per cent of net earn-

---

[1] United States *vs.* Union Pacific Railroad Company, 91 U. S. R. 72.

ings received increased attention. The words of the statute of 1862 are: "And after the said road is completed, until said bonds and interest are paid, at least five per centum of the net earnings shall be annually applied to the payment thereof."[1] Two questions were raised in determining the amount due to the government : (1) When was the road completed? (2) What was meant by the term "net earnings?" (1) The government claimed that the Union Pacific was completed in November, 1869; the company, in October, 1874.[2] In fact, part of the bond subsidy and land grant had been withheld by the government because the roads were not completed according to law. Yet the Union Pacific and the Central Pacific had been operated over their entire length since July, 1869. However, the companies and the government maintained their separate views of the question, and neither was entirely consistent. (2) In defining the term "net earnings," the companies insisted on determining them by deducting from the gross earnings interest on bonded indebtedness, expenses of land grant, new improvements and equipment, and the government's half compensation—items that the government insisted were part of the "net earnings," and ought to be paid out of them. By the Act of June 22, 1874, the Secretary of the Treasury was directed to require the payment by the companies of "all sums of money due, or to become due, the United States for the five per centum of net earnings," and "in case . . . . said railroad companies shall neglect or refuse to pay the sum within sixty days after demand therefor, ... the Attorney General . . . . shall . . . . institute the necessary suits and proceedings to collect and otherwise obtain redress in respect of the same in the proper circuit courts of the United States." Demand was made on each of the companies for the payment of the amounts claimed, being computed on the earnings since 1869,[3] but the demands met with no response. Suits were begun against the several Pacific railway companies in the proper circuit courts

[1] Supra, page 106.
[2] Supra, page 159.
[3] Ibidem.

and eventually reached the Supreme Court, where they were decided in the October, 1878, term. The Court held (Justice Bradley delivering the opinion) that the "net earnings" were to be ascertained by "deducting from the gross earnings all the ordinary expenses of organization and of operating the road, and expenditures made *bona fide* in improvements, and paid out of earnings, and not by the issue of bonds or stock, but not deducting interest paid on any of the bonded debt of the company,"[1] nor the government's half compensation.[2]

But before the "net earnings cases" were passed upon by the Supreme Court, Congress seemed to tire of waiting for the determination of the rights of the Pacific railway companies in the courts and passed the Thurman Act, in May, 1878. Of all the remarkable legislation on the Pacific railways, this act, under which the government and the companies have plodded on to the present (1894), is by no means the least remarkable.

IV.

After the decision of the Supreme Court on the "interest case" in the fall of 1875, Congress became alarmed for the security of the debt to the government of the Pacific railways. The half compensation fell far short of the current interest on the government bonds and the companies were refusing to pay the five per centum of net earning ; on the most liberal calculations, if they should pay the five per centum, the amount realized from

[1] Syllabus in Union Pacific Railroad Company *vs.* United States, 99 U. S. R. 402.

[2] Union Pacific Railroad Company *vs.* United States, 99 U.S.R. 402 ; United States *vs.* Central Pacific Railroad Company, 99 U.S.R. 449 ; United States *vs.* Kansas Pacific Railway Company, 99 U.S.R. 455; United States *vs.* Sioux City and Pacific Railroad Company, 99 U. S. R. 491. In these cases it was also decided—a point not very material in this connection—that the priority of the lien of the first mortgage bonds over the lien of the government bonds "authorized the payment of the interest accruing on the [former] out of the net earnings of the road, in preference to the five per centum payable to the government, which [latter] is only demandable out of the excess in each year." (Syllabus in Union Pacific Railroad Company *vs.* United States). Justices Strong and Harlan dissented on this point in each case.

the two sources would be quite inadequate to reimburse the government for its payments of interest, not to speak of the principal debt. The companies were laying by no means for the extinguishment of their debt to the government at its maturity, and in 1875, with apparent audacity (really as a business necessity) were distributing their surplus earnings in dividends among their stockholders. Popular condemnation seemed to be in store for Congress unless something should be done at once, and Congress had no desire for a repetition of the experience of the Credit Mobilier scandal. In each House, the Committee on the Pacific Railroad was set to work ; as the relations of the companies with the government were almost entirely matters of legal interpretation of the Charter Acts of 1862 and 1864, the two Committees on the Judiciary were asked for recommendations. The companies, perhaps fearing more arbitrary legislation and always suffering on the stock market from apprehensions of " what Congress might do," were at one with Congress as to the necessity of a " sinking fund" for the future payment of the debt to the government. The means with which the fund should be filled caused the differences of opinion. The companies proposed to return the unsold balance of their land grant (the best part having been disposed of) to the government, and have the sinking fund credited with its value computed at $2.50 per acre, and to have it credited further with the amount due to the companies for services and withheld by the government ; to these credits they proposed to add each year an amount sufficient to equal, at their maturity, the amount due on the government bonds. All the amounts in the sinking fund were to bear interest at six per cent compounded semi-annually, while simple interest was to be computed on the government bonds. The propositions of the companies were presented in the bills reported by the Committees on the Pacific Railroad. The Committees on the Judiciary made exhaustive reports accompanied by proposed bills ; the one proposed in the Senate was called (from the chairman of the committee) the " Thurman bill," and concerned only the Union Pacific Railroad Company and the Central Pacific Railroad Company (the latter

a consolidation of the original Central Pacific and Western
Pacific). Its discussion in the Senate was prolonged, and the
views of the constitutional lawyers among its members were
widely divergent. The bill, proposing "to alter and amend
the acts [of 1862 and 1864,"] became law May 7, 1878, with the
following provisions :

"Net earnings . . . shall be ascertained by deducting
from the gross . . . earnings . . . the necessary expenses actually paid . . . in operating the [road] and keeping the same in . . . repair, and the sum paid . . . in
discharge of interest on . . . first-mortgage bonds . . .
and excluding all sums paid . . . for interest upon any other
indebtedness."

A sinking fund was established in the Treasury of the United
States, into which should be paid each year the one-half compensation for government services payable by the act of 1864 to the
companies, together with such sum, not in excess of $850,000.00
(in the case of the Union Pacific) or of $1,200,000.00 (in the case
of the Central Pacific), as added to the whole compensation for
government services and five per cent of net earnings, should
make them equal to twenty-five per cent of the net earnings of
each company ; unless the remaining seventy-five per cent should
be "insufficient to pay the interest [on the first-mortgage bonds]
. . . and such interest [should have] been paid out of such
net earnings," in which case the Secretary of the Treasury [was]
authorized . . . to remit so much of the twenty-five per
centum of net earnings required to be paid into the sinking fund
. . . as may have been thus applied and used in the payment
of interest as aforesaid." As required by the Act of 1864, one-
half of the compensation for services for the government were
still to be applied directly on the payment of the bonds and interest.[1] The sinking fund should be invested in (preferably five per

---

[1] This somewhat intricate provision caused much confusion in the debates
in Congress. The amount paid on the government bonds and into the sinking
fund could not exceed twenty-five per cent of net earnings unless the twenty-
five per cent of net earnings should be less than the total compensation for

cent) bonds of the United States, and the income should semi-annually be likewise invested.[1] Dividends were prohibited as long as either company should be in default of payment of either the interest on its first-mortgage bonds, the contributions to the sinking fund, or the five per cent of net earnings. Illegally paid dividends might be recovered by suit and paid into the sinking fund. "And every . . . officer, person, or stockholder who shall knowingly vote, declare, make, or pay any such dividend, contrary to the provisions of this act, shall be deemed guilty of a misdemeanor, and, on conviction thereof, shall be punished by a fine not exceeding ten thousand dollars, and by imprisonment not exceeding one year."

"Said sinking fund . . . shall . . . be held for the protection, security, and benefit of the lawful and just holders of any mortgage or lien debts of [the] companies, . . . lawfully paramount to the rights of the United States, and for the claims of other creditors, if any, lawfully chargeable upon the funds so . . . paid into said sinking fund, according to their respective lawful priorities, as well as for the United States, according to the principles of equity, to the end that all persons having any claim upon said sinking fund may be entitled thereto in due order ; but the provisions of the section shall

government services plus five per cent of net earnings; nor could it exceed the total compensation for government services plus five per cent of net earnings, plus $850,000.00 (or $1,200,000.00). There is an apparent incongruity in the provision that if seventy-five per cent of net earnings should not be sufficient to pay the interest on the first-mortgage bonds, part of the twenty-five per cent in the sinking fund should be used for that purpose ; the *amount of net earnings is determined by deducting from the gross earnings* the operating expenses and *interest on first mortgage bonds;* the interest on the first-mortgage bonds is paid before there are net earnings ; according to the definition of net earnings in the act, interest on first-mortgage bonds could not be paid out of *net* earnings in any case.

[1] By the Act of March 3, 1887, this provision was so amended that in addition to the five per cent bonds, the Secretary of the Treasury might invest the sinking fund in any of the government bonds issued in aid of the Pacific railways or in their first-mortgage bonds, having priority of lien over the government bonds. 24 Statutes, 488.

not . . . impair the existing legal right . . . of any mortgage, lien, or other creditor of . . . said companies, ... nor excuse [them] from the duty of discharging, out of other funds, its debts to any creditor but the United States."

"All sums due the United States from . . . said companies . . . whether payable presently or not, and all sums required to be paid to the United States or into the Treasury, or into said sinking fund . . . are hereby declared to be a lien on all the property . . . of every description granted . . . by the United States to . . . said companies . . . . . and also upon all the estate and property, real, personal and mixed, assets, and income of the . . . . companies . . . . from whatever source derived, subject to any lawfully prior and paramount mortgage, lien, or claim thereon."

"If either of said railroad companies shall fail to perform . . . the requirements of this act and of the acts [of 1862 and 1864], and of any other act relating to said company, . . . for the period of six months next after such performance may be due, such failure shall operate as a forfeiture of all the rights, privileges, grants and franchises derived . . . by it from the United States."

"This act shall be subject to alteration, amendment or repeal, . . . as justice or the public welfare may require. And nothing herein contained shall be held to deny, exclude or impair any right or remedv in the premises now existing in favor of the United States."[1]

[1] 20 Statutes, 56.

By the Act of June 19, 1878, the important office of Auditor of Railroad Accounts was established as a bureau of the Interior Department, for the purpose of attaining closer control of the government aided railways and promoting the successful operation of the Thurman Act.

"The duties of [the] Auditor, under and subject to the direction of the Secretary of the Interior shall be to prescribe a system of reports to be rendered to him by the railroad companies whose roads are in whole or in part west, north, or south of the Missouri River, and to which the United States have granted any loan or credit or subsidy in bonds or lands; to examine the books

Cases were soon made up in the Court of Claims and Circuit Court for the District of California to test the constitutionality of the Thurman Act. They reached a decision in the Supreme Court in the fall of 1878, and the act was declared constitutional so far as it provided for the establishment of a sinking fund (no other question being necessarily raised). The Court (Chief Justice Waite delivering the opinion) held that the power to alter and amend the Acts of 1862 and 1864 had been reserved by Congress, and that the reserved power could be exercised by it so far as the regulations imposed by it on the corporations were not unreasonable or arbitrary, or destructive of vested rights. "It is sufficient now to say that we think the legislation complained of may be sustained on the ground that it is a reasonable regulation of the administration of the affairs of the corporation and promotive of the interests of the public and the corporators. It takes nothing from the corporation or the stockholders which actually belongs to them. It oppresses no one, and inflicts no wrong. It simply gives further assurance of the continued solvency and prosperity of a corporation in which the public are so largely interested, and adds another guaranty to the permanent

and accounts of each of said companies once in each fiscal year, and at such other times as may be deemed by him necessary to determine the correctness of any report received from them ; to assist the government directors of any of said railways in all matters which come under their cognizance ; . . . . to see that the laws relating to said companies are enforced ; to furnish such information to the several departments of the government in regard to tariffs for freight and passengers and in regard to the accounts of said railroad companies as may be by them required, or . . . as he may deem expedient for the interest of the government ; and to make an annual report to the Secretary of the Interior, . . . on the condition of each of said railroad companies their roads, accounts, and affairs. . . .

"Each and every railroad company aforesaid which has received from the United States any bonds of the United States, issued by way of loan to aid in constructing or furnishing its road or which has received from the United States any lands, granted to it for a similar purpose, shall make to the said Auditor any and all such reports as he may require from time to time, and shall submit its books and records for the inspection of said Auditor . . . . at any time that the said Auditor may request." 20 Statutes, 169.

and lasting value to its vast amount of securities."[1] But the decision was reached by a bare majority of the Court, Justice Hunt not sitting, and Justices Bradley, Strong and Field dissenting. Justice Bradley was of the opinion that "the power of Congress, even over those subjects upon which it has a right to legislate, is not despotic, but is subject to certain constitutional limitations. One of them is, that no person shall be deprived of life, liberty, or property without due process of law ; another is that private property shall not be taken for public use without just compensation ; and a third is that the judicial power of the United States is vested in the supreme and inferior courts, and not in Congress. It seems to me that the law in question is violative of all these restrictions, of their spirit at least, if not their letter ; and a law which violates the spirit of the constitution is as much unconstitutional as one that violates its letter. . . . . The case before us . . . . is a direct abrogation of a contract, and that, too, of a contract of the government itself, a repudiation of its own contract."

As a matter of abstract justice, it was perhaps right that the Union Pacific and Central Pacific were required to make some reasonable provision out of their surplus earnings for the payment of their debts, when due ; if that were not done, the United States appeared likely to lose the greater part of their claim, as the original property of the companies would be inadequate security, and the accumulations would be dissipated in dividends ; if the United States agreed that the interest of its loan should not be paid before the maturity of the principal, because the enterprise was regarded as unusually hazardous, and if afterwards it proved very profitable, the companies ought not to have objected to laying by only one-fourth of their net earnings to pay their debts, which otherwise would not be paid ; it is true, the government and public were saving immense sums each year by the improved

---

[1] Sinking Fund Cases, Union Pacific Railroad Company *vs.* United States, and Central Pacific Railroad Company *vs.* Gallatin, 99 U.S.R. 700. Compare the decision in these cases with the decision in the "interest case," United States *vs.* Union Pacific Railroad Company, 91 U.S.R. 72, cited supra, pages 211–212.

facilities of transportation, but that was merely an incident, and would not justify a failure on the part of the companies to pay their debt to the United States. The contract read that "at least five per centum" of net earnings should be paid over each year, [1] but the fair implication that more than five per centum might be required was not taken into consideration in either enacting the Thurman Law, or passing on its constitutionality. It was at first supposed that the half compensation for services and five per cent of net earnings would more than pay the current interest, and for that reason no other provision was made for its payment; but if the government fortunately did not need all the services expected, was it a moral hardship for the companies to have to make up the deficit in money, if they were able?

But from a purely legal standpoint, it is hard to say that the decision is " good law." In its relations with the companies, the United States acted in two capacities, that of sovereign and that of individual ; in the former, it granted a charter ; in the latter, it loaned bonds, payable, with accrued interest (less the credits realized from services and percentage of net earnings), at the end of thirty years. As sovereign, the United States could compel the performance of certain public duties by the corporations, as defined in the charter ; as individual, it was entitled to the repayment of its loan at the time and in the manner specified in the contract (charter). The United States had no lien on the income or earnings of the corporation, except to the extent of the five per cent provided for, and no reserved right to alter or amend the charter could arbitrarily give to an individual creditor security in addition to what he had taken by his contract. The Supreme Court admit that the payment of the balance of accrued interest and principal could not be required before the maturity of the bonds, and particularly insist that the sinking fund remains the property of the companies until applied in payment of some or all of the debts. The Thurman Act is a statutory order for a receivership, in a case in which the United States is plaintiff, and the Union Pacific and Central Pacific defendants, Congress assum-

[1] See page 106 supra.

ing to act as judge. Congress could no more lawfully sit in deter-mination of the rights of the United States, creditor, and Union Pacific and Central Pacific, debtors, than it could try an ordinary mortgage foreclosure case and order a receivership; that is not "due process of law," and Congress is not a court. Again, the corporations had a vested right in their earnings until their debt to the United States should be due ; if at that time its property should be insufficient for the payment of its debts, improvident creditors, who had not obtained adequate security, would have to suffer ; if the corporation should be wasting its substance and approaching insolvency, a proper proceeding for a receivership, supported by a sufficient showing of the facts, would be available ; but that is entirely a matter for the courts, and not for Congress. Congress undoubtedly has power to make reasonable regulations for the Union Pacific in the use of its franchise and performance of its public functions, as in restricting its tariff for freight and passengers, exacting periodical reports of its operations, requiring due care in the control of its trains, or compelling it to operate the Omaha bridge as a part of its continuous line, and not as a stub ; but Congress could not compel it to pay to the United States, or any other creditor, a debt, or to put a fund in the hands of a third party for that purpose, before its maturity. The decision sanctions the usurpation by the legislature of the functions of the judiciary.

V.

By careful computations it had been determined that if the maximum amounts required by the Thurman Act to be paid into the sinking fund should be promptly and fully paid and invested in government bonds and the interest on the bonds compounded semi-annually at five per cent, the amount accumulated in the sinking fund by the time the subsidy bonds matured would be sufficient to pay the government's claim. But several causes have conspired to make the scheme, to a great extent, a failure. In the first place, the definition of "net earnings" in the act has been very materially modified by the Supreme Court in the "net earnings cases"[1] by requiring that expenditures for "new construction and new equipment" be deducted from the gross earnings, though interest on first-mortgage bonds should not be so deducted, as required by the Thurman Act. The Central Pacific has complied with the provisions, probably because its expenditures for new construction and new equipment were insignificant ; but the Union Pacific, under its policy of constructing branch lines, has insisted on deducting such expenditures from its gross earnings. The railways have had "hard times," too, and the maximum limit of the contributions to the sinking fund has not been attained. In investing the sinking fund in government bonds, the Secretary of the Treasury has been unable to obtain the bonds in the market, except at a high premium ; for example, April 6, 1881, $198,000.00 was invested in currency sixes at a premium of 35, $76,000.00 at a premium of 34.95, and $220,000.00 at a premium of 33.9. For considerable times large sums of money have lain in the sinking fund uninvested ; in June, 1881, the amount of such unproductive money was $935,328.52. In 1887, when some of the bonds had been called, it was estimated[2] that the proceeds were actually less, including interest, than had been originally paid out of the fund for the bonds. In 1880, the average rate of interest earned by the sinking fund was only from two and a half to three per cent.

After a few years operation showed that the sinking fund of the Thurman Act was doomed to failure as a means of discharging the companies' debt to the government at its maturity, efforts were made to substitute for it some plan that would make the government secure. All the plans suggested were in two classes, the one maintaining the sinking fund feature of the Thurman Act, with the requirement of a larger percentage of net earnings, the other contemplating the extension of the time of payment by from forty to one hundred years, and the division of the gross debt into annual or semi-annual payments ; opposed to both

[1] See pages 213–214, supra.

[2] See Report of United States Pacific Railway Commission, cited infra, page 224.

plans was the demand by a large western, anti-monopolistic contingent for proceedings by the government for the immediate forfeiture of the charters of all the bond aided Pacific railway companies, and the assumption of their property and duties by the government, if necessary in enforcing the payment of the debt. But the Thurman Act has been supplemented by no further legislation.

March 3, 1887, an act was passed creating the United States Pacific Railway Commission, and in the following month Robert E. Pattison, of Pennsylvania, E. Ellery Anderson, of New York, and David F. Littler, of Illinois, were appointed by President Cleveland as its members. The commission were to investigate fully the affairs of the bond aided railways, their relations to one another, to the people, and to the government, and their internal condition, management, and financial responsibility ; they were to report the evidence taken, their findings, and recommendations. Their report was exhaustive, but as to their recommendations, Pattison (chairman) urged immediate proceedings for the forfeiture of the companies' charters and a "winding up" of their affairs, while Anderson and Littler proposed legislation extending the time of payment of the debts to the government, if agreed to by the companies, otherwise requiring a larger percentage of net earnings each year for the sinking fund.[1]

[1] See Reports of United States Pacific Railway Commission, Senate Executive Documents, 50th Congress, 1st Session, No. 51.

CHAPTER VIII.

PRESENT AND FUTURE.

UNDER the operation of the Thurman Act, contributions to the sinking fund assumed to be payments to the United States, the debt of the Pacific railway companies to the nation is increasing at the rate of nearly two million dollars a year. The amount received from them in 1892 was only a little more than half the amount paid out by the United States in interest on the subsidy bonds, not to speak of their principal.[1] The subsidy bonds will mature from January, 1895, to January, 1899, and the several series of first-mortgage bonds issued by the companies will

[1] According to the Statement of the Public Debt, May 1, 1893, the indebtness of the companies is in the following condition:

NAME OF RAILWAY.	Principal outstanding.	Interest accrued and not yet paid.	Interest paid by the United States.	INT. REPAID BY COMPANIES.	
				By transportation service.	By cash payments: 5 p. ct. net earnings.
Central Pacific..........	$25,885,120 00	$517,702 40	$38,207,073 67	$6,754,238 5	$658,283 26
Kansas Pacific..........	6,303,000 00	126,060 00	9,722,043 09	4,129,697 49	....
Union Pacific..........	27,236,512 00	544,730 24	40,482,662 25	13,697,345 85	438,409 58
Central Branch U. P....	1,600,000 00	32,000 00	2,461,808 26	550,028 57	6,926 91
Western Pacific..........	1,970,560 00	39,411 20	2,791,468 14	9,367 00	....
Sioux City and Pacific	1,628,320 00	32,566 40	2,392,439 89	200,954 35	....
Totals..........	64,623,512 00	1,292,470 24	96,057,495 30	25,341,631 31	1,103,619 75

NAME OF RAILWAY.	Balance of interest paid by the United States.	SINKING FUND.		
		Bonds.	Cash.	Total.
Central Pacific..........	$30,794,552 36	$4,859,500 00	$587 76	$4,860,087 76
Kansas Pacific..........	5,592,345 60	....	....	....
Union Pacific..........	26,346,906 82	12,286,500 00	3,852 90	12,290,352 90
Central Branch U. P....	1,904,852 78	....	....	....
Western Pacific..........	2,782.101 14	....	....	....
Sioux City and Pacific..	2,191,485 54	....	....	....
Totals..........	69,612,244 24	17,146,000 00	4,440 66	17,150,440 66

mature in equal amounts and *pari passu* with the subsidy bonds.[1]
While the interest on the first-mortgage bonds has been kept
down, the un-reimbursed interest on the subsidy bonds will
amount, it is estimated, to at least $60,000,000.00 in 1899, and
added to the principal of $64,623,512.00 will make the total debt
of the companies to the United States about $125,000,000.00.
Of course, the companies will be unable to pay the debts when
they mature. And it hardly becomes a prudent creditor to wait
until his debtor's debt is due to determine what he will do on his
failure to pay the debt, particularly when the debtor is sure to
be in default. What shall Congress do? It seems plainly
necessary to take some action with little further delay. There
are three ways open to Congress by which to dispose of the
matter :

I. When the debt matures, the United States may foreclose
the lien reserved as security for the repayment of its debt, and if
the debt be not thus satisfied, direct proceedings may be resorted
to for the collection of the deficiency.

II. The sinking fund may be maintained, and a larger percentage of net earnings required to be paid into it, so that not
only current interest may be met, but even the principal of the
bonds may be gradually reimbursed.

III. The debt may be refunded at any time and definite

[1] The amounts of subsidy bonds maturing each year, for each company, are
as follows:

	1895.	January 1, 1896.	January 1, 1897.	January 1, 1898.	January 1, 1899.	TOTAL.
Union Pacific..............	......	(Feb. 1) 4,320,000	3,840,000	15,919,512	3,157,000	27,236,512
Central Pacific..............	(Jan. 16) 2,362,000	1,600,000	2,112,000	10,614,120	9,197,000	25,885,120
Kansas Pacific..............	(Nov. 1) 640,000	1,440,000	2,800,000	1,423,000	......	6,303,000
Central Branch Union Pacific.	......	640,000	640,000	320,000	......	1,600,000
Sioux City and Pacific.......	......	.....	.. ....	1,628,320	......	1,628,320
Western Pacific..............	......	......	320,000	......	1,650,560	1,970,560
Total...........	3,002,000	8,000,000	9,712,000	29,904,952	14,004,560	64,623,512

The amounts of companies' bonds maturing each year will be the same as
those of government bonds, except in 1899, when the amount will be about
$7,000.00 less for the Union Pacific.

periodical payments may be received from the companies in liquidation of it.

In determining which of the three courses is best to follow,
several general considerations must be kept in mind :

1. The case is not exactly an ordinary one of creditor and
debtor, of lender and borrower, in which the rights of one and
the obligations of the other, are distinct and definite. The
United States thought, in 1862 and 1864, that only one thing was
more needed than the suppression of the Rebellion, and that was
a railway from the Mississippi Valley to the Pacific Ocean. When
the inducements offered by the Act of 1862 were found to be
insufficient to attract individual effort to the enterprise, the new
inducements of the Act of 1864 were added. The opinion was
entertained by many capitalists and members of Congress that
the enterprise would never be a financial success and that the
loan of bonds would prove to be virtually a bonus. If the railway had proved unable to earn expenses, Congress would
undoubtedly have come to its assistance, as a national necessity.
If no payment had been made on the principal or interest of the
bonds by reason of the vast expense of constructing and operating the line, the public disappointment would have been slight.
The strongest argument with Congress was that if the United
States expended no more in interest on subsidy bonds than it was
then costing the government to transport its troops, mails, and
munitions of war over the plains and mountains, there would
be nothing lost. If that view should be taken now, the nation
would be found to have driven a shrewd bargain, and to be now
saving each year in expenses of transportation more than enough
to overbalance both principal and interest of the subsidy bonds
at their maturity.[1] Though the argument was fallacious, yet if
Congress was influenced by it and made its contract in consid-

[1] According to a special report of the Secretary of War in 1861, the average
annual expense to the government of the transportation of its mails, troops,
supplies and munitions of war from the Mississippi to the Pacific was in excess
of $7,000,000.00. The annual interest on the subsidy bonds is $3,877,400.00 ; the
principal maturing in thirty years after issuance, $64,623,512.00,—an annual
average of $2,154,100.00.

eration of it, ought it now to complain if it can not get all its debt from the Pacific railway companies, when it was ready to say in 1862 and 1864 that it would be satisfied if it should never receive any of it? If the builders of the Pacific railway had waited ten years before they began their work, they could have done it at only one-half of the expense it cost them from 1864 to 1869 ; labor and material were expensive and gold at a premium in 1865 ; the cost of the road was consequently inflated, to the extent, at least, of the principal of the subsidy bonds ; as compared with competing lines, the road would have been at a disadvantage, if it had had to repay current interest on the subsidy bonds.   If the United States insisted on having a Pacific railway just when and where it was most expensive to build it, ought the nation not to be willing to pay for having its whim humored, instead of requiring its convenient debtor to yield back dollar for dollar of his loan?   If the enterprise proved more profitable to its managers than had been expected, were the national interests less fully subserved by supplying what the Republican party called the " imperative demand of the whole people?"

On the other hand, the companies must remember that the government subsidy was very liberal, much more liberal than it would have been if Congress had known how exaggerated were the difficulties of building the roads.   If the railways were very expensive, the companies made them more expensive by their excessive haste in constructing them, when Congress had given them ample time.   They were amply compensated for their work, unparalled though it was, by the enormous profits that they received from it.   The granting the subsidy was the result of a highly excited state of the public mind, and the charter-contract was inspired rather by sentiment than by reason ; the early relations of the government and companies were not on a basis of strict business, a view emphasized by the Supreme Court in the " interest case." [1]   Moreover, the companies, in their disagreements with the government, have always exhibited an unusual

[1] United States vs. Union Pacific Railroad Company, 91 U. S. R., 79.   See pages 210–212, supra.

willingness to rely on the strict letter of the law, and have bested
the government because the courts would not permit it to read
between the lines of its contract an expression of the sentiments that prompted its execution ; the spirit and letter of the
Acts of 1862 and 1864 are neither identical nor in harmony ; may
the companies now ask in good conscience to be permitted to
rely on the spirit, and reject the letter of the contract?

2. The course that Congress ought to take depends much on
what general attitude the national government ought to sustain
to railways and railway corporations. It was generally conceded
before 1860 that the connection of the government with the
industries of the people should not be intimate ; " state interference " with industries was not favored. The preceding chapters
have shown the evils of such intimacy and interference ; most of
the tribulations of the Union Pacific (and of the government, too)
have come, not from its being worse managed or more dishonest
than other railway companies, but from the constant intermed-
dling of the government and the resultant contumacy of the corporation. One Congress has legislated without regard to the
spirit in which its predecessors have legislated on the same subject matter ; while the congressmen of 1862 and 1864 saw in the
Union Pacific only a national project to be accomplished through
the agency of patriotic individuals, the congressmen of 1873 saw
hardly more than a corrupt ring of men guiltily thriving at the
expense of a magnanimous government. Interference with industries for the purpose of fostering them, on the theory that they
are necessary elements of national prosperity, has done more to
undermine the foundations of the republican government of the
United States than any other policy it has sought to enforce.
The natural tendency of a democratic government to intermeddle
continually with the affairs of an enterprise that it has created, is
a serious impediment to its healthy prosperity. " Tinkering with
the tariff " (or apprehensions of it) causes a periodical stagnation
in many branches of industry, because it can not be foreseen what
a change of administration or overthrow of a party at the polls
will bring forth at Washington ; a large percentage of the people

of the United States waste a good part of their time and substance
in " waiting to see what Congress will do," or " trying to make it
do." But this is a " large question." Suffice it to say that whatever legislation Congress may enact in settlement of the relations
of the Pacific railways to the government, it should be final, if
possible, and leave no further legislation necessary ; it should,
moreover, if possible, make the relations so remote that they will
be nearly the same as those of railways that have received no government bonds in aid of their construction. By all means, the
sovereign United States ought to avoid the future necessity of
frequent contests with its subjects in the courts, and the possible
humiliation of defeat, as in the past. The United States should
not attempt to operate a railway in competition with corporations
of citizens, unless it be absolutely necessary ; if ever American
social ideas be ripe for the ownership and operation of railways
by the state, then it will be time for a change of policy ; at present, the ideas of the public are not compatible with state socialism
as applied to railways. If the United States will do justice
between railway corporations and between them and the people,
it will do all that society expects for a while.

3. In dealing with the Pacific railways, Congress must not be
too much affected by recollections of the Credit Mobilier, Jay
Gould, and the "Big Four" monopoly. The Pacific railway
companies are no worse than others. All railways, unfortunately,
have had their Credit Mobiliers, and all have had their Jay
Goulds. Watered stock and excessive incumbrances are unfortunately not peculiar to the Union Pacific. If the United States
has been a sufferer, it is only because, in a moment of over-
heated sentiment, it put itself on a level with individual creditors
of railway corporations ; if the logic of the situation were to be
consistently applied, it would probably, like the average second-
mortgage bondholder, see the stale water boiled out of the Union
Pacific obligations over the heat of a receivership and fresh water
added by a "reorganization committee " of first-mortgage bondholders. If the United States has to suffer the consequences of
being in bad company, it is only what is expected of an individ-

ual. The Union Pacific never could be the ideal railway that Congress expected it to be; it is only real now. The question of the payment of its debt must be answered in the light of the economic history of railways during the past thirty years.

4. It is a popular impression that the Pacific railway companies are wholly iniquitous, and that they have avoided doing their duty whenever they could ; that moreover they have taken unfair advantages of a liberal government. This is not strictly true. The courts have usually decided that the companies rightly interpreted the law, and when not, the companies have always yielded ready compliance. They have certainly not been more unreasonable than the government. The occasions on which the government has violated the letter and spirit of the Acts of 1862 and 1864 are as numerous as those on which the railway companies have violated them. Failure to make voluntary provision for the payment of the debt to the United States at its maturity was culpable, while the demand by the government of the payment of current interest was unwarranted. Perhaps earnings ought to have been put into a sinking fund for the payment of debts instead of into branch lines, but the branch lines were absolutely necessary, and in securing them the companies performed a duty not imposed upon them. Likewise, in constructing the main lines, the companies provided even better facilities for the accommodation of the public than had been contemplated by their charter. If such lines as the Oregon Short Line and Southern Pacific seem to be competitors of parts of the Pacific railway and thus afford ground for a suspicion that the managers have not done their duty to the creditor United States by building competing lines, it will yet be found that they have protected the Pacific railway, as a whole, from worse competition. Nor must it be assumed that the Pacific railway companies have had so much greater aid from the government than others. The land grant of the Northern Pacific was better in quality and twice as large, and those of the Illinois Central and other lines east of the Missouri will be found (their superior quality being considered) to be even more liberal. Compared with tariff protected

lumbermen, mine owners, manufacturers, sugar planters, and sheep raisers, the United States ought to cancel the debt of the Pacific railways and refund them what they have paid in on it.

5. The United States must preserve its sovereign dignity in its dealings with the Pacific railway companies. Though the courts have held that its rights under a contract must be subject to the same construction as those of an individual in the same position, it is yet a sovereign. Its dealings with these companies must not degenerate into a squabble. It must act deliberately, even liberally, but firmly, and with a full knowledge of all material facts. There must be no " bickering." When the United States discovers what policy is right, it must enforce it consistently and without hesitation. If finally it should be necessary to take possession of the Pacific railways and operate them rather than to submit to the contumacious conduct of its creatures and subjects, let it be done, even at great cost and expense ; a few millions of money are of no consequence to the United States, when compared with the preservation of the respect and obedience of its subjects and creatures. The question is not merely of dollars and cents ; the political question of the attitude of the United States to its subjects is greater.

I.

When the debt matures, the United States may foreclose the lien reserved for the payment of its debt, and if the debt be not thus satisfied, direct proceedings may be resorted to for the collection of the deficiency.

When the first series of bonds mature, the debt will be about $120,000,000.00, and the lien securing it will be subject to a first mortgage securing $63,615,000.00 of companies' bonds. If the subsidized lines should be sold under decree of court, they would not bring more than enough to pay the first-mortgage bonds,[1] and

---

[1] In October, 1887, Richard P. Morgan, Inspecting Engineer for the United States Pacific Railway Commission (supra, page 224), estimated the "cost of reproducing" the Pacific railway substantially as follows :

the United States would either have to lose its claim or buy in the lines and pay off the first-mortgage bonds.[1] If it should buy in the lines, (1) What would it get? and (2) What would it do with it after it got it?

1. In January, 1880, the Union Pacific, Kansas Pacific, and Denver Pacific were consolidated under the name of the Union Pacific Railway Company,[2] the stock of the consolidated company

	Miles.	Cost of Reproduction.	Average Cost per Mile without Terminals.	Average Cost per Mile with Terminals.
Union Pacific, Omaha to Ogden............	1039	$27,857,500		
Terminals, Omaha and Ogden..............		10,300,000		
Total............................		$38,157,500	$26,814	$36,728
Kansas Pacific, Kansas City to Denver............	639	$14,907,870		
Terminals, Kansas City and Denver...		7,000,000		
Total..................... .		$21,907,870	23,315	34,263
Central Branch Union Pacific..	100	$2,004,000	20,040	20,040
Central Pacific and Western Pacific, Ogden to Oakland, via Sacramento, Stockton, Lathrop and Niles, also Niles to San José......	892	$31,972,920		
Terminals, Sacramento, Oakland and San Francisco.....................		7,000,000		
Total.`.....		$38,972,920	35,845	43,693
Sioux City and Pacific............................	104	$2,372,700	22,814	22,814
Grand Total, Lines...................	2774	$79,114,990		
Terminals.....................		24,300,000		
		$103,414,990	$28,520	$37,280

See Reports of United States Pacific Railway Commission, Senate Executive Documents, 50th Congress, 1st Session, No. 51, pages 4437 – 4468.

[1] If the United States should buy in the properties and assume the payment of the first mortgages, the nation's investment would stand about as follows :

	Miles of Aided Line.	Average per Mile of First Mortgage Debt.	Average per Mile of Subsidy Mortgage Debt and Interest.	Total Average Cost per Mile to United States.	Morgan's Estimated Cost per mile of Reprod'ction.
Union Pacific..................	1038	$26,232	$40,306	$66,538	$36,728
Kansas Pacific.................	394	16,000	30,511	46,511	34,263
Central Pacific................ .	737	35,119	71,013	106,132	} 43,693
Western Pacific................	123	16,000	38,959	54,959	
Sioux City and Pacific..........	102	16,000	37,768	53,768	22,814
Central Branch Union Pacific....	100	16,000	35,368	51,368	20,040
Total......	2494	$25,907	$47,465	$73,372	$37,280

[2] The name of the original corporation was the Union Pacific Railroad Company.

being made equal in amount to the combined stock of the three constituent companies. The stock of the Kansas Pacific and Denver Pacific had been of little value, while the stock of the Union Pacific had earned a good reputation in the stock market. The two weak companies were controlled by Jay Gould, who was also a director in the Union Pacific. Consolidation was in favor with the majority of the Union Pacific management, but only on the condition that shares of Union Pacific stock should be exchanged for shares in the consolidated company at a higher ratio than shares of the two other companies, while Gould wanted the exchange of stock to be share for share. Gould brought his fellow directors in the Union Pacific to his terms by purchasing the Missouri Pacific and threatening to extend the Kansas Pacific from Denver to Salt Lake City and to a connection with the Central Pacific, thus forming a transcontinental competing line that would probably ruin the Union Pacific. The Union Pacific then inaugurated the policy of building branch lines and feeders for the main line and leasing and controlling other lines until now, while the main lines have a mileage of 1,777 miles and the branch lines of 45 miles, the auxiliary lines aggregate 6,326 miles, controlled through ownership of stock, leases, and a variety of relations.

In 1869, almost as soon as completed, the Western Pacific (having absorbed the San Francisco Bay Railroad Company, with a line from San José to San Francisco) was consolidated with the Central Pacific under the name of the Central Pacific Railroad Company.[1] Lines were built by the Central Pacific syndicate until California and Oregon were under their control and the Southern Pacific stretched across Arizona and New Mexico to El Paso. All the new lines were leased to the Central Pacific. But in 1885, a division was made of the California railroads, part of them being retained by the Central Pacific and part being turned over to the Southern Pacific Railroad Company ; then both sys-

[1] The name of the original corporation was the Central Pacific Railroad Company of California.

tems were leased to a new corporation chartered by the state of Kentucky and called the Southern Pacific Company.

The Central Branch Union Pacific (formerly the Atchison and Pike's Peak, the assignee of the Hannibal and Saint Joseph) was built to a point (Waterville) one hundred miles west of Atchison, and there it ended without connections ; later a small system of six branch lines aggregating about 290 miles was spread out from the western terminus, consolidated, and leased to it ; in 1880, the whole, having come under the control of Jay Gould, was unloaded on the Union Pacific in the consolidation, and by the latter then leased to the Missouri Pacific, probably to prevent its becoming, directly or indirectly, a competitor of either line. The intention of Congress in 1862 and 1864 had been to have this line connect with the Kansas Pacific, but the latter was permitted by the Act of 1866 to change its course westward,[1] and the Central Branch failed to reach either the Kansas Pacific or the Union Pacific.

The Sioux City and Pacific[2] was built for the sole purpose of earning the government subsidy of land and bonds. Since 1884 it has been a local branch of the Chicago and Northwestern.[3]

All the branch lines have been built on the pattern of the Union Pacific, in such a manner as to heap up bonded indebtedness, stock indebtedness, and obligations under leases and other arrangements in a bewildering and incomprehensible mass. In nearly all cases, the first-mortgage indebtedness is as much as the lines have cost. Without the branches the main lines would be bankrupt, and except as feeders of the main line, the branches are of no value.

Since 1885 competition has affected nearly every part of the original Pacific railway system. The California octopod, of which the Central Pacific is a tentacle, has kept out competition by covering all the competitive territory with lines that under other control would be competitors for trans-continental traffic.

[1] See page 108 and Note, supra.
[2] See page 107 and Note, supra.
[3] See map (2) showing the Pacific railway branches as planned and built.

The consolidation of the Union Pacific with the Kansas Pacific, so onerous to the former, was the means of putting an end to existing competition and preventing worse competition in the future. The miserable Central Branch Union Pacific and Sioux City and Pacific are mere appendages, for local business, to other trunk lines, and have only the slightest connection with transcontinental traffic. Immense sums have been paid by the Union Pacific to the Northern Pacific to keep it out of its territory, and the Oregon Short Line was built as a protection from the same competitor, though it also incidentally diverts traffic from the Central Pacific. Meanwhile the Burlington, Rock Island, Chicago and Northwestern, Missouri Pacific and Great Northern have projected their lines westward into Union Pacific territory to the material detriment of the latter's earnings.

Of the lines aided by the government, all, with the possible exception of the Central Branch Union Pacific, are maintained in good condition and well equipped.

In the case of the United States *vs*. the Kansas Pacific Railway Company,[1] it was decided that the lien of the United States for the reimbursement of its subsidy attached only to such lines or portions of lines as were built by the aid of it. Under this ruling the Omaha bridge, and the stub of which it is a part, would probably not be subject to the lien ; likewise the lines from San José to San Francisco, and from Sacramento to Oakland ; the Denver Pacific and Kansas Pacific west of the 394th mile-post, would not be subject to the government's lien. Even the Sioux City and Pacific forms its principal connection with the Chicago and Northwestern over an unsubsidized link of five miles. The lines covered by the lien would be as follows :

(*a*) Union Pacific, from Omaha to a point five miles west of Ogden, . . . 1038 miles.

(*b*) Kansas Pacific from Kansas City to a point 394 miles west, . . . 394 miles.

(*c*) Central Pacific, from a point five miles west of Ogden, to Sacramento, . . . 737 miles.

[1] 99 U. S. R. 455.

(*d*) Western Pacific, from Sacramento to San José, . . . 123 miles.

(*e*) Sioux City and Pacific, from Sioux City to California Junction, Iowa, and thence to Fremont, Nebraska . . . 102 miles.

(*f*) Central Branch Union Pacific, from Atchison to Waterville, Kansas . . . 100 miles. Total, 2,494 miles.[1]

What else would the companies have to which the United States could resort for the collection of the inevitable deficiency judgment ? In building up their branch systems, the Union Pacific and Central Pacific have in some cases built the lines themselves; in others, they have become the holders, for the purpose of controlling the branches, of a considerable amount of their stocks and bonds. The stocks have no substantial value, but some of the first-mortgage bonds would be available.

In the case of the Union Pacific, all of its branch line stocks and bonds, amounting to about $100,000,000.00 (face value), estimated by competent financiers at a market value of $42,000,-000.00, have been deposited with Drexel, Morgan and Company as security for the company's floating debt of $20,000,000.00 and future obligations not to exceed (together with the present floating debt) $24,000,000.00. The owned branches could be bought in under judicial sale, and the equities and rights of the companies in controlled lines could be secured in the same way, by the purchase under judicial sale of the means through which the control is exercised.

2. When the United States had thus become a full fledged railway owner and operator, it might proceed to business. A commission or board of managers would probably be necessary, and Congress would probably average two investigating committees each session. It could not well compete with private citizens for traffic, yet it would have to do it. It would also need some branch lines for an inlet to San Francisco, and for connections with other railways, as with the Chicago & Northwestern at Missouri Valley, or possibly over the Omaha bridge, but with its

[1] See map (3) for relation of aided lines to main lines and branch lines.

unlimited means and credit, it could have what it needed. It is generally assumed that the United States would have only a disjointed main line, without connections and branches, and would have to operate it at a loss. But that is not necessarily true. Many of the branches could be profitably lopped off, and many of them would have no natural outlet except over the government road. The business management of the government is not so bad as it used to be, and perhaps the government railway would be as well managed as the post-office. It is also assumed that the corruptions of the civil service would even be aggravated on a railway operated by the government; such a danger has been happily much lessened during the past ten years, and possibly the management might be sufficiently removed from "politics" to reduce the danger to a minimum. Nor is it necessarily true that the road would be much more extravagantly managed by the government than by a corporation. There would certainly be a material saving in legislative incidentals, interest on excessive bonded indebtedness, discounts and free transportation. It is urged that all the states and municipalities that have dabbled in railways have always failed to attain success in the railway business and have sold out at a loss. A state cannot successfully build railways in a settled community; that is clearly shown by the history of the Union Pacific, as well as by the experience of Canada, American states and European nations. But state management of railways already built, has never been tried under favorable conditions in the United States. If the United States must operate the Pacific railway, either "to maintain its dignity," or "to get even," let it give the experiment of state railway management a fair trial; failure is not inevitable.

But again, possibly it would be better for the United States to lose the entire Pacific railway debt than to get "mixed up" with the transcontinental railways through the management of the Pacific railway and its branches. Certainly such a step could be justified only as a last resort, in the event of a want of any other satisfactory solution of the vexatious problem. The legislation of 1862 and 1864 was a questionable departure from the settled policy of the government, and public sentiment has not fully approved it ; certainly there has been no tendency to follow it as a fixed change of policy. Public sentiment is not prepared for state ownership of railways, though it would probably approve the state operation of the Pacific railway in a case of necessity. In any event, such a necessity, in an extremity, must not be permitted to be such a bugbear as to justify the government in accepting unconscionable terms from the companies.

II.

The sinking fund may be maintained, and a larger proportion of net earnings required to be paid into it, so that not only current interest may be met, but even the principal of the bonds may be gradually diminished.

The sinking fund in itself is a clumsy and unwieldy piece of machinery ; instead of maintaining it, the money deposited should go into the general funds of the Treasury of the United States, and credit be given for it, with or without simple or compound interest, as justice may demand. The railway companies should not be made to suffer for the unskillful management of the Thurman Act sinking fund ; whatever arrangement is made, they should be allowed by the United States compound interest at six per cent for the sums heretofore paid in from time to time. After the subsidy debt has matured, a sinking fund will hardly be necessary, and the payments in money or transportation may be directly applied or set apart for the benefit of all creditors ; the time is now so short, that the sinking fund would be available only in case of a definite extension of the time of payment of the debt after its maturity. The use of the net earnings as a basis of payments involves too many intricate questions of accounting, even if the term can be defined ; the troubled past experience of the government, courts and railway companies with the term justifies its rejection as a basis of payments. In some respects, it may appear fairer to the companies to expect of them payments only in proportion to their earnings, but like most business men, they themselves would prefer to make payments of definite amounts; then they may always know what they have to meet and make preparations accordingly. Besides, in the past, the very natural suspicion that the companies were purposely keeping their earnings down by diverting traffic to allied lines and by distributing earnings on the basis of constructive mileage for branch lines, has caused no end of ill feeling; future trouble would doubtless be avoided by making payments no longer dependent on net earnings.

III.

The plan that has found most favor with financiers is the ascertainment of the worth of the debt at the time of settlement, on some just basis, and the provision for its payment in annual or semi-annual installments (usually in bonds) either equal or in an ascending or descending ratio, all secured by a lien or mortgage upon the present subsidized lines and upon as much more property as the companies can offer for security.

The fairest plan for the ascertainment of the worth of the debt is by adding all amounts overdue (of which there will be none until after the maturity of the first series of bonds, in January, 1895) with interest at two[1] per cent per annum, compounded semi-annually, to such amounts as, with interest at six per cent per annum, compounded semi-annually, will equal the payments not yet due, at their maturity. The amounts paid into the sinking fund (except reinvested interest) at various times, should then, with interest at six[2] per cent compounded semi-annually, be deducted from the amount first found. The remainder would be the present worth of the debt.

After the present worth were determined, it could be paid by several series of bonds of equal amounts, bearing interest payable annually or semi-annually, one series of bonds maturing each

---

[1] It is assumed that the government could borrow money at two per cent; the rate paid by the companies should be only sufficient to reimburse the government.

[2] The rate should be only two per cent on so much of the sinking fund as should be equal to the amount of debt to the government already matured at any time, and computed only after such maturity.

year or each half year. As each succeeding year would find one series of bonds less on which to pay interest, a scale of decreasing payments would be the result. The first payments would, however, be so much larger than the last, that they might prove embarrassing to the companies, and on that account would be objectionable. A scale of increasing payments, represented by bonds, would be better, as giving the companies time and opportunity to adjust their management to the new conditions. But better still would be a number of series of bonds, maturing semi-annually, and so arranged in number or amount as to make equal the semi-annual payments (including interest) by the companies. As the government can obtain money at two per cent per annum, it ought not to expect a higher rate on the companies' bonds; if the subsidy bonds had not yet matured, the difference between two per cent and six per cent could be easily compensated for. The several series of bonds should extend over a long time, from sixty to one hundred years, according to the ability of the companies to make payments.

Any such arrangement would have to be made conditional on acceptance by the companies, but there is no difficulty apprehended in that regard. The best method of arrangement would be by the appointment of a commission of responsible citizens for conference with the companies and the recommendation to Congress of one or more refunding plans, or some other plan, in case no reasonable refunding plan could be agreed on with the companies or any of them.

The execution of trust deeds or mortgages by the companies (covering not only their subsidized lines but all their other present and future real and personal property) to the Secretary of the Treasury or some other public officer as trustee would provide the most convenient form of security, much better than the indefinite statutory lien now provided.

The taking a new lien from the companies would either have to be consented to by inferior lienees or mortgagees,[1] or it would

---

[1] See tables of funded indebtedness of Union Pacific and Central Pacific, infra, pages 246 and 247.

16

have to be taken conditionally in place of the present lien.   All
present rights in the United States ought to be preserved for use
in the case of the failure of the new arrangement; else the
present lien might be subordinated to some other liens now inferior to it.

If some plan such as the above may be dévised, consistently
with the dignity of the United States, it is best that it be done.
The nation would lose nothing by it, but might gain much ; it
would avoid the dangerous necessity of trying to operate the
lines, and it would be just to the companies.   If, however, some
such plan cannot be devised, it is folly to consider sinking fund
schemes and plans that contemplate the continued management
of the lines by the companies; then it will be time for the
national government to assert its strength, foreclose its lien, take
possession of the lines, and operate them to the best possible
advantage, even at a loss.

If some settlement should be reached by the United States
with the bond aided Pacific railway companies, and its terms
should be fully complied with, their future course would probably
be very similar to those of other American railway companies ;
but if the United States should have to take possession of their
lines and operate them, the experiment, if successful, might be
productive of far reaching results.   As for their past history, the
Union Pacific, as a type of them, has furnished the student of
American politics, history and economics more material for
study and reflection than any other factor of American industrial life.

NOTE.

THE RECEIVERSHIP AND REORGANIZATION.

SINCE the foregoing chapters were written, the general business depression of 1893, most keenly felt in the West, has made the burdens of Union Pacific obligations too heavy to be borne, and has forced the system into the hands of receivers. On the 13th of October, 1893, on application of security holders, an order was made in the the United States court at Omaha for the appointment of S. H. H. Clark, of Saint Louis, Oliver W. Mink, of Boston, and E. Ellery Anderson, of New York, as receivers ; in the following month, on application of counsel for the United States, two additional receivers were appointed in Frederick R. Coudert, of New York, and J. W. Doane, of Chicago. Clark is president, and Mink vice-president of the Union Pacific ; Anderson and Doane are government directors, and Coudert also represents the interests of the United States, and is likely to be appointed government director to fill an existing vacancy. The interests of the government seem to be amply protected in the provisional management of the property.

Most of the Colorado lines and the Texas line (Fort Worth and Denver City Railway), aggregating about 1500 miles of lines and consolidated in 1890 under the subsidiary control of the Union Pacific, Denver and Gulf Railway Company, have been placed by the United States court at Denver in the hands of separate receivers.

The concomitant "reorganization committee" of security holders has also been formed (with Senator Calvin S. Brice, chairman of the Senate Committee on Pacific Railroads, as chairman) to devise a new basis for the management of the property and an adjustment of the indebtedness to the government of such a nature, if possible, as to leave some crumbs of future revenue for inferior lien holders. As the Union Pacific system, under foreclosure sale, could not be sold for enough to satisfy the debt to the government and the first mortgage debt superior to it, whatever participation other lien holders may be accorded in the future earnings of the system will be a gratuity to them, and the reorganization ought to be effected, if at all, with little reference to their desire to perpetuate their fictitious interests in the property; the extreme solicitude of first mortgage bond holders for the welfare of holders of securities inferior to the government lien is traceable to the considerable identity of the two classes and their mutual interest in the leased, operated and controlled lines of the system. But while the Union Pacific system is an admirable property and fully capable of earning an ample return on an unwatered valuation, it will hardly be abler in the future than in the past to yield dividends and interest on watered stocks, bonds, and guaranteed obligations five times the actual value of its assets; it is now in the hands of receivers not because it is incapable of sustaining itself on its legitimate traffic, but because, like the great majority of American railways, it has been burdened with obligations in such outrageous excess of its earning power that it is unable to carry them in a season of general depression. Every dollar of future revenue expended in payment of dividends and interest on watered stock and bonds will make the government's security for its claim more scant and necessitate a longer extension of the time for its payment, while the commercial efficiency of the system will tend to bear a direct ratio to its financial ability, and an inverse ratio to the financial obligations imposed on it. The holders of watered stock and bonds of the Union Pacific, not reflected in the value of the property of the system, have no rights in its revenue deserving of protection at the expense of the nation as creditor, the public as patrons, or the system as an instrument of social activity and prosperity. Whatever plan of reorganization Congress may be called on to endorse, it is plainly its public duty to demand that the amount of stock, bonds and other obligations on which the system will have to pay future returns be approximated to the reasonable value of its property.

Perhaps, too,—the hope will be indulged—each senator and congressman will be able to consider that in the adjustment of the future relations of the Pacific railway to the government, the nation, not some section, locality or business class, is his constituency, and that the details of the adjustment may be more safely arranged by Congress and the United States courts than by "reorganization committees," even when they have United States senators for chairmen.

INTRODUCTION.   II

to have been offered a new and strange definition in response to the demand of a dangerous industrial outgrowth. In the uncertain groping of statesmen, jurists and "industrial captains," manifestoes and edicts in place of laws and judgments, and "manipulations" in place of free individual activity, have afforded convincing proof of the obscurity in which the relations of social principles are involved.

The present practical question of the Pacific railway debt is of the highest importance in that it involves the possible loss to the United States of one hundred and twenty-five millions of dollars, with the dangerous alternative of a radical departure from the previous industrial policy of the government and people of the United States. If one hopes to discover a true solution of the question, it is only by a scientific study of the subject in its origin, development and present status.

Character of Bonds.	Term of Bonds. Years.	Term of Bonds. Date of Maturity.	Rate of Interest. Per ct.	Amount of bonds outstanding June 30, 1893	Lien on
Union Pacific (Original.)					
Union Pacific, first mortgage..	30	1896–1899	6	$27,229,000	Road and franchise, Omaha to Ogden.
United States subsidy, second mortgage..	30	1896–1899	6	27,236,512	Do.
Sinking-fund mortgage, coupon..	20	1893	8	4,712,000	Road and franchise, Omaha to Ogden, third mortgage: granted lands, second mortgage.
Sinking-fund mortgage, registered..	20	1893	8	450,000	
Collateral trust, 6 per cent..	29	1908	6	3,724,000	Bonds of branch lines held by trustees.
Omaha Bridge..	25	1896	8	565,000	Omaha Bridge, first mortgage.
Land-grant mortgage..	20	1887–1889	7	8,000	Granted lands.
Kansas Pacific.					
Eastern division, first mortgage..	30	1895	6	2,240,000	Road and income, Kansas city to a point 140 miles west.
Middle division, first mortgage..	30	1896	6	4,063,000	Road and income, one hundred and fortieth mile post to three hundred and ninety-fourth mile post.
United States subsidy, second mortgage..	30	1895–1898	6	6,303,000	Road and franchise, Kansas City to three hundred and ninety-fourth mile post
Denver extension, first mortgage..	30	1899	6	5,887,000	Road and lands, three hundred and ninety-fourth mile post to Denver.
Leavenworth branch, first mortgage..	30	1896	7	15,000	Leavenworth branch.
Income..	50	1916	7	11,400	Income.
Income, subordinated..	50	1916	7	23,100	Do.
Consolidated mortgage..	40	1919	6	11,724,000	Blanket mortgage, 779 miles of road and 394 miles of land grant.
Denver extension, coupon certificates..	12	1886	6	385	Income.
Denver Pacific.					
Cheyenne branch, first mortgage..	30	1899	7	4,000	Cheyenne branch, road and lands.
Union Pacific (Consolidated).					
Trust, 5 per cent. coupon..	24	1907	5	4,724,000	Bonds of branch lines held by trustees.
Trust, 5 per cent. registered..	24	1907	5	18,000	Do.
Omaha Bridge renewal, second mortgage.	21	1906	5	1,056,000	Omaha bridge.
Equipment trust, series A..	1 to 10	1888–1897	5	358,000	Equipment held by the American Loan and Trust Company of Boston, as trustees.
Equipment trust, series B..	1 to 10	1889–1899	5	1,052,000	
Equipment trust, series C..	1 to 10	1891–1900	5	671,000	
Collateral trust, 4½ per cent..	29	1918	4½	2,030,000	Bonds of branch lines held by trustees.
Kansas div'n, and collateral mortg. coupon	30	1921	5	5,000,000	Road and lands and bonds and stocks held by trustees.
Collateral trust, 6 per cent. notes..	3	1894	6	11,433,000	Bonds and stocks held by trustees.
Total funded debt..				$120,537,397	

CHARACTER OF BONDS.	TERM OF BONDS. Years.	TERM OF BONDS. Date of Maturity.	Rate of Interest. *Per cent.*	Amount of bonds outstanding June 30, 1893	LIEN ON
Central Pacific.					
First mortgage, series A..........	30	1895	6	$2,495,000	Road and franchise, Sacramento to State line.
First mortgage, series B..........	30	1896	6	1,000,000	Do.
First mortgage, series C..........	30	1896	6	1,000,000	Do.
First mortgage, series D..........	30	1896	6	1,483,000	Do.
First mortgage, series E..........	30	1897	6	3,997,000	Road and franchise, California State line to 5 miles west of Ogden.
First mortgage, series F..........	30	1898	6	3,999,000	Do.
First mortgage, series G..........	30	1898	6	3,999,000	Do.
First mortgage, series H..........	30	1898	6	3,999,000	Do.
First mortgage, series I..........	30	1898	6	3,511,000	Do.
United States subsidy, second mortgage......	30	1895–1898	6	25,585,120	Road and franchise, Sacramento to 5 miles west of Ogden.
First mortgage, series A, California and Oregon division, extended.	30	1918	5	5,982,000	Road and franchise, Roseville Junction to Oregon State line.
First mortgage, series B, California and Oregon......	20	1892	6	6,000	Do.
First mortgage, series B, California and Oregon, extended......	26	1918	5	4,358,000	Do.
Land-grant bonds, extended........	10	1900	5	2,908,000	First mortgage, Central Pacific and California and Oregon lands.
Fifty-year bonds..........	50	1936	6	56,000	Lands granted by United States and all other property except aided.
Fifty-year bonds..........	50	1939	5	11,000,000	Lands granted and all other property.
Western Pacific.					
Old issue........	30	1895	6	111,000	Road and franchise, Sacramento to San José.
First mortgage, series A........	30	1899	6	1,359,000	Do.
First mortgage, series B........	30	1899	6	765,000	Road and franchise, Niles to Oakland.
United States subsidy, second mortgage......	30	1895–1898	6	1,970,560	Road and franchise, Sacramento to San José.
San Joaquin Valley.					
First mortgage........	30	1900	6	6,080,000	Road and franchise, Lathrop to Goshen.
Total........				$86,863,680	

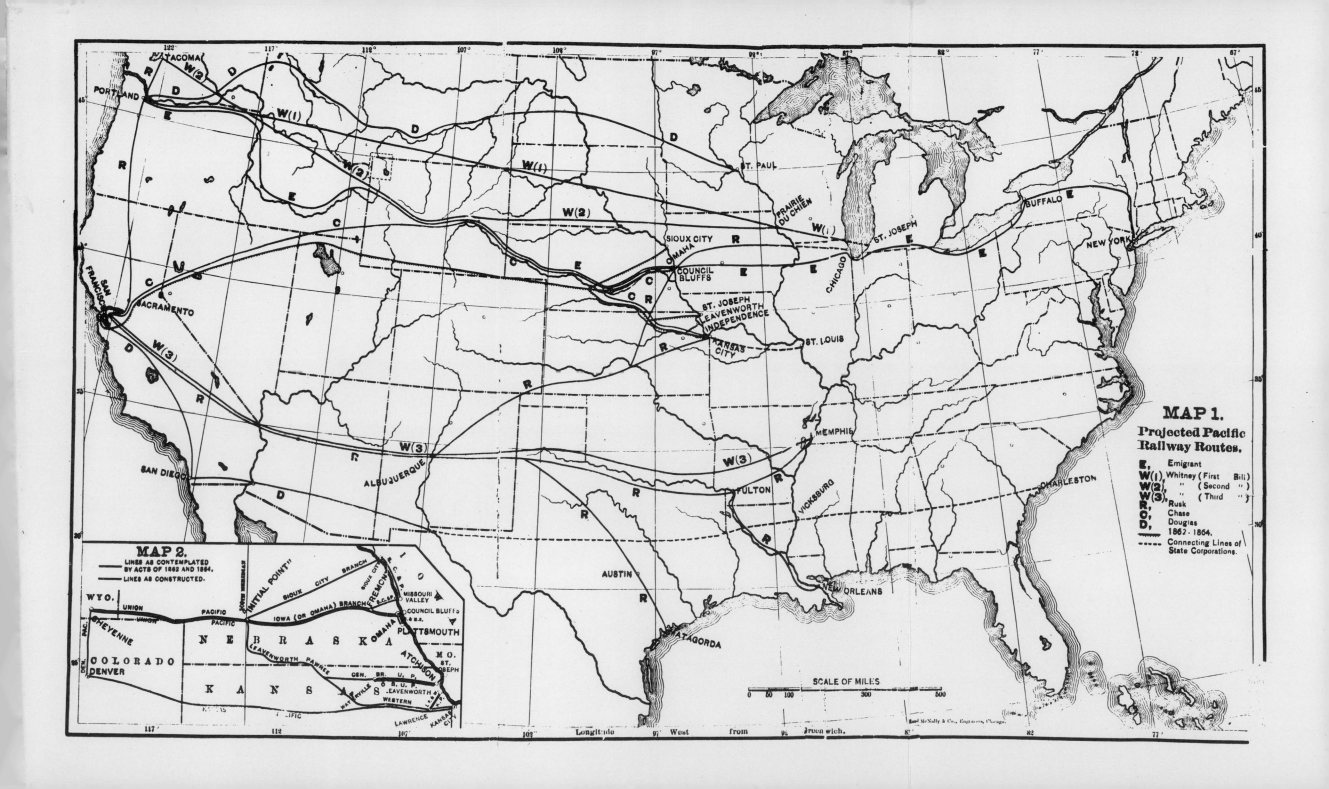

MAP 1.

Projected Pacific Railway Routes.

E, Emigrant
W(1), Whitney (First Bill)
W(2), " (Second ")
W(3), " (Third ")
R, Rusk
C, Chase
D, Douglas
1862 - 1864,
---- Connecting Lines of State Corporations.

MAP 2.

---- LINES AS CONTEMPLATED BY ACTS OF 1862 AND 1864.
— LINES AS CONSTRUCTED.

WYO.
UNION PAC. CHEYENNE
DEN. PAC.
COLORADO
DENVER
KANS.

NEBRASKA

INITIAL POINT
SIOUX CITY BRANCH
SIOUX CITY
IOWA (OR OMAHA) BRANCH
PACIFIC
LEAVENWORTH PAWNEE
GEN. BR. U. P.
WATERVILLE
LEAVENWORTH WESTERN
LAWRENCE
K. P. R.

IOWA
FREMONT
MISSOURI VALLEY
COUNCIL BLUFFS
OMAHA
PLATTSMOUTH
ATCHISON
MO.
ST. JOSEPH
KANSAS CITY

SCALE OF MILES
0 50 100   300   500

Rand McNally & Co., Engravers, Chicago.

PORTLAND
TACOMA
W(2)
D
E
R
W(1)
D
W(2)
D
E
C
U
R
D
SAN FRANCISCO
SACRAMENTO
W(3)
D
R
SAN DIEGO
D
ALBUQUERQUE
W(3)
R
R
R
R
AUSTIN
MATAGORDA
NEW ORLEANS

ST. PAUL
PRAIRIE DU CHIEN
W(1)
SIOUX CITY
OMAHA
COUNCIL BLUFFS
C
C R
R
E
ST. JOSEPH
LEAVENWORTH
INDEPENDENCE
KANSAS CITY
ST. LOUIS
R
R
MEMPHIS
FULTON
W(3)
R
VICKSBURG

ST. JOSEPH
CHICAGO
E
E
E
E
BUFFALO E
NEW YORK
CHARLESTON

Longitude   West   from   Greenwich.

Big Business

Economic Power in a Free Society

An Arno Press Collection

Alsberg, Carl L. **Combination in the American Bread-Baking Industry:** With Some Observations on the Mergers of 1924-25. 1926

Armes, Ethel. **The Story of Coal and Iron in Alabama.** 1910

Atkinson, Edward. **The Industrial Progress of the Nation:** Consumption Limited, Production Unlimited. 1889

Baker, John Calhoun. **Directors and Their Functions:** A Preliminary Study. 1945

Barron, Clarence W. **More They Told Barron:** Conversations and Revelations of an American Pepys in Wall Street. 1931

Bossard, James H. S. and J. Frederic Dewhurst. **University Education For Business:** A Study of Existing Needs and Practices. 1931

Bridge, James H., editor. **The Trust:** Its Book. Being a Presentation of the Several Aspects of the Latest Form of Industrial Evolution. 1902

Civic Federation of Chicago. **Chicago Conference on Trusts.** 1900

Clews, Henry. **Fifty Years in Wall Street.** 1908

Coman, Katharine. **The Industrial History of the United States.** 1910

Crafts, Wilbur F. **Successful Men of To-Day:** And What They Say of Success. 1883

Davis, John P. **The Union Pacific Railway:** A Study in Railway Politics, History, and Economics. 1894

Economics and Social Justice. 1973

Edie, Lionel D., editor. **The Stabilization of Business.** 1923

Edwards, Richard, editor. **New York's Great Industries.** 1884

Ely, Richard T. **Monopolies and Trusts.** 1912

Ford, Henry. **My Life and Work.** 1922

Freedley, Edwin T. **A Practical Treatise on Business.** 1853

Hadley, Arthur Twining. **Standards of Public Morality.** 1907

Hamilton, Walton, et al. **Price and Price Policies.** 1938

Haney, Lewis H. **Business Organization and Combination.** 1914

Hill, James J. **Highways of Progress.** 1910

Jenks, Jeremiah Whipple and Walter E. Clark. **The Trust Problem.** Fifth Edition. 1929

Keezer, Dexter Merriam and Stacy May. **The Public Control of Business.** 1930

La Follette, Robert Marion, editor. **The Making of America:** Industry and Finance. 1905

Lilienthal, David E. **Big Business:** A New Era. 1952

Lippincott, Isaac. **A History of Manufactures in the Ohio Valley to the Year 1860.** 1914

Lloyd, Henry Demarest. **Lords of Industry.** 1910

McConnell, Donald. **Economic Virtues in the United States.** 1930

Mellon, Andrew W. **Taxation:** The People's Business. 1924

Meyer, Balthasar Henry. **Railway Legislation in the United States.** 1909

Mills, James D. **The Art of Money Making.** 1872

Montague, Gilbert Holland. **The Rise and Progress of the Standard Oil Company.** 1904

Mosely Industrial Commission. **Reports of the Delegates of the Mosely Industrial Commission to the United States of America, Oct.-Dec., 1902.** 1903

Orth, Samuel P., compiler. **Readings on the Relation of Government to Property and Industry.** 1915

Patten, Simon N[elson]. **The Economic Basis of Protection.** 1890

Peto, Sir S[amuel] Morton. **Resources and Prospects of America.** 1866

Ripley, William Z[ebina]. **Main Street and Wall Street.** 1929

Ripley, William Z[ebina]. **Railroads:** Rates and Regulation. 1912

Rockefeller, John D. **Random Reminiscences of Men and Events.** 1909

Seager, Henry R. and Charles A. Gulick, Jr. **Trust and Corporation Problems.** 1929

Taeusch, Carl F. **Policy and Ethics in Business.** 1931

Taylor, Albion Guilford. **Labor Policies of the National Association of Manufacturers.** 1928

Vanderlip, Frank A. **Business and Education.** 1907

Van Hise, Charles R. **Concentration and Control:** A Solution of the Trust Problem in the United States. 1912

The Wealthy Citizens of New York. 1973

White, Bouck. **The Book of Daniel Drew.** 1910

Wile, Frederic William, editor. **A Century of Industrial Progress.** 1928

Wilgus, Horace L. **A Study of the United States Steel Corporation in Its Industrial and Legal Aspects.** 1901

[Youmans, Edward L., compiler] **Herbert Spencer on the Americans.** 1883

Youngman, Anna. **The Economic Causes of Great Fortunes.** 1909